Commodity
Strategies

Founded in 1807, John Wiley & Sons is the oldest independent publishing company in the United States. With offices in North America, Europe, Australia and Asia, Wiley is globally committed to developing and marketing print and electronic products and services for our customers' professional and personal knowledge and understanding.

The Wiley Trading series features books by traders who have survived the market's ever-changing temperament and have prospered—some by reinventing systems, others by getting back to basics. Whether a novice trader, professional or somewhere in between, these books will provide the advice and strategies needed to prosper today and well into the future.

For a list of available titles, please visit our Web site at www.WileyFinance.com.

Commodity Strategies

High-Profit Techniques for
Investors and Traders

THOMAS J. DORSEY

TAMMY F. DEROSIER, SUSAN L. MORRISON, PAUL L. KEETON
OF DORSEY, WRIGHT & ASSOCIATES
WITH JOSHUA B. PARKER

BICENTENNIAL
1807
WILEY
2007
BICENTENNIAL

John Wiley & Sons, Inc.

Published by John Wiley & Sons, Inc., Hoboken, New Jersey
Published simultaneously in Canada.

Wiley Bicentennial Logo: Richard J. Pacifico

Limit of Liability/Disclaimer of Warranty: While the publisher and author have used their best efforts in preparing this book, they make no representations or warranties with respect to the accuracy or completeness of the contents of this book and specifically disclaim any implied warranties of merchantability or fitness for a particular purpose. No warranty may be created or extended by sales representatives or written sales materials. The advice and strategies contained herein may not be suitable for your situation. You should consult with a professional where appropriate. Neither the publisher nor author shall be liable for any loss of profit or any other commercial damages, including but not limited to special, incidental, consequential, or other damages.

For general information on our other products and services or for technical support, please contact our Customer Care Department within the United States at (800) 762-2974, outside the United States at (317) 572-3993 or fax (317) 572-4002.

Wiley also publishes its books in a variety of electronic formats. Some content that appears in print may not be available in electronic books. For more information about Wiley products, visit our web site at www.wiley.com.

Library of Congress Cataloging-in-Publication Data:

Commodity strategies : high-profit techniques for investors and traders/
   Thomas J. Dorsey . . . [et al.].
      p. cm.—(Wiley trading series)
   Includes index.
   ISBN 978-0-470-12631-8 (cloth)
   1. Commodity exchanges. 2. Speculation. 3. Investment analysis.
   4. Commodity futures. I. Dorsey, Thomas J.
   HG6046.C662 2007
   332.64′4—dc22   2007012415

Printed in the United States of America

10 9 8 7 6 5 4 3 2 1

Contents

Preface

F or those who were investing at the time, it was the most remarkable, previously unfathomable, day in market history. For those who were not yet investing, it was still a day of mythical proportions. The day I am referring to, naturally, is Monday, October 19, 1987. At Dorsey, Wright & Associates (DWA), we came to work expecting business as usual, but by day's end we experienced the largest one-day percentage drop in the Dow Jones Industrial Average ever recorded. The Dow Jones dropped roughly 23 percent in one day, and after that the media began proclaiming a replay of 1929. DWA had been in business exactly 9 months and 19 days when this happened.

That day was significant to our corporate history because that single session changed the entire direction of DWA. It was as if we were moving from one train track to another. You see, we started out as an "Outsourced Options Strategy Department," primarily servicing firms that did not otherwise have this type of department in-house. The blame for the crash of 1987 was initially placed squarely on the shoulders of the options market, however, and in particular portfolio insurance strategies and naked put sellers. Some firms were said to be on the verge of going under because of the options liability exposed on that fateful day. For most firms, though, things worked out. The market eventually rebounded, and today the tales of that one market session are legendary. Most advisers haven't been in the business long enough to have firsthand knowledge of October 19, 1987, but for those of us who have, it is a day that will not soon be forgotten.

That day could be looked at as Wall Street's "Big Bang." It marked the financial end for some, but the beginning for others. DWA survived, just as most firms on Wall Street did, but that one day marked a new beginning for Dorsey, Wright & Associates. For us, it meant moving away from the options business almost entirely, as I knew wholeheartedly at the end of that session that the options business would never be the same again. I knew many firms would be enmeshed in litigation for years to come, that I was likely to become an expert witness for my clients during this period, and that few firms would be increasing their options resources in the near-future. That one day caused us to turn DWA around 180 degrees, pushing the options business from the engine to the caboose of our train, and the Point & Figure technical work to the front as our locomotive. It was a natural move for us, as we had employed the Point & Figure technical work in my Options Strategy Department at Wheat First Securities for years prior. But on that day, we were forced to begin marketing ourselves as technical analysts instead of options strategists.

On October 20, 1987, I created the first Dorsey, Wright & Associates commodity report. I knew that if we were going to move out of the options business, we would need to fill that hole with something. Commodity prices are governed by the irrefutable law of supply and demand, making it a seamless application for our Point & Figure work. I look at most things in both life and business in the most simple of terms. Copper is, quite simply, a hunk of metal. Cocoa is simply a bean that grows, primarily on the Ivory Coast, and from time to time the locusts will come and wreak havoc. Coffee is similarly a bean that Juan Valdez and others cultivate down in Colombia. By the same token, IBM is simply a stock that moves about on the New York Stock Exchange, its prices governed by supply and demand imbalances. What makes the movement of cocoa's price different from the movement of IBM's price? One could offer that there are no cocoa CEOs to be carried out of their offices in handcuffs for various improprieties. There are no claims of corporate malfeasance thrust upon live cattle. But in terms of what causes a change in price, there is nothing different between a share of IBM and a contract of coffee. IBM is to cocoa as coffee is to copper, and so on.

There is no question in my mind that the Point & Figure method of analysis is best suited to evaluating those basic imbalances between supply and demand. Charles Dow himself popularized this methodology in the late 1800s because he wanted a logical, sensible way of recording supply and demand in the market. This was the case in spite of the fact that he was a fundamentalist at heart. The Point & Figure chart fit beautifully with commodities and in very short order our company was in the commodity business nearly 20 years ago.

At the time, I had never seen a soybean, or a cocoa bean, or even a coffee bean that wasn't already ground. Armed with the Point & Figure chart, I was an expert in their price movement just the same. I knew that if there were more buyers than sellers willing to sell gold, the price of gold would rise. Conversely, if there were more sellers than buyers willing to buy gold, the price would decline. If supply and demand for gold was in perfect balance, the price would remain the same. There is nothing else to consider. In October 1987, I created our first commodity report and had it marketed to a firm by the name of Interstate Securities. They had one of the most progressive commodity departments in the country and immediately liked what we had to offer.

Still, it turned out to be the right product at the wrong time. The stock market was in the middle of a 20-year bull market, while commodities were amidst a 20-year bear market. The report we had created didn't take off as we would have hoped; it was, quite simply, 13 years early.

Had we hung our hat on this single product, or any single product really, we would have ended up in Wall Street's graveyard, as Mr. Hamilton suggests in Chapter 1. The beauty of Point & Figure is that it is adaptive to any free market, and while the commodity business was ready to contract significantly for the next 13 years, the Point & Figure Technical Analysis skill we had developed for many years prior to Watson's and my starting Dorsey, Wright & Associates was applicable to many other facets of Wall Street.

There was one more act to the commodity show before we allowed it to atrophy back in 1987. There was a hedge fund manager in Europe who was a client of ours on the equity side. I talked to him one day and told him that his temperament was more suited to commodity trading. I offered him our commodity report for free so that he could get familiar with trading commodities on paper before venturing into the real world of platinum and pork bellies. This began a long and intriguing story at DWA, much of which I can only look back on and shake my head. It took this client about three months to get used to commodities and then one day I received a call from him, "Tommy, I'm ready." I replied, "Ready for what? " Unabashedly, he offered, "Commodity trading." Well, the rubber hit the road that second, and I was immediately called upon to advise this large hedge fund on commodity trading, and I had never traded the first commodity in my life. I had a disciplined methodology to fall back on, but very little else at that time.

I set up this client with an introducing broker to clear through and we were off and running. If you can recall the last time you sat down to watch the Kentucky Derby, the horses are all in the gates, the bell rings, the commentator then offers heartily, "And they're off." Well, that was us. This hedge fund manger had the intestinal fortitude of either a gladiator or one of those "lovely apprentices" that allows someone to throw knives at them. We started trading 500 lots of currencies at a time. A 500-contract position in something like the euro today is still a massive position, over 83 million US dollars worth of euros. At that time I either didn't or couldn't fully conceptualize the scope of these positions; it was simply colossal. Come to think of it, I don't think we ever had a calculator that would quantify that amount of leverage back then, so we just didn't get the full flavor of the risk we were taking. Today, I would break out into a cold sweat with a position that size. But back then, we did it, did it regularly, and didn't flinch. Buying 600 gold contracts for this client became commonplace. At this writing, each contract controls 100 ounces, or $50,000, worth of gold. Six hundred contracts is then $30,000,000 in leverage. Still, this client didn't even breathe heavily with a position of this magnitude, and so eventually, neither did I. At any given moment, we could have been long 500 yen, 500 British pounds, or 500 Canadian dollars, and I vividly remember at one time being long 2,000 contracts of various currencies.

My entire day and night was devoted to this account. He required me to have one of the first cell phones available at the time so that we could be in constant contact. This phone would be called a "suitcase" by today's standards but it was cutting edge at the time. He would have me take the Concorde to Europe to simply have dinner with him. It was the wildest time I have ever experienced in my 31 years in the business; and just as many stories of excess unfold, this did not end well. Strangely enough, it was not the commodity trading that eventually caused his fund to hemorrhage; it was actually a risk arbitrage trade in United Airlines. He was, as today's Texas Hold'em player might say, "all in." To this day I am reluctant to even consider "deal" stocks, as I have witnessed someone hold out for the last drop of a merger deal that eventually fell through. The fund imploded as a result.

Seeing this type of thing take place firsthand is surreal, and after that our commodity research took its place on the back burner of what we do here at DWA. There just wasn't the demand present to suggest otherwise. We focused on our stock research and this is where we built a strong business that finished its twentieth year in 2006. The key to our success over time has been our ability to adapt to the changing landscape. The Point & Figure methodology is one of the few forms of analysis that truly allows one to do so in such a seamless fashion. Five years ago we were able to correctly identify a new positive trend developing in the broad commodity markets, and thus we dusted off the old commodity charts and began actively trading a corporate commodity account. Even employing very little of the potential leverage available within a commodity account, this portfolio has performed exceptionally well, which we will discuss in more detail later in this book. While my experiences trading currency futures 500 lots at a time makes for a good story, the comfort I feel today in the commodities market is far more a function of simply having a logical, disciplined approach toward managing risk to fall back on. I feel as comfortable trading commodities as I do stocks. I still don't know what a soybean or a cocoa bean looks like, but I have been very successful trading them nonetheless.

What we will aim to do in this book is teach you what we know about trading the commodity markets using the Point & Figure method. We would suggest that you familiarize yourself with some of the basics of commodity trading, such as hours of trading, contract sizes, and other environmental influences. All of this information is readily available on the Internet or in other various commodity books. We won't rehash that work, but will rather focus specifically on using the Point & Figure tools to develop a disciplined trading plan for commodities. We will also examine the many commodity-related vehicles that are present in today's markets outside that of strictly futures contracts. I think you will be both amazed and delighted to see the various instruments available to you in today's market.

For a handful of reasons, this book is unique for Dorsey, Wright & Associates when compared to the many others we have authored to date. First, this book is a collaboration of all my analysts who participate in managing and advising our very successful Corporate Commodity Account. The collaboration doesn't end there. We also teamed up with Josh Parker on this book. Josh is a partner of Gargoyle Asset Management LLC and is the manager of their Hedged Value Fund, which I have participated in for many years. Josh is a past trader on the AMEX floor and one of the authorities on trading whose input I respect greatly. Second, this book is the first book we've written that is totally devoted to commodity trading using the Point & Figure method of analysis. We have found over the last 30 years that the irrefutable law of supply and demand governs all prices whether it is cocoa, Japanese yen, or IBM. The simpler one keeps trading, the better the results. In this book, we present our results from the DWA corporate commodity account, which adheres to the principles of Point & Figure charting, which in its simplest form is a logical organized method of recording the imbalances between supply and demand. The leverage we used was so low, one might even consider our commodity investing account to be on a cash basis.

With this book, we have strived to give anyone interested in commodity trading, a logical, organized, sensible method of managing such an account utilizing the Point & Figure methodology. To help you in continuing to manage a commodity account, whether through futures, exchange-traded funds, or mutual funds, you will find all the charts, relative strength analysis, and commentary you need at www.dorseywright.com. If you are not already a client, you can take advantage of a three-week free trial of the largest Internet charting system in the world at www.dorseywright.com.

CHAPTER 1

Developing a Trading System

"If you bet on a horse, that's gambling. If you bet you can make three spades, that's entertainment. If you bet cotton will go up three points, that's business. See the difference?"
—Blackie Sherrod (b. 1922), U.S. sportscaster and sports writer

There are only two reasons to trade—because you enjoy the "game" or because you want to make money. There is absolutely nothing wrong with trading for fun. Everyone has a hobby. If yours is golf or tennis or bridge, you are not primarily concerned with the cost of your hobby, except to the extent that it should not adversely affect your (or your spouse's) present or future lifestyle. If your hobby is investing or trading, the same rules should apply. You need to know that it is a hobby, that it will likely cost you money, and that you will need to take precautions to ensure that it will not affect your present or future lifestyle.

Since you are reading this book, my guess is that your approach to trading is not that of a hobbyist. While you may enjoy trading, as I do, you want to win at the "game," and that means making money. But do not start trading with the idea that it is an easy way to get rich. Like any other endeavor, it requires hard work. The good news is that it is a lot easier to learn to trade or invest like a pro than it is to learn to play golf like Tiger Woods.

"There are no secrets to success. Don't waste your time looking for them. Success is the result of perfection, hard work, learning from failure, ... and persistence."
—Colin Powell (b. 1937), former U.S. Secretary of State and Chairman of the Joint Chiefs of Staff
"No profession requires more hard work, intelligence, patience, and mental discipline than successful speculation."
—Robert Rhea, U.S. Dow theorist and author, *The Dow Theory*, 1932

Anyone can make money in the markets. All it takes is (1) the willingness to work hard to find a profitable approach and (2) the patience and discipline to adhere to that approach. Unfortunately, too many people either cannot or will not take the time to develop a profitable approach or, worse yet, having developed one, they find excuses to override it (e.g., "It's different this time").

"Charts not only tell what was, they tell what is; and a trend from was to is (projected linearly into the will be) contains better percentages than clumsy guessing."
—R. A. Levy

Since its inception in 1987, Dorsey, Wright & Associates (DWA) has been providing its clients with the tools to develop a solid game plan for profitably trading. Their tools of choice are Point & Figure charts, which dispassionately record the tug and pull between supply and demand. This dispassion is important because it permits you to analyze a stock, a commodity, a sector of a market or the market at large without the fog of emotion. Unlike bar chart patterns, such as their head-and-shoulder or cup-and-saucer formations, which are notoriously subjective, Point & Figure signals are objective and unambiguous and can therefore be back tested for profitability, a necessary prerequisite for developing a winning approach to the markets.

"If you are not willing to study, if you are not sufficiently interested to investigate and analyze the stock market yourself, then I beg of you to become an outright long-pull investor, to buy good stocks, and hold on to them; for otherwise your chances of success as a trader are nil."
—Humphrey B. Neill, U.S. editor of *The Neill Letter of Contrary Opinion, Tape Reading and Market Tactics*, 1931

If your background is stock investing—long-term buying and holding that seeks appreciation over time and, perhaps, dividends—you will need to change your time horizon and focus. Commodities are about trading, not investing. One could invest in commodities, for example, by collecting art or coins for long-term appreciation or by buying and holding gold or gold futures as a hedge against inflation or by buying and holding foreign currency or foreign currency futures as a hedge against adverse changes in the exchange rate. But most people (other than hedgers) trade commodities for the purpose of profiting from relatively short-term swings either directly or by investing with a commodity-trading adviser (CTA) or in a commodity pool. In the latter case, the CTA or commodity pool operator does not invest in commodities either; he trades commodities for the purpose of profiting from relatively short-term swings.

> "Wall Street's graveyards are filled with men who were right too soon."
> —William Hamilton (1867–1929), U.S. editor
> of the *Wall Street Journal* and chief popularizer of
> the Dow theory in the 1920s

> "It isn't as important to buy as cheap as possible as it is to buy at the right time."
> —Jesse Livermore (1877–1940), legendary
> stock trader immortalized in *Reminisces of a
> Stock Operator* (Edwin Lefèvre, 1994)

Why does this make a difference? Because the shorter your time horizon, the more critical it is to select the correct entry point and the more important it is to pay attention to the technical characteristics (as opposed to the fundamental characteristics) of a stock or commodity. If you are buying a stock or commodity this week with the intention of holding it for, say, 20 years, your exact entry point will have little impact on your ultimate rate of return. For example, suppose XYZ is "worth" $20 per share and will grow at the long-term stock market rate of return of 10 percent per year. At the end of 20 years, XYZ will be "worth" $134.55. If you missed your entry by 5 percent and bought XYZ at $19 per share or $21 per share, your ultimate compound annual rate of return would not be much different than 10 percent to 10.28 percent and 9.73 percent, respectively. If, however, you are a trader looking for your stock or commodity to appreciate to $25 within six months, now your entry point makes a huge difference (see Exhibit 1.1).

Bought at	Rate of return if sold at $25 after 6 months	Annualized Rate of return
19	31.58%	73.13%
20	25.00%	56.25%
21	19.05%	41.72%

EXHIBIT 1.1 Rate of Return.

In short, the shorter the time horizon, the more critical it is to get in (and out) at the "right" price.

A word of caution: If you want to trade the commodities market as part of your overall asset allocation plan, you may be making a grave mistake; trading commodities is not investing in commodities. An "asset class" is a category of investments, all of which share similar risk/reward characteristics and are used to address similar risks. For example, the grains—wheat, rye, corn, and so on—have similar risk/reward characteristics and help address the risk of core inflation. Since trading commodities does not hedge you against commodity inflation, it should not be included with those assets that you have earmarked for the commodities asset class. To put it another way, the objective of asset allocation is to spread your investments among different asset classes either to reduce the volatility of your overall portfolio or to target those areas of risk to your long-term financial health. While the reward/risk profile of trading commodities may justify its inclusion in your overall asset allocation plan, it is not a substitute for an investment in commodities for the purpose of protecting you against some commodity-specific risk (such as inflation or change in exchange rate).

Returning from my brief digression of technical analysis, there is nothing I could add to a DWA discussion of Point & Figure charting. But whether (and when) a particular stock or commodity is a good buy (or sale) is only part of a successful trading approach. A successful trading approach also requires, at a minimum:

- Rules for determining how much of your assets you will invest on any particular trade.
- Rules for exiting a trade both (a) if the trade is going in your favor and (b) if it goes against you.

It is amazing how many people have good ideas as to when to enter a trade, but no idea as to when to exit the trade or how big to trade. The good news is that, as I've learned over the years, the keys to successful trading are universal. As such, I hope that the broader principles that have guided my professional and personal trading over the past 20 years will help you discover for yourself how you can trade the commodities markets successfully.

> "It may be that the race is not always to the swift nor the battle to the strong—but that is the way to bet."
> —Damon Runyon (1884–1946), U.S. journalist,
> sports columnist, and short-story writer

There is one and only one way to make money in the markets and that is by applying a strategy with positive mathematical expectancy. This is the secret to casinos and insurance companies. Sure, a casino or insurance company can lose money on any given day or to one or another customer (or hurricane) but they "can't" be beaten over the long run. For example, say someone walks into your casino with $100 in his pocket to play craps. Even if he were to employ his best strategy, you still have a 1.36 percent edge. This means that, after he has bet his $100, you "expect" to earn $1.36. But it is even better than that. Your edge is based on the amount of money he wagers, not the amount of money he earmarked for the craps table, a fact frequently overlooked by casino customers, to the glee of many a casino. So, if a customer arrives at your casino with $100 in his pocket and things go as expected, you will earn $1.36 only if he manages to limit his wagering to just $100. If he is like most people, he will keep wagering as long as there is still money in his pocket. If, because of his occasional wins, he is able to stretch his $100 so that he can place one hundred $5 bets, the entire $500 is subject to your edge, and you "rate" to earn $6.80 ($500 × 1.36%) before the customer leaves your casino.

Also, entering a trade is only half the battle. Too many traders pay an inordinate amount of attention to finding an approach with a high winning percentage for entering trades and pay absolutely no attention as to when to exit a trade. This is one of the two biggest mistakes traders make in constructing a trading strategy. (The other is not knowing how much to invest in a given trade.) A successful strategy requires both an entry strategy and two different exit strategies—one for exiting if the trade moves against you ("cut your losses short") and the other for exiting winning trades. Without entry *and* exit rules, you cannot determine whether your strategy is sound.

> "In investing money, the amount of interest you want should depend on whether you want to eat well or sleep well."
> —J. Kenfield Morley (1838–1923), British
> journalist, *Some Things I Believe*

> "If you don't know who you are, the stock market is an expensive place
> to find out."
> —George J. W. Goodman (b. 1930), U.S.
> portfolio manager and author (under the nom de
> plume Adam Smith)

What particular approach should you employ? That depends on *you*.
How you invest or trade is as personal as your choice in clothes, food, and
spouse. It is a reflection of your personality. Do you prefer a high chance
of success with low payoff or a low chance of success with a high payoff?
Do you prefer investing in out-of-favor stocks or commodities (so-called
value investing) that may take a while to turn profitable or investing in "hot
stocks" that could make or lose your money quickly (so-called momentum
trading). Based on your (reasonable) preferences, you *will* be able to fashion a positive mathematical expectancy strategy. So, for example, if you
like buying the "hot" stock or commodity, you should fashion your trading
around a breakout system. A number of years ago, DWA conducted several
studies showing that certain bullish patterns have a very high probability of
trading higher by a significant percentage. Several more recent academic
studies show that relative-strength stocks from one year tend to outperform the next year.

> "The time to buy is when blood is running in the streets."
> —Baron Nathan Rothschild (London
> financier, 1777–1836)

I, however, am a contrarian by nature. It was key to my success as an
"options market maker" on the American Exchange (AMEX) floor. To me,
it is logical that different stocks, commodities, real estate, art, widgets, or
anything else you can think of, fall in and out of favor. The market is emotional, not rational, in the short term. At times and for a time, everyone
"needs" to own a particular investment or be involved in a particular fad.
As a contrarian, I watch for those times when something is irrationally in
or out of fashion and apply Point & Figure charts to determine when the
sentiment may be turning. To be more concrete, in my hedge fund, I quantify the various fundamental criteria—price-to-earnings (P/E) ratio, price-
to-book, price-to-sales, and so on—to determine when a stock is underval-
ued and use Point & Figure charts to help me determine when the "knife
has stopped falling." Value determines what to buy; charts determine when
to buy.

In a similar vein, I am a contrarian in my commodity investing. Since I
have enough on my plate managing my hedge fund, I do not trade the commodity markets directly. Instead, I trade the commodity markets by invest-

ing with commodity trading advisers. I do this for several reasons. First, most CTAs charge the same amount, typically a 1 percent management fee and a 20 percent incentive fee. Thus, I can invest with a good trader for the same price as I can invest with a not-so-good trader. This appeals to my sense of value.

Second, the commodity markets have been very difficult to trade over the past several years (2004 was an exception). Many CTAs have left the commodity markets for the greener pastures of hedge funds. Those CTAs who stayed have spent, and spend, exhaustive amounts of time developing and evolving their systems. The CTAs who are left have proven, in true Darwinian fashion, that they are the best. From a logical point of view, this appeals to me.

Third, most CTAs are trend followers. Sometimes a CTA's system is in step with the markets, and sometimes it is not. As a contrarian, I wait for a CTA to experience a significant loss, and then I invest. ("Significant" will vary from CTA to CTA, depending on a CTA's particular risk tolerance.) By taking this approach, I lower the cost of entry, improve the percentage chance of success, and gain the benefit of the CTA's experience in handling difficult times in the past. It's not foolproof. It's not a sure thing. But it has served me well over time.

Contrarian investing is not for everyone, however, and it is not nearly as sexy as momentum investing. Being a value investor during the tech bubble of the 1990s was not fun. It seemed that everyone I met at neighborhood parties was crushing the market. I don't know how many friends, family, and neighbors told me how, with Yahoo at, say, $340, they had "shrewdly" purchased it only weeks earlier at $150. I knew that the greater-fool theory of trading works for only so long, but it seemed that the laws of nature were being suspended for an exceedingly long time.

> "In this game, the market has to keep pitching, but you don't have to swing. You can stand there with the bat on your shoulder for six months until you get a fat pitch."
> —Warren Buffet (b. 1930), legendary U.S.
> investor, philanthropist, and second richest man in
> the world

> "There's nothing wrong with cash. It gives you time to think."
> —Robert Prechter Jr. (b. 1949), Elliott Wave
> theorist and guru of the 1980s (according to
> Financial News Network)

Finally, and perhaps more importantly, select a time horizon that matches how frequently you like to trade. If you are already comfortable with trading, you probably know how easy it is to put on a trade dictated by your system. What frustrates most traders is waiting for a signal. The worst thing that a trader can do—and I've seen it many times on the floor of the AMEX—is to trade out of boredom. Your system works only when you put on the trades that are dictated by the proven system that you created. If you force trades, you are lowering the positive expectancy of your system, thereby simultaneously reducing your long-term profitability and undermining your confidence in your system. Don't do it.

> "Those who cannot remember the past are condemned to repeat it."
> —George Santayana (1863–1952), U.S.
> (Spanish-born) philosopher, *The Life of Reason*,
> Volume 1, 1905

> "In the stock market those who expect history to repeat itself exactly are doomed to failure."
> —Yale Hirsch, U.S. publisher, *Stock Trader's
> Almanac*

You can never know for certain whether your strategy will be profitable in the future. The best you can hope for is that your strategy is logical and that it has been historically profitable. So, if your strategy is logical, but your back test shows that it was a loser historically, do not trade it. Assuming the past is relevant to the future, you will be trading a losing system. Conversely, regardless of past results, if your strategy is illogical (e.g., going long or short the stock market based on who won the Super Bowl, a particular alignment of the stars, the length of women's skirts, the width of men's ties, etc.), do not trade it.

> "There are three kinds of lies: lies, damn lies, and statistics."
> —Benjamin Disraeli (1804–1881), English
> statesman and prime minister

In my youth, I would let the numbers alone dictate my trading. I did not do anything as foolish as let the winner of the Super Bowl determine my trades, but I did not give enough weight to the logic behind a particular trading approach. One of peculiarities of statistics is that with enough data—price, volume, time, Super Bowl winners, celestial patterns, the length of women's skirts, the width of men's ties, and on and on—you can always find two completely unrelated items that show a high degree of statistical correlation. In fact, it can be statistically proven that out of 500 studies, each of which is over 99 percent accurate, it is more than 99 percent certain that at least one of the studies is wrong. I hope you will learn from my mistake and select a trading approach that is both logical and has a historically verifiable positive mathematical expectancy.

> "This year I invested in pumpkins. They've been going up the whole month of October and I got a feeling they're going to peak right around January. Then bang! That's when I'll cash in.
> —Homer Simpson (b. 1955 or 1956, depending on episode), U.S. cartoon character

So, if you cannot trust the back tests and you cannot trust your common sense, what do you do? Actually, the prior two paragraphs do not contradict each other. I use back tests to disprove the validity of a trading strategy, not to create a trading strategy. In other words, I do a lot of reading and thinking about a particular market that interests me. The goal is to get an understanding of what makes the market move. I then form a testable entry-rule hypothesis (such as buy above the bullish support line on a double top) and a testable exit-rule hypothesis (exit the position if there is a subsequent double bottom break or if the horizontal or vertical price target is met). Finally, I test the enter-and-exit strategy for profitability. If all goes according to my thinking, I will now have a logical, profitable, historically verified approach.

> "The less a man knows about the past and the present the more insecure must be his judgment about the future."
> —Sigmund Freud (1856–1939), Austrian psychologist

There is another reason you want a logical strategy that is historically verifiable. Whatever approach you select, there will come a time when it seems that it will never signal another winning trade. Unless you are confident in your reasoning and "know" what to expect, you will find it exceedingly difficult, if not impossible, to weather this inevitable bad patch. By reexamining your thinking and reexamining (and continually updating) your back test, you can see whether the bad patch is within the range of "normal" or a cause for concern.

> "It is not how right or wrong you are that matters, but how much money you make when right and how much you do not lose when wrong."
> —George Soros (b. 1930), U.S. (Hungarian-born) billionaire fund manager and philanthropist

> "Markets can remain irrational longer than you can remain solvent."
> —John Maynard Keynes (1883–1946), British economist and author, considered by many to be the leading economist of the twentieth century

I hate to tell you this but just having a logical, historically verifiable profitable strategy is not enough. You also need good money management skills. There are two sides to this coin. First, you do not want to invest more than you could comfortably lose. When I was on the floor of the AMEX, there was a trader who would frequently say "good for a one lot, good for a 1,000 lot." In other words, if a trade met his reward/risk parameters, he would be willing to put on that particular trade as large as the other side was willing. When things were going well for him, they were going very, very well. Unfortunately, the inevitable occurred. He put on a high-probability stock-and-options play in Yahoo when Yahoo was trading at $187. Believe it or not, had he never touched the position, he would have made $250,000. Unfortunately, Yahoo immediately ran up to almost $400, at which time he was forced (he wasn't eating *or* sleeping well) to hedge the position. His hedge then came back to bite him when the stock cracked. All in all, he *lost* over $250,000 because the initial position was just too big.

Avoiding playing too big is not the whole battle, however. If your goal is to maximize your rate of return (as opposed to just make a certain amount of money), it is also important not to play too small, although the repercussions are not nearly as dire. This means trading a portion of your investable assets at each and every opportunity. So, for example, suppose we agreed to play the following game: I will flip a fair coin. For every dollar you wager, I will pay you $1.25 for a head and you will pay me $1.00 for a tail. Clearly, this is a game that you want to play, but what is your money management strategy for maximizing the size of your investable assets?

Let's say you start with $1,000. If you bet it all every time, you will lose as soon as one tail comes up—and you will not be able to continue to play the game to win back your bankroll. However, if you invest, say, $50 each time, barring a run of 20 initial tails or subsequent strings that are predominantly tails, after 1,000 coin flips, you "expect" to make $6,250. If more than half the flips are heads, you will do better than that; if more than half are tails, you will do worse. All in all, not a bad return.

Your optimal strategy, however, is to invest 10 percent of your assets every time. First, since you never invest your last dollar: you cannot lose it all. Second, after 1,000 coin flips, you "expect" to make $49,732.88. This is a clear winner over even the best equal-dollar money-management strategy. Interestingly enough, underinvesting or overinvesting by the same amount produces the same (suboptimal) result.

You needn't remember all this. The important point is that, while a strategy that has a positive mathematical expectancy is necessary to your success, it is not sufficient; you also need good money management. Or, to put it another way, bad money management can make a good strategy a loser, but good money management cannot make a bad strategy a winner.

> "Compound interest is the eighth wonder of the world, the greatest mathematical discovery of all time."
> —Albert Einstein (1879–1955), U.S.
> (German-born) physicist and Nobel laureate

Investing is not a get-rich-quick scheme. It is a slow, consistent process that takes advantage of what Albert Einstein (yes, that Albert Einstein) called the eighth wonder of the world—compound interest. If Peter Minuet, who supposedly paid $24 in beads to purchase Manhattan Island from the local Canarsee Indians in 1624, had instead invested the $24 at 10 percent—the long-term rate of return of the stock market—his $24 would have been worth almost $142 quadrillion (that's 142 followed by 15 zeroes) today. Since all of Manhattan is worth only a fraction of a fraction of that amount, one wonders who got the raw deal!

Compound interest has many fascinating features. For example, a 10 percent compound annual rate of return is far more than twice as good as a 5 percent compound annual rate of return. If you were to invest $100,000 for 10 years at a 10 percent compound annual rate of return, you would have made almost $160,000, while at a 5 percent compound annual rate of return, you would have made closer to one-third of that amount—or a little over $60,000. The longer you do this, the more meaningful the difference.

The difference in the rate of return needs not to be so dramatic. Adding just 1 percent to your compound annual rate of return can have an outsized impact on the size of your account after a number of years. For example, increasing your compound annual rate of return from 5 percent to 6 percent will increase your profitability by almost 50 percent after 30 years (see Exhibit 1.2).

Compound Rate of Return	Profits after 5 Years	Profits after 10 Years	Profits after 20 Years	Profits after 30 Years
5%	$ 27,628	$ 62,889	$ 165,330	$ 332,194
6%	$ 33,823	$ 79,085	$ 220,714	$ 474,349
10%	$ 61,051	$ 159,373	$ 572,750	$ 1,644,940

EXHIBIT 1.2 The Wonder of Compounding.

> "Slow and steady wins the race."
> —Aesop, c. 620 B.C.E.–564 B.C.E., Greek
> fabulist

How do you achieve a high compound rate of return? By looking for strategies that produce less fluctuation in the trade-to-trade rate of return. Most traders would see no difference between alternately making and losing 3 percent per month for one year versus alternately making and losing 10 percent per month for one year. In each case the arithmetic average is 0 percent, but arithmetic averages are misleading. Both traders are losers. The 10 percent-per-month trader would be out $5,852 after one year or more than *10* times as much as the 3 percent-per-month trader's loss of $539. In fact, the 3 percent-per-month trader is even better off than a trader who alternately makes 11 percent but loses only 10 percent (an arithmetic average of +1/2 percent per month), for the latter would still lose $599 after one year. So, when you are evaluating your trading strategy, be sure not to look at just the arithmetic average rate of return. You also need to examine how volatile the individual component returns are.

I know I have covered a book's worth of material in one chapter, and a short chapter at that. Don't lose heart. The rules are simple and can be taken a step at a time:

1. Decide on a trading approach that makes sense to you and is consistent with your personality.
2. Establish rules for entering and exiting the trades selected by your approach.
3. Test the approach to ensure that it is historically sound.
4. Determine how much of your investable income you want to devote to this approach as well as to each trade mandated by the approach. Do not base it on the prior worst losing streak. My own personal rule is that the worst losing streak is yet to come.
5. Stick to your approach. After spending all the time and energy on steps (1) through (4) do not override your approach for *ad hoc* reasons.
6. Have fun.

CHAPTER 2

Patterns, Trends, and Price Objectives

A s with any educationally geared book, like this one, it is important to start by laying a foundation. Just as with building a house, you must start block by block when laying the house's foundation. If this process is not properly done, then the house has little chance of sheltering you from the elements, let alone standing. The same can be said with respect to trading stocks, or commodities, with the Point & Figure method. So we begin this book with the basics—the building blocks of the Point & Figure methodology: patterns and trend lines. For some, this will likely be a review; for those new to technical analysis, and in particular Point & Figure, you will want to take your time working through this chapter, because everything to follow will build on this chapter's discussion. I have used this old saying in my life and it works: "Life's a cinch by the inch; life's hard by the yard." Take this subject inch by inch and you will catch on very quickly. Try to bite off too much at a time and, like anything else, it becomes overwhelming.

The cornerstone of the Point & Figure (P&F) methodology is the irrefutable law of supply and demand. It is this simple economic concept that is responsible for the formation of the chart—in essence, the battle that is waged between supply and demand, and its related price changes, results in the different patterns being formed, and ultimately the overall trend of the commodity. I have found that commodity trading is actually easier than stock trading; it is pure supply and demand. Copper is just copper—it's a hunk of metal, nothing more, nothing less. There is no chief executive officer, earnings, fundamental reports, product acceptance, or competition. It is what it is. I guess you could say there are fewer moving parts in trading commodities than in trading stocks.

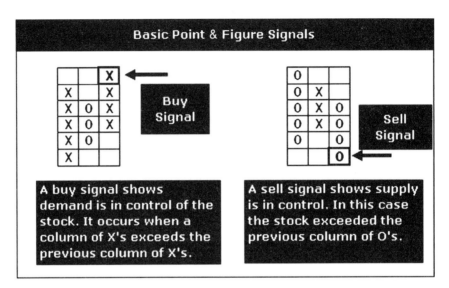

EXHIBIT 2.1   Basic Point & Figure Signals.

CHART PATTERNS

In the P&F methodology there are 11 types of patterns. But for all intents and purposes, nine of these patterns are merely derivatives of the two most basic patterns—the double top and double bottom. And you know what? You will see the double top and double bottom more than any other pattern in commodities. Commodities don't spend much time in one place moving back and forth like a stock can (see Exhibit 2.1).

Now as we have said, all patterns build from the basic double top (buy signal) and double bottom (sell signal). In Exhibits 2.2 and 2.3, we have laid out static examples of the remaining nine P&F patterns. You will want to take some time to review these patterns, to understand which are bullish and which are bearish, and to learn the main characteristics of each. The ultimate goal, of course, is for you to be able to recognize these specific chart patterns, and by doing so make informed buy and sell decisions. (For more information on P&F chart patterns and the basics of charting, we would recommend Thomas J. Dorsey, *Point & Figure Charting*, 3rd ed. Hoboken, N.J.: John Wiley & Sons, 2007.) Once you have a good feel for the patterns, the easy part is simply to have our database charting system search the commodity constituents for specific patterns. We have taught our system to do the work for you. For example, you can ask our system to pull or search for all the bullish catapult formations in the commodity universe (Exhibit 2.2). It helps to cut to the chase when you actually begin trading.

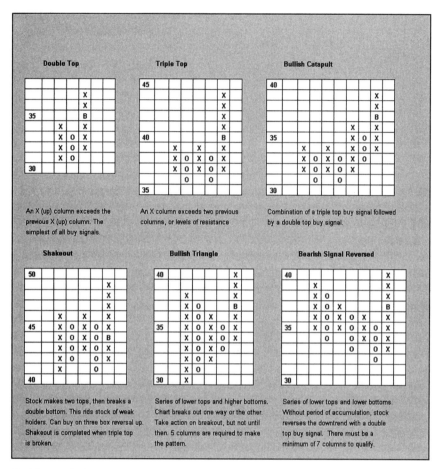

EXHIBIT 2.2 Bullish Point & Figure Patterns.

Now let's take our newly learned knowledge of chart patterns and apply it to a real-life situation. In the two commodity charts in Exhibits 2.4 and 2.5 (cotton, March 2005 [CT/H5] and the Canadian dollar, June 2005 [CD/M5]), see if you can identify the different patterns that appear within each chart. The main point to remember is that when a "bottom" is broken, or exceeded, it is considered a sell signal, whereas when a "top" is broken, or exceeded, it is considered a buy signal.

TREND LINES

Now that you have a good handle on the different P&F patterns, let's turn our discussion to trend lines. One of the main premises of technical

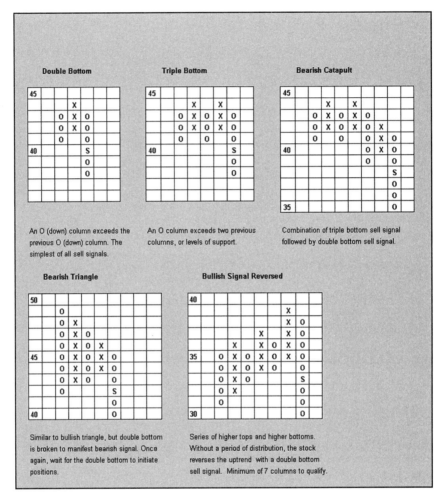

EXHIBIT 2.3 Bearish Point & Figure Patterns.

analysis is that prices tend to trend. Therefore, one of the main purposes of a chart is to help in the identification of the overall trend of a given commodity—and to then play the direction of that trend for as long as it stays in force. Trend lines aid in the determination of the overall trend of a financial instrument, be it a stock, mutual fund, or commodity. You can't imagine the money that could have been made by simply following the U.S. dollar's downtrend the past few years, and then just as importantly knowing when that trend changed to positive.

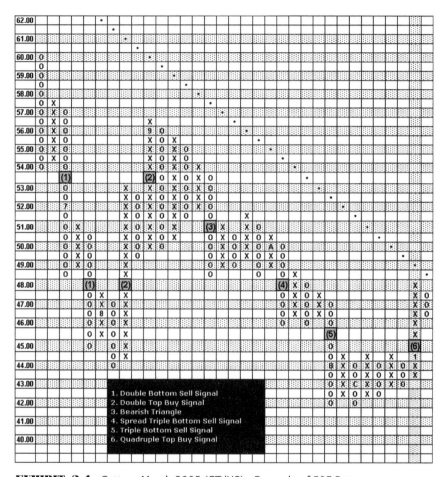

EXHIBIT 2.4 Cotton, March 2005 (CT/H5)—Example of P&F Patterns.

In the P&F methodology, two main trend lines are used: the bullish support line and the bearish resistance line. It is these trend lines that allow us to easily identify whether a commodity is in an overall "uptrend" or whether its main trend is negative and in a "downtrend." Trend lines are very easily drawn using the P&F method, whereas bar charts and other methods can be very subjective in nature. In the case of either of these two lines, it is uncanny how they can act like brick walls, with the commodity able to repeatedly bounce off the line and resume its trending bias. As well, the overall trend of a commodity, be it an uptrend or downtrend, can stay in force for months, if not years.

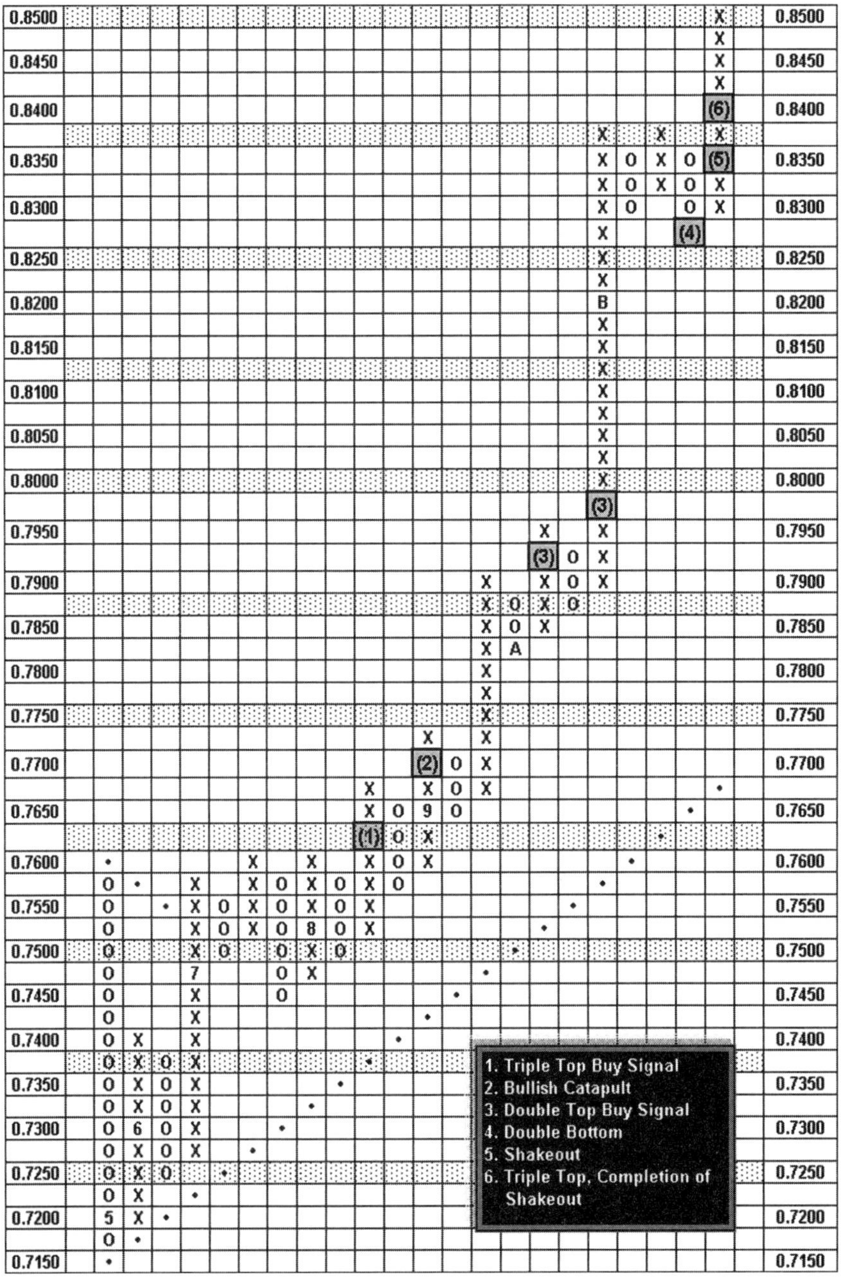
0.8500
0.8450
0.8400
0.8350
0.8300
0.8250
0.8200
0.8150
0.8100
0.8050
0.8000
0.7950
0.7900
0.7850
0.7800
0.7750
0.7700
0.7650
0.7600
0.7550
0.7500
0.7450
0.7400
0.7350
0.7300
0.7250
0.7200
0.7150
1. Triple Top Buy Signal
2. Bullish Catapult
3. Double Top Buy Signal
4. Double Bottom
5. Shakeout
6. Triple Top, Completion of Shakeout

EXHIBIT 2.5 Canadian Dollar, June 2005 (CD/M5).

The bullish support line is similarly known as the uptrend line. In other words, if your commodity is trading above its bullish support line, it is said to be in an overall uptrend. I've often referred to this line as Interstate 95 North; and as you might have guessed, the opposite, which we will discuss below, is Interstate 95 South. It stands to reason, then, that over time the only way a given commodity will stay in an overall uptrend is from recording higher prices. The bullish support line is always a 45-degree line, which is upward sloping to the right. Drawing this uptrend line is very easy—once the first buy signal is given, off the bottom or after a period of accumulation (moving sideways), you then go to the lowest-reaching column of O's in that pattern on the chart and begin drawing the trend line by placing a mark in the box directly below the lowest O. You then move up and over a box and place a second mark, and repeat this process, which will result in an upward sloping 45-degree-angled line—this is your bullish support line. In P&F charting this will always be the same.

As a general rule of thumb, if a commodity is trading above its bullish support line, in an overall uptrend, your trades should be limited to long positions. This is hard to do sometimes—it's like having to swing "easy" in golf to get the farthest drive. Of course, shorter-term trend lines can alter this posture, which we will discuss shortly, but your overall bias, long or short, will be determined by whether the commodity is trading above or below its bullish support line. Therefore, it is crucial for you to watch for a violation, or penetration, of the bullish support line, as that would be a sign that the overall trend is changing from positive to negative—or from an uptrend to a downtrend. A violation of the bullish support line, coupled with a sell signal (recall the discussion on chart patterns) on the commodity chart is a "call to action." It is a sign that you must change your current course of action with that particular commodity. Long positions, generally speaking, should be sold, or some type of protective action should be taken; short positions could then be considered as well. That's the interesting thing about commodity trading, unlike stock trading; once a commodity proves you are wrong in the direction of the trade, you should close it and execute an opposite trade going in the right direction. With stocks there is a ton of baggage that goes along with the thought process. You might be stopped out of a long position in a stock, but you would never go short for a whole host of reasons, so investors tend to simply search for another one of the 8,000 stocks that trade for their next venture. There are relatively few commodities that trade versus the number of equities that trade.

Exhibit 2.6 shows an example of a bullish support line on the chart of sugar, March 2005 (SB/H5). Notice how sugar "trended" higher for the better part of a year, continuing to show a series of higher tops and higher bottoms, while trading above its bullish support line. Therefore, when considering March sugar for a trade during this time frame, your bias would

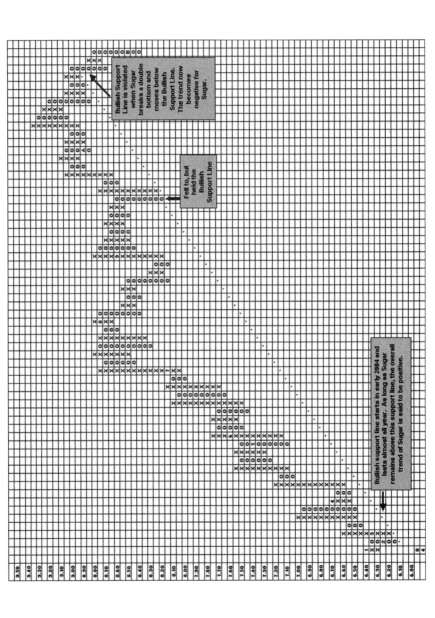

EXHIBIT 2.6 Sugar, March 2005 (SB/H5)—Example of Bullish Support Line.

have been to the long side given the uptrend in place. Also notice how the contract sold off to 8.20 in September 2004, yet managed to hold right at its bullish support line—it fell right to the trend line, yet did not penetrate it. For a trend line "violation" to occur, the line must be pierced, or penetrated, not merely touched. Sugar subsequently bounced back up off this trend line and resumed its upward bias. It wasn't until a month later that sugar violated its bullish support line at 8.85, as marked on the chart in Exhibit 2.6. At this point, long positions in sugar should have been stopped out and short positions considered.

The bearish resistance line is just the opposite of what we discussed above. As I mentioned above, it's Interstate 95 South. This particular trend line is also called the downtrend line, and as the word suggests, a commodity that is trading below its bearish resistance line is trending lower and is in what we would consider an overall negative or bearish trend. This obviously happens as a result of sustained lower prices. The bearish resistance line is basically a 45-degree line, well, actually the reciprocal of the 45-degree line. I think it's a 135-degree line. Since this is not a geometry course, suffice to say it's just the opposite of the bullish support line and is a downward sloping line to the right. Drawing this downtrend line is equally simple—you merely go to the highest column of X's on the chart, after a sell signal has been given, and place a mark in the box directly above that highest X. From there you go down and over a box, make another mark, then continue this process until your bearish resistance line has been drawn.

Conversely (to a commodity trading above its bullish support line), if the given commodity is trading below its bearish resistance line, in an overall downtrend, we would tend to restrict positions taken to shorts. Similar to the bullish support line, it is paramount that you monitor whether a commodity has penetrated its bearish resistance line, as this would signal a change from what had been a negative trend, to a bullish trend; this would then prompt a change from focusing on shorts to one focused on longs. In other words, the commodity would have changed direction from heading down Interstate 95 South to being on Interstate 95 North, headed up toward Bar Harbor, Maine.

Exhibit 2.7 is an example of a bearish resistance line on the chart of wheat, March 2005 (W/H5). As you can easily see, this commodity topped out in April 2004 at 440. After violating its longer-term bullish support line in May 2004 at 394, the bearish resistance line came into force and March wheat was considered to be trading in an overall downtrend. This downtrend persisted for many months, with wheat continuing to make lower tops and lower bottoms, falling in price to lows of 296. Short-term rallies have occurred for wheat, but all within the confines of an overall negative trend, and with the commodity always failing to make any headway on any approach to the line. So, in looking at Exhibit 2.7, it would take a move

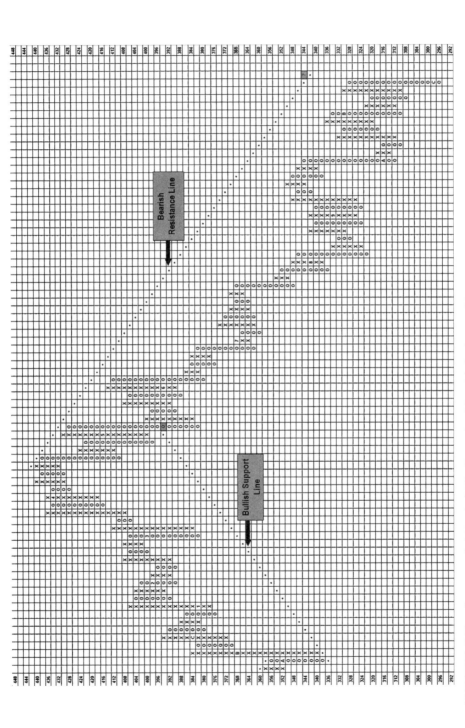

EXHIBIT 2.7 Wheat, March 2005 (W/H5)—Example of Bearish Resistance Line.

to 344 to penetrate the bearish resistance line, and thus suggest a change in trend (to positive) has transpired. Until such a violation occurs, though, your general posture with respect to wheat would be bearish, suggesting short positions. One last point we want to make on trend lines is that only one line is in force at any given time—a commodity is either trading above its bullish support line or trading below its bearish resistance line.

In sum, as a result of drawing trend lines, you are able to determine the overall trend of a commodity, and from this ascertain your trading posture, be it long or short. These trend lines easily quantify for you whether sugar, or wheat, or any other commodity is trending up or down, and allows you to "let the trend be your friend." By adapting your posture to the overall trend, you can let your winners run, staying with and catching a long-term trend. Or, should a trend change, it allows you to, more importantly, cut your losses short. Over time, this is one of the keys to success in trading both stocks and commodities.

According to Michael Marcus, "Ed Seykota is a genius and a great trader who has been phenomenally successful. . . . One time, he was short silver and the market just kept eking down, a half penny a day. Everyone else seemed to be bullish, talking about why silver had to go up because it was so cheap, but Ed just stayed short. Ed said, "The trend is down, and I'm going to stay short until the trend changes." (quoted in *Trend Following* 18)

Before finishing our discussion on trend lines, we want to talk about something we alluded to above: the raising and lowering of trend lines. Basically, here we are talking about drawing shorter-term trend lines. This is an equally easy process and serves to provide guidance as to what the trend of a commodity is on a short- to intermediate-term basis. The same general rules apply—you look to go long when the given commodity is trading above its bullish support line, and your posture is slanted toward shorts when trading below the bearish resistance line.

To illustrate how we can raise or lower a trend line, let's look again at the cotton, March 2005 (CT/H5) chart (Exhibit 2.8). At first glance, you can quickly see that the overall trend of cotton is bearish as the contract continues to trade below its long-term bearish resistance line. This longer-term downtrend line dates back to January 2004, when cotton was trading at 72.50. But, as this chart displays, you can draw subsequent shorter-term bearish resistance lines. In order to be able to do this, however, you must first see a buy signal followed by a sell signal. The process is the same in that you go to the highest column of X's just prior to the sell signal and then draw the line downward at a 45-degree angle. So we first were able to lower

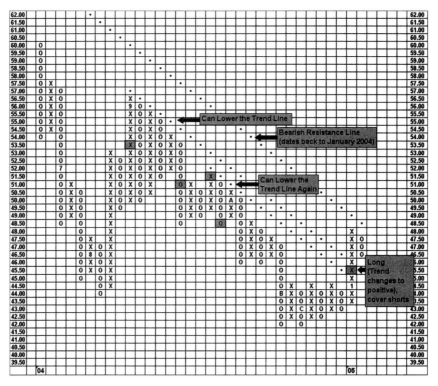

EXHIBIT 2.8 Cotton, March 2005 (CT/H5)—Example of Short-Term Bearish Resistance Line.

the bearish resistance line for cotton in September once the double bottom sell signal was given at 51.00 (in fact, this pattern was a bearish triangle). The highest X prior to the sell signal, but after a buy signal, was at 56.50, so we start drawing our new bearish resistance line at 57.00, then downward to the right. But we were able to lower the bearish resistance line one more time in this example. A double top buy signal was given at 51.50, then a double bottom sell signal at 48.50. This action allowed us to draw yet another, lower bearish resistance line, as the chart shows. In keeping with the posture we laid out earlier, any trades taken in cotton should have been relegated to shorts, even despite lowering the downtrend line. Why? The answer is that cotton continued to trade below its short-term bearish resistance line. A bias toward short positions would have been maintained until cotton penetrated its short-term bearish resistance line at 45.50 (following the quadruple top buy signal). Only then would you change your posture from having a short bias to one of considering long positions.

```
107.0 |                                                                      | 107.0
106.5 |                                                                      | 106.5
106.0 |                                                                      | 106.0
105.5 |                                                      •               | 105.5
105.0 |                                          X     X   •                 | 105.0
104.5 |                                          X O X O •                   | 104.5
104.0 |                                          X O X O     •               | 104.0
103.5 |                                          A O     O           •       | 103.5
103.0 |                            X     X     X       O          •          | 103.0
102.5 |                            X O X O X           O                     | 102.5
102.0 |                      X     X O X O X           O                     | 102.0
101.5 |                      X O X O X O               O                     | 101.5
101.0 |                      X O X O X                 B                     | 101.0
100.5 |                      X O X O X                 O                     | 100.5
100.0 |                X     X O X O X                 O                     | 100.0
 99.5 |          X     X O X 8       O X         •   O X                     | 99.5
 99.0 |          X O X O X           O X           •   O X O X               | 99.0
 98.5 |          X O X O X           9           •     O X O X O             | 98.5
 98.0 |          X O X O X                   •         O X O X O             | 98.0
 97.5 |          X O 7 O X                 •           O X O     O           | 97.5
 97.0 |      X   X O X O X                •             O         O          | 97.0
 96.5 |      X O X O X O X              •                 O                  | 96.5
 96.0 |      X O X O   O              •                     O   O            | 96.0
 95.5 |  X   X O X           •   ← Raised the bullish support      •   O     | 95.5
 95.0 |  X O X O X         •                                 •   O           | 95.0
 94.5 |  X O X O         •                                       •           | 94.5
 94.0 |  O X 6 X       •                                   •                 | 94.0
 93.5 |  O X O X     •                                         •             | 93.5
 93.0 |  O   O X   •                                       •                 | 93.0
 92.5 |  O   •                                           •                   | 92.5
 92.0 |      •                                     •   ← Bullish support line| 92.0
 91.5 |                                          •                           | 91.5
 91.0 |                                      •                               | 91.0
 90.5 |                                  •                                   | 90.5
 90.0 |                              •                                       | 90.0
```

EXHIBIT 2.9   Feeder Cattle, March 2005 (FC/H5)—Example of Short-Term Bullish Support Line.

Raising the bullish support line is done in a similar fashion, except that you must first see a sell signal followed by a buy signal. An example of this can be seen in Exhibit 2.9 with feeder cattle, March 2005 (FC/H5).

PRICE OBJECTIVES

Price objectives are a key component in determining the risk-reward ratio of a trade, and proper analysis of risk versus reward in any trade is imperative to your long-term success in trading commodities. In a later chapter, we discuss in detail how to calculate the risk-reward ratio, and how this applies to your trading.

With P&F charting, we use two different methods for calculating price objectives—the vertical count and horizontal count. Suffice to say, the concept behind calculating price objectives resides in the science of ballistics—how far a bullet will travel after its initial impulse, based on the size of its powder keg, the size and attitude of its barrel, air temperature, and other germane factors. These same principles can be applied to commodities by looking at such characteristics as the size of the base of accumulation or distribution, and the length of the move "off the bottom" (or top). By no means is a price objective a guarantee as to where a given commodity will rise or fall, but it does provide a guideline as to where you might expect to see it travel. And, as we alluded to, this is a crucial component to know when ascertaining the risk versus reward of a given trade.

As stated earlier, there are two types of counts—the vertical price objective and horizontal price objective. With each type, you can determine a bullish and bearish price objective. Below, we walk you through how to calculate both of these types of counts. Typically, we use the vertical count when calculating a price objective, yet when afforded the opportunity of a big base of accumulation or distribution, we will turn to the horizontal count to provide us with a price target. When both methods are available on the chart, use the more conservative of the two counts.

Vertical Price Objective

Upside, Bullish Target Using a Vertical Count   Look to the column that has the first buy signal off the bottom (following the last sell signal) and count the number of X's in it. You wait for the reversal down into a column of O's before counting the number of X's to ensure there will be no more X's added to the column (otherwise, the count is considered to be "incomplete").

Once you have counted the X's, multiply by 3 (for the P&F three-box reversal method; see Thomas J. Dorsey, *Point & Figure Charting*, 3rd ed. for further explanation) and then multiply that product by the value per box. Add this result to the bottom X, and that is your count or price target (see Exhibit 2.10).

Downside, Bearish Target Using a Vertical Count   The process is very similar to that outlined above, yet there is one minor difference. You are counting the number of O's in the column after the first sell signal off the top, then multiplying that by 2 (instead of 3), and then multiplying by the value of each box. Then *subtract* that number from the top O's price, and that is your bearish price objective.

Horizontal Price Objective

When a notable base has formed on a chart, we prefer to calculate the price objective using a horizontal count. That, of course, does not preclude

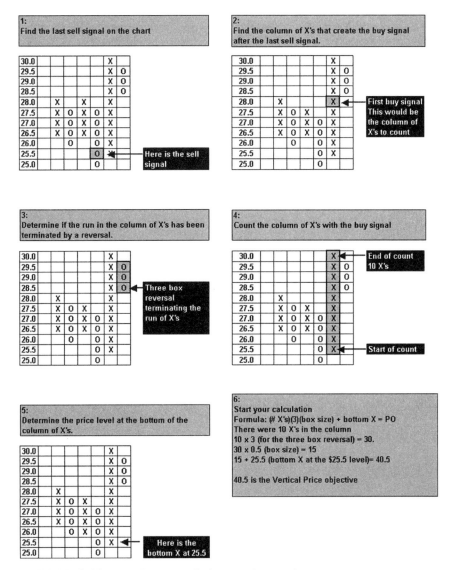

EXHIBIT 2.10 Calculating a Bullish Vertical Price Objective.

you from also using the vertical count. The horizontal price objective is determined by measuring the size of the base that a commodity has created and broken out from—basically, by measuring the width of this base. The base of the formation must be unbroken. In other words, you must be able to count horizontally across the columns filled with X's and O's without any spaces in between. So you find the widest part of the base that is unbroken

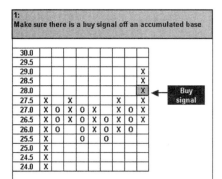

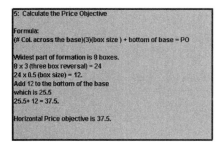

EXHIBIT 2.11   Calculating a Bullish Horizontal Price Objective.

to count. There are no minimum columns required, but you will see many charts where a large area of accumulation was created and then the chart broke out. It is these types of charts where a horizontal count is most effective. In essence, the base acts as the powder keg—the more it builds up, the more explosive the breakout can be; or, as the saying goes, the bigger the base, the bigger the move up (or down) out of that base.

Upside, Bullish Target Using a Horizontal Count   Once a buy sig-nal is given, count across the base the commodity has built. Multiply the number of columns across the formation by 3, and then multiply that prod-uct by the value per box. Add this number to the bottom, or lowest point of the base formation. This is your horizontal price target (see Exhibit 2.11).

Downside, Bearish Target Using a Horizontal Count   The pro-cess is exactly the same as the bullish price objective using the horizontal count, with one exception. Instead of multiplying the number of columns in the base by 3, you multiply by 2. Then, after multiplying that product by the box size, the end result is subtracted from the highest point on the base formation.

That concludes our discussion on the basics of the P&F methodology. By understanding chart patterns, trend lines, and price objectives, you now have a good foundation from which to build. Remember to read Tom's book, *Point & Figure Charting*, 3rd ed. It goes into detail on the basics of the P&F methodology. There are also a number of other educational re-sources on our web site, www.dorseywright.com, including an online uni-versity.

Most of the tactics of commodity trading will come from the principles outlined in this chapter. Always keep it simple and trade with the trend. I can recall numerous instances when I've seen a triple top or a bullish catapult broken from below the trend line. I've been tempted, sometimes very tempted, to take a shot at those trades, but because the trend was negative, I stayed on the sidelines. Adhering to that principle has saved me from disastrous trades many times.

CHAPTER 3

Using Spot Charts

Now that we have covered the basics of the Point & Figure method, and have learned how the same concepts that are applied to equity analysis are transferable to the analysis of commodities, we now want to present you with another tool that can help in your commodity trading: the use of spot and continuous charts.

For edification, "spot" refers to a cash market price for a physical commodity that is available for immediate delivery. The "spot month" is basically the futures contract month closest to expiration, and is also referred to as the "nearby delivery month." A "continuous" chart uses the current nearby futures contract price data, continually rolling to the next near month as the earlier one expires. So, the price of a futures contract at expiration and the cash or "spot" price of the underlying asset must be the same, because both prices refer to the same (physical) asset.

Spot and continuous charts are particularly useful in the analysis of the longer-term trend of a given commodity because of the amount of the historical price data included on such a chart. I always check the continuous chart before I go to the contract month I want to trade, as it helps with my perspective. You will recall that we just finished a discussion on trend analysis and how this is an integral part of technical analysis. So it goes to reason that by consulting a spot or continuous chart, you will be provided perspective as to what the longer-term trend of a given commodity is, thereby directing your overall trading posture. Not only can such charts aid in overall trend determination, but we can also use the historical price data to generate pertinent relative strength charts. It is this type of analysis that can serve to pinpoint specific outperformance by one commodity over another, allowing you to zero in on the best opportunities for success.

As we work through this chapter, we will be returning to our discussion on trend analysis and the use of the bullish support line and bearish resistance line; in Chapter 4 we will also be introducing in more detail the subject of Relative Strength and how it can be applied to the commodities market. Before doing so, we want to spend a little time discussing some of the specific spot and continuous charts we use and the nuances of each.

COMMODITY MARKET INDEXES

As we mentioned earlier in this book, commodities have shed a great deal of the stigma previously associated with them, and instead have now gained respect as an asset class in and of itself. So, just as you would chart the Dow Jones Industrial Average (DJIA) or the Standard & Poor's 500 Equal Weighted Index (SPXEWI) to gain perspective on the broad equity market, the same can be done for the commodities market.

There are several commodity market indexes that we turn to when evaluating the general picture for the commodities market. The one we have focused on the most over the years has been the Reuters/Jeffries CRB Index (CR/Y on our system); more recently, we have also paid attention to the Goldman Sachs Spot Return Index (GN/X), which tends to be favored by institutional money managers, and the Dow Jones–AIG Commodity Index (DJAIG). Other measurements exist, such as the Journal of Commerce Index, and the Deutsche Bank Liquid Commodities Index (DBLCIX); and as more and more attention gets paid to this alternative asset class, there will be additional commodity indexes created.

The Reuters/Jeffries CRB Index (CR/Y) is the standard in the industry. It has been in existence for 50 years, first being calculated by the Commodity Research Bureau, Inc. in 1957. The CRB Futures Index was originally designed to reflect, in a dynamic fashion, the broad trends in overall commodity prices and to serve as a price measurement for macroeconomic analysis. To accomplish this, the index, from time to time, has been adjusted. In all, there have been 10 revisions to the components, the first occurring in 1961, and the last one in 2005.

Prior to this most recent change in the CRB, the Index was made up of 17 commodities, all equally weighted. Some may have thought this was a weakness, questioning why cocoa should have the same weight as crude oil, when crude oil has greater importance to our economy. Yet others may reason that an equal-weighted commodity index is just as pertinent as, say, an equal-weighted S&P 500 in providing a true, unbiased picture of

2005 Revisions to Reuters/Jefferies CRB Index Component List	
1995	**2005**
1. Cocoa	1. Aluminum
2. Coffee 'C'	2. Cocoa
3. Copper	3. Coffee
4. Corn	4. Copper
5. Cotton	5. Corn
6. Crude Oil	6. Cotton
7. Gold	7. Crude Oil
8. Heating Oil	8. Gold
9. Live Cattle	9. Heating Oil
10. Live Hogs	10. Lean Hogs
11. Natural Gas	11. Live Cattle
12. Orange Juice	12. Natural Gas
13. Platinum	13. Nickel
14. Silver	14. Orange Juice
15. Soybeans	15. Silver
16. Sugar No. 11	16. Soybeans
17. Wheat	17. Sugar
	18. RBOB Gasoline*
	19. Wheat

The 2005 change to the CRB Index, on a component-basis, was to remove Platinum and to add Aluminum, Nickel, and Unleaded Gas.

* = Unleaded Gas was changed to RBOB Gasoline in late 2006

EXHIBIT 3.1 CRB Index 2005 Revisions.

the broad health of the commodity market or equity market, as the case may be. Be that as it may, the CRB lost its equal-weighted status with the most recent revision. The good news is the "old" CRB Index can still be followed, and charted, under the name "Continuous Commodity Index" using the symbol UV/Y on the Dorsey, Wright & Associates (DWA) web site, www.dorseywright.com.

The CRB revision in 2005 brought notable changes—most important was the move away from an equal-weighted status to one that takes into account relative significance and liquidity of the various commodities markets. Secondarily, the components changed, with three being added and one deleted. Exhibit 3.1 reflects the changes in the components.

As mentioned, the CRB changed its component weightings in 2005 and is now constructed with 19 "front month" commodity contracts weighted using a four-tier system. The top tier now reflects the most liquid and most economically significant commodity—crude oil. While the previous construction of the index gave every component an equal weighting, the new construction overweights the tier in descending order, and equal weights

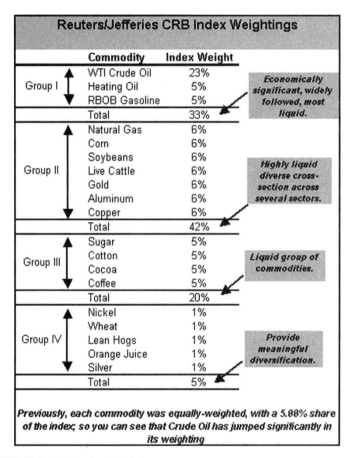

EXHIBIT 3.2   CRB Index Weightings.

the components within tiers 2, 3 and 4. Clearly, the price action in the CRB is now affected more dramatically by the action in the energy markets due to the 23 percent weighting now afforded to crude oil. Exhibit 3.2 shows the 2005 change in member weightings for the CRB, and Exhibit 3.3 is a pie chart showing the sector weightings for the CRB. As of January 2007, the member components and weightings remain the same as those listed here.

Over the years, we have placed great emphasis on the CRB Index (CR/Y), relying on its Point & Figure chart for insight into the potential direction of the commodity market as a whole. The spot chart for the CRB has consistently trended, often for years on end. By monitoring this trend, aided by the bullish support and bearish resistance lines, we have been able to provide consistent investment guidance for our clients on this all-

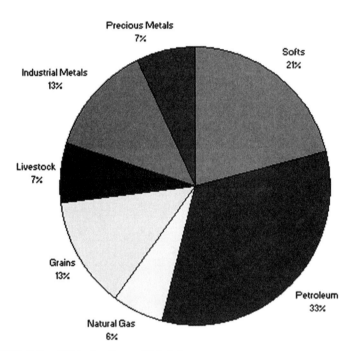

EXHIBIT 3.3   CRB Index Sector Weightings.

important asset class. Let's take a look at an example (these examples below are based on the CRB as it was trading then—as an equal-weighted index). In November 2001 and again in June 2002, we featured the CRB Index in our *"Daily Equity & Market Analysis Report,"* wanting to bring to the attention of our clients a significant change that was taking place in the CRB, and by doing so, providing insight into the broader commodity market. From our analysis, a major bottom and trend change was taking place in the CRB, and the prospects existed for higher prices in the commodity market. You can view the CRB Index chart (CR/Y) from these time periods, and an excerpt from this important inflection point in Exhibit 3.4.

> *The CRB Index has fallen to a low of 182. This basically put the index back just below the same level where it bottomed out in 1999, and in fact took it to lows not seen since 1975!!! But since putting in that low, we have seen some back and forth action on the chart, a higher bottom, and the potential for a double top buy signal at 192. This*

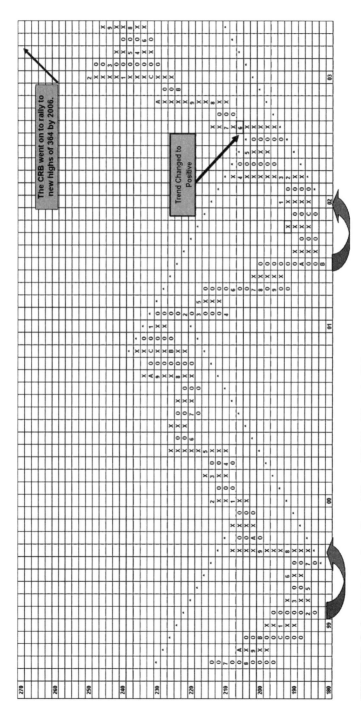

EXHIBIT 3.4 CRB Index Spot Trend Chart (CR/Y)—Historical View.

would be the first buy signal off the bottom. But realize that the CRB Index trends extremely well. In line with that, the CRB Index's longer term monthly momentum has been negative for 14 months, having turned so in October of 2000. Conversely, the monthly momentum is now getting less and less negative, and could well turn back to positive with Monday night's calculation . . . it, too, trends very well, and often times leads the trend chart by a month or two.

So what does all this mean? . . . [I]t is suggesting that the economy could well have put in its bottom. That interest rates may well have bottomed out, and that instead of a deflationary environment, we have an inflationary environment on the horizon. So, what do you do? Consider buying the CRB as an inflation hedge. You can buy futures contracts on the index. Before buying it, we would wait for the first buy signal off the bottom and for the momentum to turn positive. Or take a look at some of the other commodities futures charts as plays.

—Excerpt from November 28, 2001, Daily
Report

Recall that we featured this particular index back in late November, 2001, alerting you to what looked like a potential change in trend for the CRB. This has come to fruition, as you will see in the discussion below.

Since putting in that low in early November, we have seen the CRB show an overall series of higher tops and higher bottoms. The first buy signal was given in late November at 192, then two consecutive buy signals were given before the index spiked up in March and April to the bearish resistance line. This was a huge initial move off the bottom for the CRB, carrying from a low of 182 to 208. During that time we saw the bond indexes falter and give sell signals, while interest rates eked higher, at least temporarily. Then with the CRB hitting resistance and failing at the bearish resistance line, it backed off and spent a couple of months consolidating the initial spike up off the bottom. . . . [T]he CRB Index (CR/Y) has just penetrated its bearish resistance line based on yesterday's action. This is a very important change in trend for this commodity index, occurring with the double top buy signal at 206. Initial support lies at 194, then much more so around 184–186. The bullish price objective is 230, basically around its highs from late 2000–early 2001. Lastly, the longer-term monthly momentum did turn back to positive a few months ago, and continues to get more positive. As we mentioned in

November's feature, both the trend chart for the CRB and its monthly momentum trends very well. So, with this important penetration of the downtrend line, it suggests higher prices in the CRB Index. . . .in all, it pays for you to be informed on these topics. The CRB Index does have futures contracts that can be traded.
                                                     —Excerpt from June 25, 2002, Daily Report

The preceding commentary allows you to see how following one simple chart can provide you with great insights into the macro-economic picture, but can also afford you an avenue for investment via the CRB futures contract. I'll tell you something else. It also allows you to avoid doing the tedious and often erroneous fundamental work most use to evaluate both stock and commodity markets—all that there is to know will show up in the chart. The CRB chart also is a great example of why you keep your foot in the stirrup as long as the ride lasts—meaning as long as the trend is in place. The CRB remained in a strong uptrend for several years, portending higher prices (as long as it continues to trade above its bullish support line). This chart clearly helped us to see that commodities had reentered a bullish phase back in 2002. It was a long, dry 13 years but it appeared to us back then that the baton was being passed back to the hard (raw materials) asset class from the paper asset class.

As mentioned, the venerable CRB Index used to be an equal-weighted commodity index, having just changed this status in 2005. Prior to the CRB changes in 2005, we had seen the advent of other commodity indexes that are structured based on open interest, liquidity, and/or the world production quantities of the index's components; the aforementioned Goldman Sachs Spot Return Commodity Index and the Dow Jones–AIG Commodity Index follow along these lines of composition.

The GN/X has become a favorite among institutions as a premier global commodity benchmark for measuring investment performance in the commodity markets. The GN/X is currently composed of 24 commodities that meet certain liquidity requirements and are weighted by the world production quantities, and the index is rebalanced annually. So for use as an economic indicator, the appropriate weight to assign each commodity is in proportion to the amount of that commodity flowing through the economy (i.e., the actual production or consumption of that commodity). (*Sources:* www.gs.com/gsci/#construction; www.cme.com/about/press/cn/printerFriendly/GSCI2005CSW10433.html.) Given this style of construction, the GN/X is currently dominated in weighting toward the energy group. As you can see in Exhibit 3.5, as of January 2007, crude oil itself accounted for roughly 31 percent of the GN/X, while energy as a group accounted for approximately 68 percent!

Goldman Sachs Commodity Index Components & Weights									
	Weight		Weight		Weight		Weight		Weight
Energy	68.21%	**Industrial Metals**	10.78%	**Precious Metals**	2.50%	**Agriculture**	13.41%	**Livestock**	5.10%
Crude Oil	31.42%	Aluminum	3.69%	Gold	2.19%	Wheat	3.21%	Live Cattle	2.90%
Brent Crude	14.61%	Copper	3.64%	Silver	0.31%	Red Wheat	1.14%	Feeder Cattle	0.65%
RBOB Gas	2.10%	Lead	0.44%			Corn	3.77%	Lean Hogs	1.55%
Heating Oil	7.57%	Nickel	1.55%			Soybeans	1.82%		
Gas Oil	4.53%	Zinc	1.46%			Cotton	0.98%		
Natural Gas	7.98%					Sugar	1.45%		
						Coffee	0.82%		
						Cocoa	0.22%		
Each commodity weighted on world production; data as of January 8, 2007									

EXHIBIT 3.5 Goldman Sachs Commodity Index Components & Weights.

You can easily deduce from these figures that the GN/X either lives or dies by the "oil sword."

The GN/X is not only a valuable commodity index to use for economic analysis, but it is also tradable via futures contracts on the Chicago Mercantile Exchange (CME). In fact, open interest in the Goldman Sachs Commodity Index (GSCI) futures, under the root "GI" dwarfs all the other index-based commodity futures. Oppenheimer Funds and Rydex Funds also use the GSCI as the benchmark for their commodity mutual funds, which we will discuss in more detail later in the book; there are currently two exchange-traded funds (ETFs) that benchmark this index, both offered by Barclays (BGI) through their iShares platform (we also will discuss ETFs in more detail later in this book). Given the extreme weightings toward energy, as listed above, any desire to invest in either the GSCI futures or the related mutual fund or ETFs, would suggest you also take the time to evaluate the prospects for crude oil and related energy commodities. But despite its massive energy weighting, the GN/X chart has, over the years, looked similar to the CRB—with both having trended decidedly up over the past few years while showing a series of higher tops and higher bottoms. In sum, they both concur that a bull market in commodities started following a late 2001 bottom, while both penetrated their downtrend lines in the summer of 2002. Because of our charts, we were able to alert our clients to this major change that started in earnest in November 2001 (see Exhibit 3.6).

The DJAIG was established in July 1998. Originally, it was available only as an over-the-counter (OTC) product, but then the Chicago Board of Trade (CBOT) introduced futures contracts on the Index, making it easier to invest in this commodity index as an asset class. The DJAIG is composed of futures contracts on 19 different exchange-traded physical commodities and uses a combination of liquidity and production data to determine its

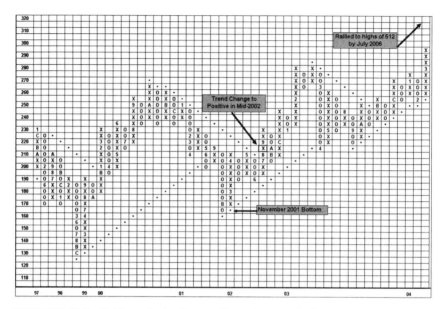

EXHIBIT 3.6   Goldman Sachs Commodity Index Trend Chart.

component weightings. Like the GN/X, the DJAIG is rebalanced annually. Unlike the GN/X, which has about 68 percent of its weight in energy, no related group of commodities may constitute more than 33 percent of the index. As well, no single commodity may constitute less than 2 percent of the index.

As Exhibit 3.7 shows, the energy group has a weighting of 33 percent, at the upper limit of what is allowed in the DJAIG. So clearly, like the GN/X the action in the energy-related commodities will have a material affect on the performance of the DJAIG (and now on the CRB), yet to a lesser extent. As is with both the CRB and GSCI, the DJAIG also has futures contracts, making it a viable investment vehicle, rather than just an economic index. These futures trade on the CBOT under the root symbol "AI." In addition to this form of investment, the DJAIG serves as the benchmark for a couple of other "real asset" mutual funds: the PIMCO Allianz Commodity Real Return Fund (PCRIX) and Credit Suisse Commodity Fund (CRSAX). At this writing, there is one ETF—or, more specifically, exchange-traded note (ETN)—that is tied to the DJAIG, the iPATH Dow Jones–AIG Commodity Index (DJP) offered by Barclays (BGI). All of these securities will be discussed further in later chapters. See Exhibit 3.8.

In sum, all three of these commodity indexes provide valuable insight into the broad commodity scene. Any and all can be used as you endeavor to evaluate the overall trend and outlook for the commodity markets as a whole. Having looked at all three of these indexes' charts, it is clear to see

Dow Jones–AIG Commodity Index Components List	
Commodity	**Weight**
Natural Gas	12.55%
Crude Oil	12.72%
RBOB Gas	3.94%
Heating Oil	3.79%
Live Cattle	6.14%
Lean Hogs	3.01%
Wheat	4.72%
Corn	5.63%
Soybeans	7.75%
Soybean Oil	2.85%
Aluminum	6.80%
Copper	6.19%
Zinc	2.80%
Nickel	2.72%
Gold	6.83%
Silver	2.29%
Sugar	3.12%
Cotton	3.15%
Coffee	3.02%

EXHIBIT 3.7 Dow Jones AIG Commodity Index Components and Weights.

that back in late 2001 and early 2002 a significant change was occurring in the commodity markets—the overall negative trend was abating, and a more constructive, bullish trend was ensuing. It is this kind of identification of trend change that is so important to your overall success in the financial markets. As we stated previously, let the trend be your friend, and rely on the chart and bullish support and bearish resistance lines to help in this determination. Also, be reminded that you need to stay aware of the specific weightings of the commodity indexes, as their price action can be greatly affected by one group in particular, such as energy (currently). Not only can these indexes provide knowledge on a macroeconomic basis, but each can be traded as an asset class via their individual futures contracts, or related vehicles, just as you would buy, say, the SPDR S&P 500 ETF (SPY) or Dow Diamonds (DIA) to gain broad equity exposure.

SPOT CURRENCY CHARTS

Just as you can study broadly inclusive commodity index charts for general knowledge on the commodity markets, you can also employ the use of spot

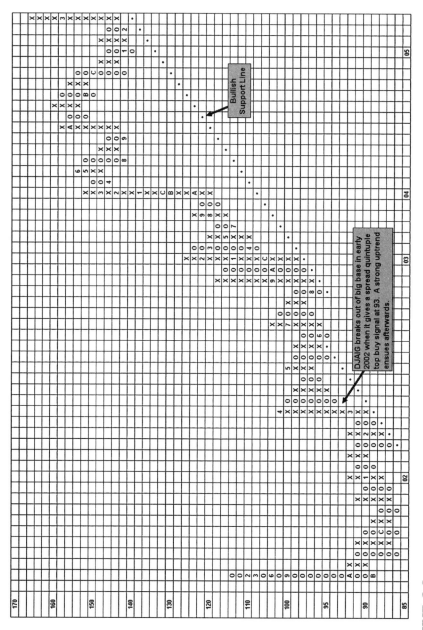

EXHIBIT 3.8   Dow Jones AIG commodity Index Trend Chart.

```
          ┌─────────────────────────────────┐
          │        Spot Currency Charts     │
          │                                 │
          │   Currency          DWA Symbol  │
          │                                 │
          │   Australian dollar    AD/Y     │
          │   British pound        BP/Y     │
          │   Canadian dollar      CD/Y     │
          │   US dollar            DX/Y     │
          │   Euro FX              EC/Y     │
          │   Japanese yen         JY/Y     │
          │   Mexican peso         M./Y     │
          │   Swiss franc          SF/Y     │
          └─────────────────────────────────┘
```

EXHIBIT 3.9 List of Spot Current Charts.

charts for long-term analysis of the currency markets. By using Point & Figure technical analysis to examine the currency markets, you can manage risk associated with currency rate fluctuations, or you can simply use these charts to take advantage of profit opportunities associated with changes in the currency rates.

At DWA we maintain spot charts on all the major currencies, as listed in Exhibit 3.9.

Of all the spot currency charts, the one we have followed most closely and probably for the longest amount of time is the U.S. Dollar Index (DX/Y). This index provides the world with a general indication of the international value of the U.S. dollar, which, of course, is helpful to importers and exporters, currency managers, and institutions, as well as investors. The DX/Y is a trade-weighted geometric average of six major world exchange rates that is calculated continuously (see Exhibit 3.10). Seventeen countries in all are represented in the DX/Y—12 from the Euro zone, plus five other nations. The current level of the DX/Y reflects the average value of the dollar relative to the March 1973 base period. Since 1973, the DX/Y has traded as high as the mid-160s and as low as the high 70s. Futures contracts based on the DX/Y are traded on the New York Board of Trade's (NYBOT's) Financial Exchange (FINEX) division, based on the March quarterly cycle (March, June, September, and December expirations). (*Source:* www.nybot.com/usdx/usdxbrochure.pdf.)

This product allows you to trade the dollar, based on your technical analysis of the chart, without having risk from exposure to just one foreign currency. More and more commodity and currency-based securities are becoming available each year, with mutual funds and ETFs being launched now with regularity. There currently are mutual funds offered by ProFunds

U.S. Dollar Index Components

Currency	Weight
Euro	57.60%
Japanese yen	13.60%
British pound	11.90%
Canadian dollar	9.10%
Swedish krona	4.20%
Swiss franc	3.60%

Source: http://www.nybot.com/usdx/usdxbrochure.pdf

EXHIBIT 3.10 U.S. Dollar Index Components.

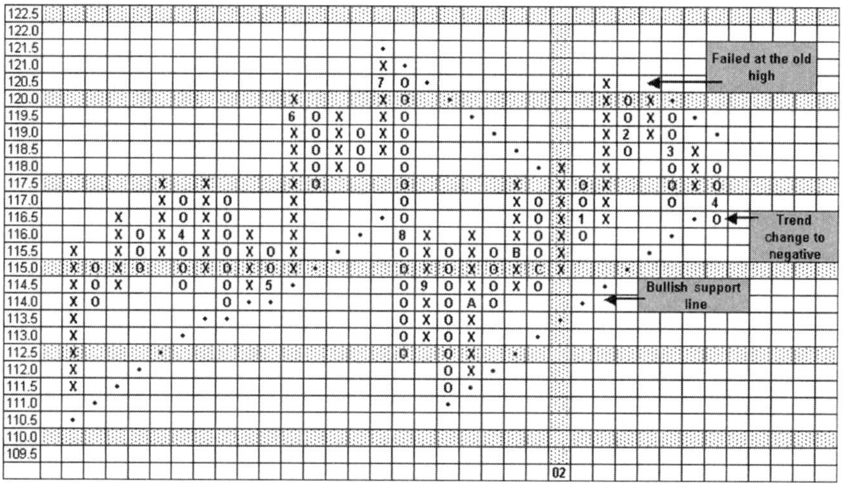

EXHIBIT 3.11 U.S. Dollar Spot Trend Chart (DX/Y) 2002.

and Rydex Investments that allow you to take a position, either long or short, in the U.S. dollar; although not yet launched, there are ETFs in registration for the U.S. dollar as well, long and short exposure in the U.S. dollar can be accomplished through ETFs from PowerShares.

In looking at the U.S. Dollar Index spot chart, you can see that it is equally easy to ascertain the overall, longer-term trend of the dollar, and therefore determine your basic trading posture toward this contract. Below is an excerpt from our *Daily Equity & Market Analysis Report* in which we lay out for you our posture on the dollar—in this case, a move to a bearish stance (Exhibit 3.11).

No Reason to Be Green(back) with Envy: Update on U.S. Dollar

As you can see in the chart below, the U.S. dollar has deteriorated on a technical basis. ...The U.S. dollar spot chart gives you a longer-term view of the dollar. As the spot chart shows, the dollar ran into significant resistance again when it spiked up in January to 120.50. This took the dollar up close to the July peak of 121.0. Since putting in that top at 120.50, the dollar has backed off and broken down. In fact, the dollar has given two straight sell signals—a double bottom break at 118, then a more recent double bottom breakdown at 116.50 (which followed a second lower top). This breakdown at 116.50 happened late last week, and it also brought with it a violation of the bullish support line. Therefore, this recent sell signal causes the overall trend to change to negative. Initial resistance lies at 118.50 ... and the bearish price objective for the spot dollar is 113.50. ... So in general, you can see the prospects for a weaker dollar exists, on a technical basis.

In summary, we are bearish on the dollar, and are short it in our commodity account. Those inclined to play the futures market, can short the dollar, especially into any rally.
—Excerpt from April 22, 2002, Daily Report

The longer-term trend for the U.S. Dollar Spot Index (using the .50 per box chart) remained bearish from April 2002—when we featured the greenback—until June 2005. Clearly visible in Exhibit 3.12, you can see how the dollar trended steadily lower, failing on every attempt to rally and test its downtrend line until mid-2005. These failed attempts can be seen in 2002, 2003, and in the first half of 2004. Such action led us to repeatedly short the dollar as the specific futures contracts allowed.

The year 2005 started off with yet another rally off the bottom, with the dollar attempting to bounce after making a nine-year low. Of no surprise to us, in December of 2004, *The Economist* magazine's cover was entitled, "The Disappearing Dollar." This was a sign to us that the dollar had probably put in its low. This was borne out, as the dollar did in fact find support around 80.50 in December 2004, the same level where it bottomed out in 1995 (and several other times in the early 1990s). Once again, a magazine cover proved to be a timely indication that you should be a contrarian and go the other way.

Finally, by June 2005, after rallying off the December 2004 bottom, the dollar was able to penetrate its bearish resistance line, causing us to change our posture and take a more bullish approach toward the dollar.

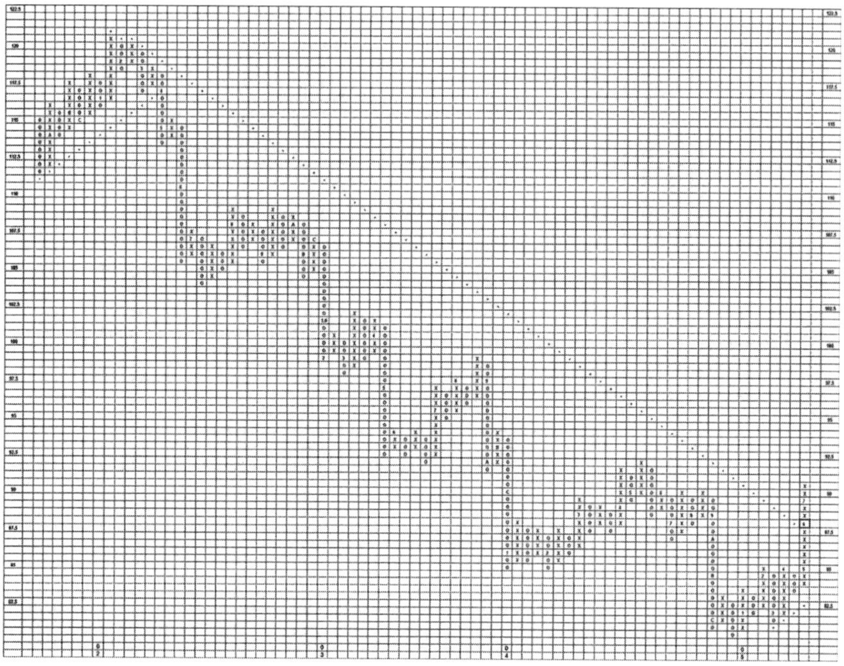

EXHIBIT 3.12   U.S. Dollar Spot Trend Chart (DX/Y) 2001–2005.

Such a stance was relatively short-lived as the dollar failed to gain much traction, as you can see in Exhibit 3.13. The rally off the December 2004 bottom petered out in November 2005 at 92.50; thereafter, a series of lower tops and bottoms were formed, with the greenback reassuming its bearish trend with the violation of its bullish support line in March 2006. As a result, our posture on the dollar once again shifted back to the bearish camp.

Another spot currency that we monitor closely is that of the Euro FX (EC/Y). Typically speaking, the dollar and euro will be exact opposites with respect to their technical picture. The Euro FX contract, like other foreign currencies, trades on the CME, and is based on the euro, the European Union's currency. The futures contracts derived from the euro, available for investment purposes, are based on the March quarterly cycle, too; and this holds true for all the foreign currency contracts we follow.

The Euro FX spot chart has been in a pronounced uptrend for a handful of years now; yet with the 2005 rally in the dollar, the euro did correct and tested its bullish support line. After multiple tests of the uptrend line, the euro's trend held and remains bullish. Not surprisingly, its chart, which is shown in Exhibit 3.14, is the inverse to the dollar. While the dollar was topping out in 2001–2002, the Euro FX spot was putting in a significant bot-

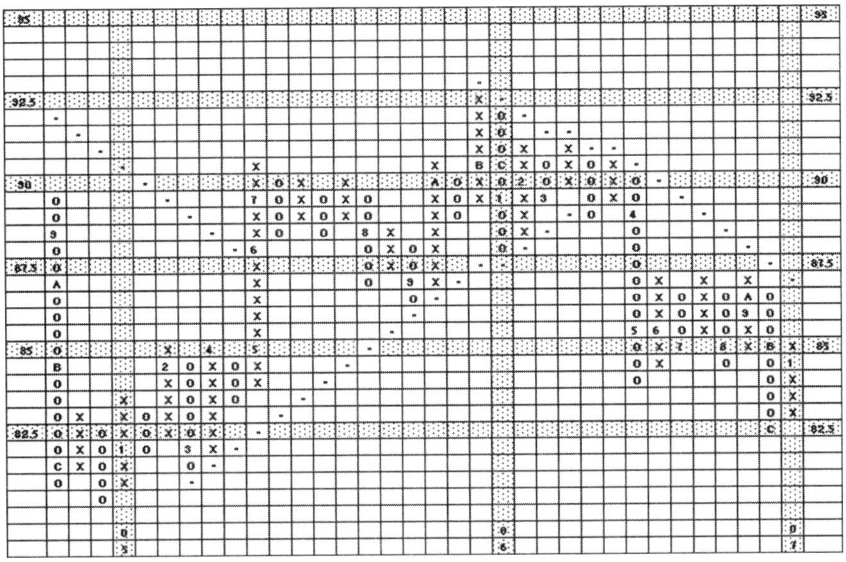

EXHIBIT 3.13 U.S. Dollar Spot Trend Chart (DX/Y) 2004–2007.

tom. As you can see, the low point for the euro spot came in October 2000 at .8300. What is so ironic about this bottom (and no surprise to us, being the contrarians that we are) is that it came shortly after the September 14, 2000, *The Economist* magazine cover entitled, "Euroshambles." This negative cover story on the euro had the picture of a gas tank gauge with the needle pointing to "E" for empty. The subtitle stated, "No fuel, roads blockaded, a vanishing currency and blundering governments." It would make most investors say, "Whoa, I'm bearish on the euro and Europe." But instead, it is this kind of negative mass media attention that often is a precursor to a significant bottom. After seeing this magazine cover, we watched both the U.S. dollar and the euro charts like a hawk, knowing that a trend change switch was likely in the offing. As both charts show, this is exactly what happened! This is yet another display of how the charts speak to the real story, compared to conventional thinking and what the mass media might be saying. Clearly, a posture of short the dollar, long the euro has paid off handsomely over the past several years and was accomplished by simply following the chart and ascertaining the long-term trend.

As mentioned earlier, we monitor numerous other spot currency charts, such as the Japanese yen (JY/Y) and the British pound (BP/Y), among others. In all cases, each has futures contracts that trade on the CME based on the March quarterly cycle. In addition, there now exists CurrencyShares ETFs, launched in 2005 and 2006, that enable the investor to play the foreign currency market via the ETF, with the transactions be-

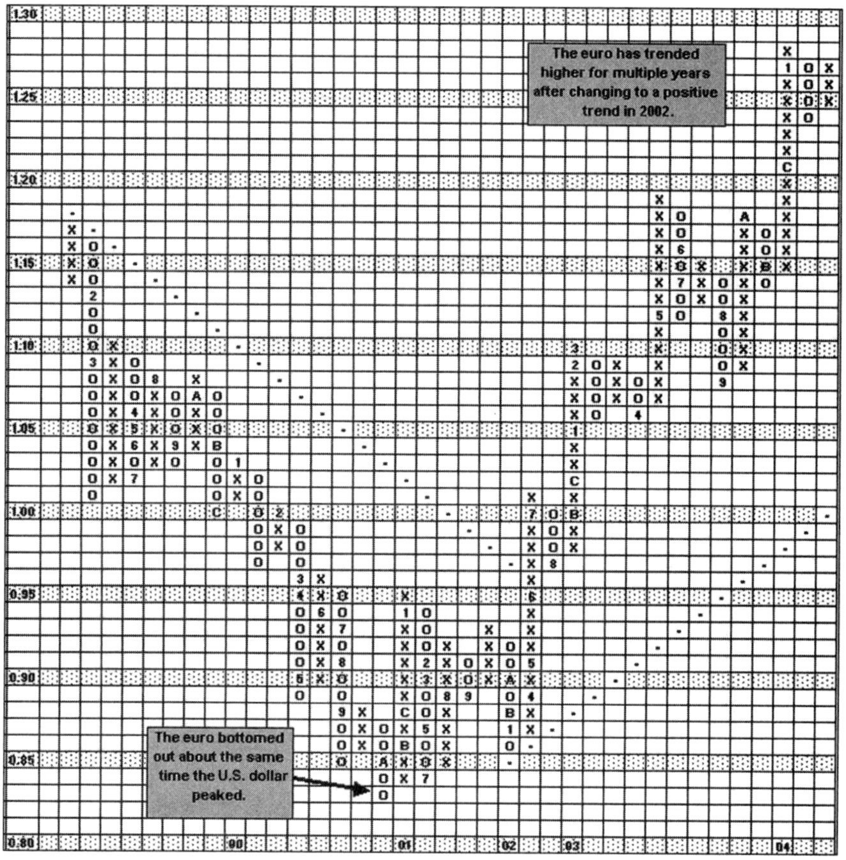
The euro has trended higher for multiple years after changing to a positive trend in 2002.
The euro bottomed out about the same time the U.S. dollar peaked.
1.30
1.25
1.20
1.15
1.10
1.05
1.00
0.95
0.90
0.85
0.80
00
01
02
03
04

EXHIBIT 3.14 Euro FX Spot Trend Chart.

ing similar and as easy as the purchase of a stock. In sum, it pays to stay abreast of how each long-term spot currency chart is developing, what the overall trend is, where significant past tops and bottoms have occurred, and what type of patterns are forming, as this will allow you to uncover potential trading opportunities, be it with the futures contract or the CurrencyShares.

OTHER USEFUL SPOT AND CONTINUOUS CHARTS

Over the years, we have also found it very helpful to follow spot charts for gold, crude oil, and copper. These specific commodities all carry notable importance on an economic basis, so close monitoring of them can serve you in more ways than one. We will be expounding on this in later chapters. For now, we merely want to introduce you to them from a commodity perspective, for purposes of trading their related underlying futures contracts. With respect to their underlying futures contracts, all three of these commodities trade on the New York Mercantile Exchange (NYMEX). The NYMEX is the largest physical commodity exchange in the world. London gold (UKGOLD) is a chart that we have been keeping since 1987, posting it by hand for many of those years. The chart is now available on our web site under the ticker UKGOLD. In essence, this chart is the London gold P.M. fixing. Therefore, it is not charted based on a high and low price for the day, but instead uses the P.M. fixing price for the day. To give you a little background information on the London fixings, it is an open process, conducted by the London Bullion Market Association, at which market participants can transact business on the basis of a single quoted price. Orders can be changed throughout the proceedings as the price is moved higher and lower until such time as buyers' and sellers' orders are satisfied and the price is said to be "fixed." The fixings, of which there are two a day (an A.M. and P.M.), are the internationally published benchmarks for precious metals (in this case, for gold). As the benchmark, many other financial instruments are priced off the fixing. The gold fixing started in 1919. (*Source:* www.lbma.org.uk/london_faq_fixings.htm.)

Our UKGOLD chart, as mentioned and as shown in Exhibit 3.15 A and B, goes back 20 years, and as a result provides an excellent long-term picture of how gold has traded over the years. This chart provides great insight into the very long-term trend of gold, and can therefore provide guidance as to how to address plays in the underlying commodity. You can easily see on this chart how gold had been in a protracted bear market for many years, following its late 1987 peak of 496. A brief rally in the mid-1990s was quashed in early 1996, only to see gold resume its downward bias for another five years. It wasn't until mid-2001 that gold finally found a bottom at 256. But since that lowly bottom in 2001, gold has strung together a six-year rally, showing a very orderly series of higher tops and higher bottoms. Suffice to say, the overall trend for gold remains bullish here, with a longer-term price objective of 724. But an important point to note here is that this is a very long-term-oriented chart for gold. It provides long-term guidance of trend; but for trading purposes, you must consult the underlying futures contracts charts to plan and refine your trading decisions. For example, UKGOLD could pull back from its January 2007 level of 648 to the 548 area without changing the longer-term trend. As a sidebar, we also follow the gold continuous chart (GC/) for guidance, similar to what UKGOLD provides. We will be coming back to this metal in a later chapter, discussing alternative ways to play gold.

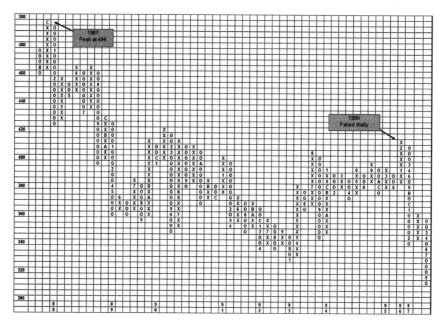

EXHIBIT 3.15A London Gold (UKGOLD) p.m. Fixing, Part I; B. London Gold (UK-GOLD) p.m. Fixing, Part II.

NYMEX crude oil (CRUDE) is another spot chart that we have kept for many years, originally plotting it by hand. The spot chart we maintain for crude oil is often referred to as West Texas intermediate (WTI), or light, sweet crude—they are one in the same, and we use the symbol CRUDE for our spot chart. Crude oil, as stated above, has futures contracts that trade on the NYMEX. According to the NYMEX, "it is the world's most actively traded commodity, and the NYMEX Division light, sweet crude oil futures contract is the world's most liquid forum for crude oil trading, as well as the world's largest-volume futures contract trading on a physical commodity. Due to its excellent liquidity and price transparency, the contract is used as a principal international pricing benchmark." (*Source:* www.nymex.com/jsp/markets/lsco_pre_agree.jsp.) Crude oil futures contracts trade monthly under the root symbol of "CL"; there now are several ETFs available for investors that allow you to purchase the underlying commodity, without the leverage of a futures contract. This will be discussed in Chapter 7.

The CRUDE chart is equally helpful in providing a long-term depiction of what the broad trend is for crude oil. Knowing this clearly has many implications, not only for trading the underlying futures, but also from an economic standpoint, an equity investment perspective, and from an infla-

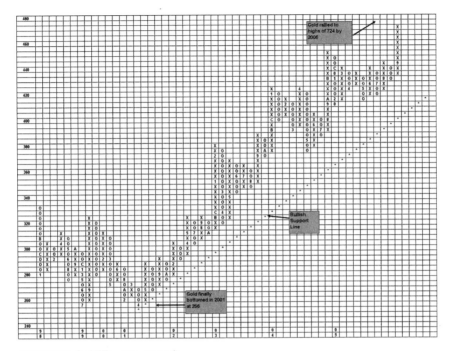

EXHIBIT 3.15B (Continued)

tionary viewpoint. Crude oil and its related products have a huge impact on our lives. Therefore, understanding the price prospects of the commodity can be very beneficial. Think back to our discussions on the Goldman Sachs Commodity Index (GN/X). This commodity index is based on world production quantities. Remember that 68 percent of the GN/X was energy, with roughly 31 percent of the index specifically being attributed to crude oil. So it should come as no surprise that the GN/X bottomed in late 1998, the same time crude oil was bottoming at $11 per barrel. Similarly, in late 2001, crude oil made another correction low bottom, this time at $17.50 per barrel, while the GN/X recorded a matching bottom. Based on the mirror-image charts shown in Exhibit 3.16, you can see how you could "play" crude oil in large part, just by using the GN/X futures.

Of course, you can purely trade crude oil using its specific futures contracts, yet rely on this NYMEX crude oil spot chart for longer-term direction. Following the late 2001 bottom, crude trended higher for over a year, until bumping up against residual resistance (from 2000) around the $37 level. A pause in the uptrend lasted a mere couple of months before crude reasserted itself. But it wasn't until a year later that crude oil managed to finally break through the critical $37–37.50 resistance (in early 2004). Then

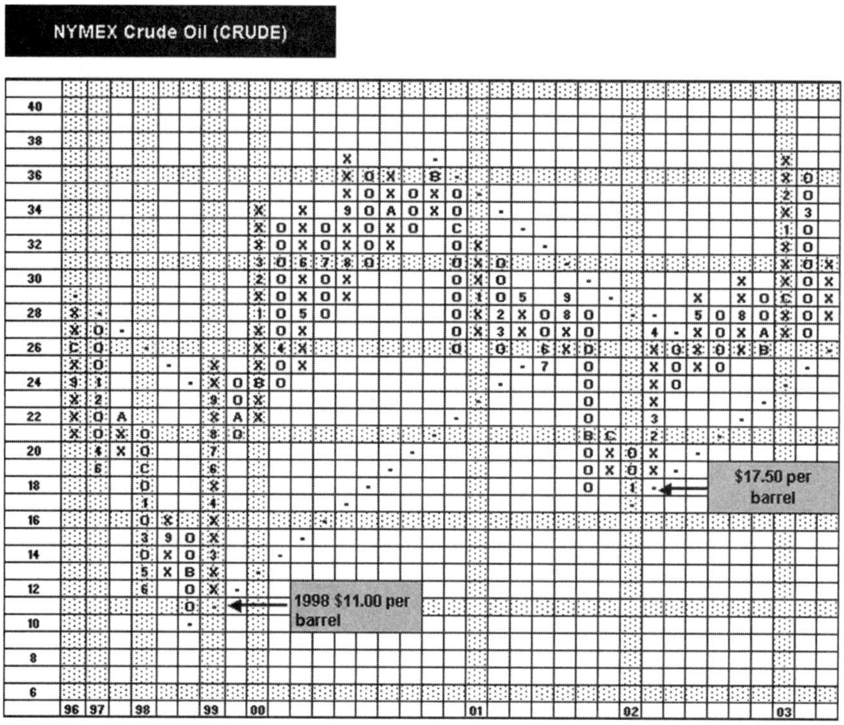

EXHIBIT 3.16 Comparison of Crude Oil and Goldman Sachs Commodity Index.

it was "off to the races." Noticing this significant breakout to new highs on the spot chart gave us conviction in further recommending crude and its related investment vehicles. This is another example of how spot charts can be very useful for technical analysis—not only are they beneficial for long-term trend determination, but also because of their illustration of noteworthy support and resistance levels (previous bottoms and tops). In early 2006, after peaking at $69, crude sold off to the $57 level again; this $57 price had become key support for NYMEX crude oil, having held this level four times. The sell-off from $68 to $57 also brought this key commodity down to its long-term bullish support line. On this test of the uptrend line, crude oil managed to hold its positive trend, and in fact from there rallied to new all-time highs of $77 by July 2006. The commodity wasn't as fortunate the next time around, just a couple of months later.

Crude oil started slipping down a slick slope in August–September 2006, violating key support at $69 when it gave a spread quadruple bottom sell signal at $68, and also violated its long-term bullish support line. This negative action was followed up with lower prices, enough so

Goldman Sachs Commodity Index (GN/X)

```
300
290
280                                                                          X        X  .
                                                                              X  O  X  O
270                                            .    .                         X  O  X  O
                                         X  .  .                              X  O     3
260                                      X  O  X  .                           X        O
                                   X     X  O  X  O  .                        2        O
250                                9  O  A  O  B  O  1  .                     X        O
                                   X  O  X  O  X  C  X  O  .            X     X        O
240                                X  O  X  O  X  O  X  O     .         X  O  X        O
                          6        X  O     O     O     O        .      X  O  X        O
230                 X     X  O  8              O  X        .      X     X  1        O
       O  .         X  O  X  O  X              2  X  O        .      X  O  X           O
220    O     .      3  O  X  7  X              3  X  O           .   X  O  C           O
       O        .   2  O  X  O                 O  X  5  9        .   X  A  X        .  4
210    O  A         X  O  5                    4     6  X  O  X     5  .  8  B  X
       O  X  O        X  O  X                        O  X  O  4  O  X  O  7  O
200    2  9  O        .  1  4  X                      .  O     O  X  O  X  O  X     .
       O  8  B           B  O                            O  X  O  X  O  X
190    O  7  O  X     X  X                         .        O  X  O     6     .
       6  X  C  2  O  9  O  X                 .              O  X
180    O  X  O  X  O  X  O  X                                O  3        .
       O  X  1  X  O  8  A                                   O  X     .
170    O     O  O  X              .                          B  X  .  ◄━━━━━━
             O  7                    .                       O  X
160          3  4              .                             .
             6  X
150          O  X           .                      ┌────────────────────┐
             7  3        .                         │ Notice how the     │
140          8  X  .                               │ bottoms correlate to│
             B  X  .  ◄━━━━━━━━━━                  │ the bottoms made in │
130          C                                     │ crude oil.          │
             .                                     └────────────────────┘
120
110
        98      99  00              01        02              03
```

EXHIBIT 3.16 (Continued)

that by January 2007 crude oil penetrated the aforementioned key support at $57. In short, crude oil had moved from strong hands to weak, suggesting that prospects for lower prices existed. By paying attention to the long-term trend chart of crude oil, we could see this notable shift had occurred (Exhibit 3.17).

Copper is another commodity we tend to follow very closely. To accomplish this, we not only analyze the futures charts, but we maintain a continuous chart for copper. A continuous chart is very similar to a spot chart, in that its prices reflect the near-month futures contract.

Copper, like gold or crude oil, is often considered a barometer of economic (industrial) health. Therefore, it can likewise provide great insights into the underlying strength or weakness in the markets. Copper is one of the oldest commodities known to man, and it is the world's third most widely used metal, after iron and aluminum, and is primarily used

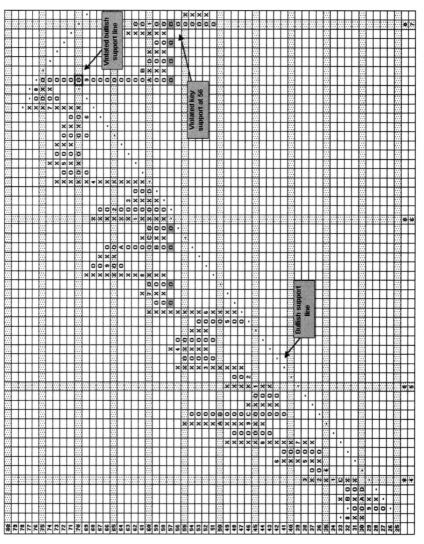

EXHIBIT 3.17 NYMEX Crude Oil Trend Chart (CRUDE).

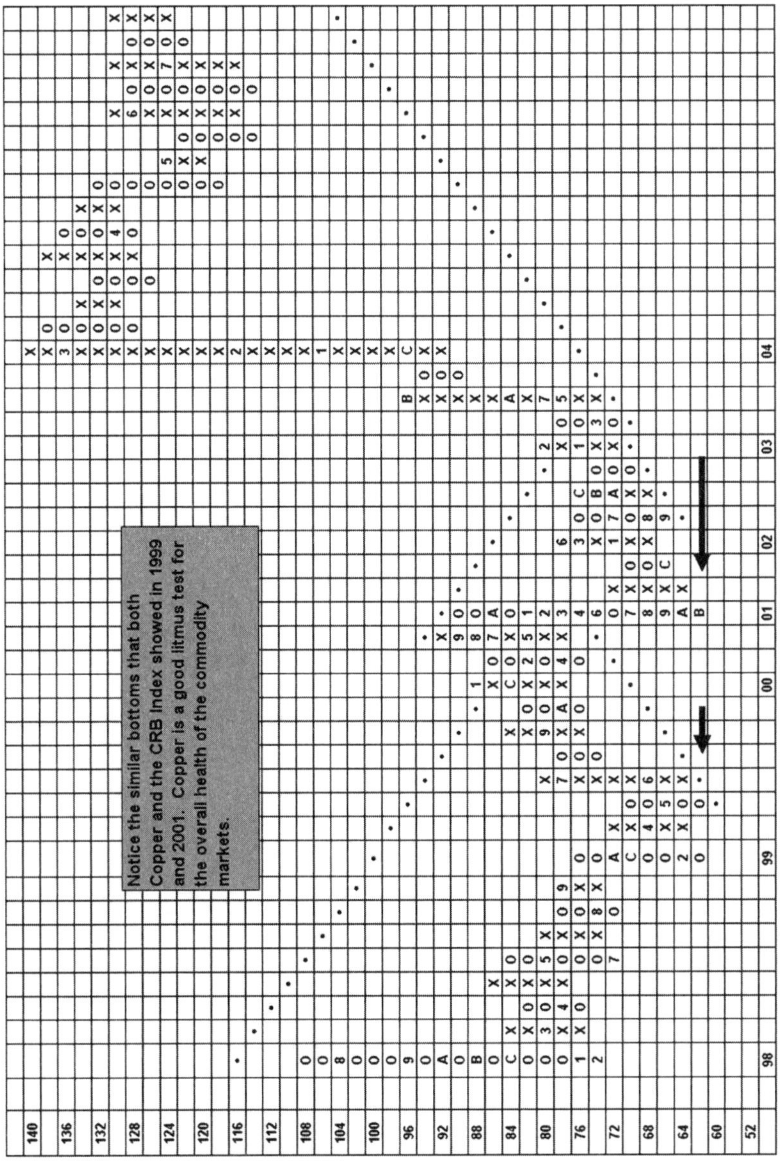

EXHIBIT 3.18 Comparison of Copper and CRB Index.

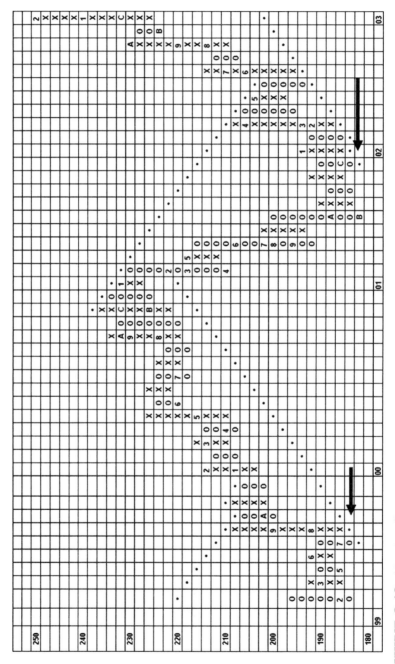

EXHIBIT 3.18 (Continued)

in highly cyclical industries such as construction and industrial manufacturing. Copper's history dates back 7,000 years, when it was first used for weapons, utensils, and tools; 5,000 years ago man learned to alloy copper with tin, which produced bronze—and the Bronze Age was born. As a result, copper was established as a commodity with commercial value. (*Source:* www.nymex.com/jsp/markets/cop_pre_agree.jsp.) Today, you can trade copper via the COMEX Division of the NYMEX with the root symbol being "HG" (for high-grade copper). The futures have a monthly expiration cycle, yet some months (March, May, July, September, and December) typically have much heavier open interest, so we would tend to focus trading on those months with the greatest open interest and trading volume.

In looking at the copper continuous chart (HG/), shown in Exhibit 3.18, it is interesting to note the striking similarities it has to the CRB Index spot chart (CR/Y). Recall that the CRB Index (prior to the 2005 revision) was an equal-weighted commodity index, known for its macroeconomic depiction. (Remember that the equal-weighted version of the CRB still exists under the name Continuous Commodity Index, available on our system under the symbol UV/Y.) Copper bottomed out in mid-1999, just as the CRB did; each tested its 1999 lows, with both putting in significant bottoms in November 2001. Both stayed in long-term, strong uptrends for numerous years after making these mirror-image bottoms. This would suggest that copper is a viable "litmus test" or gauge of prices in the overall economy—at least on a commodity basis.

CHAPTER 4

Relative Strength with Commodities

Now that we have put forth our discussion on how spot and continuous charts are very useful in long-term trend analysis, we turn our attention to the application of relative strength (RS) with commodities. Relative strength is one of the cornerstones of Dorsey, Wright's technical research—it is an integral part of our equity research, not only on a stock-specific basis, but also with our sector analysis and asset allocation. Over the years, we have continued to develop and expand our RS work. We now have numerous tools at our disposal. These same tools that work extremely well in the equity market are transferable to the commodity markets.

Relative strength, as the name implies, measures how one security is doing compared to another. For example, how Microsoft is performing compared to the Standard & Poor's (S&P) 500, or how the U.S. dollar is doing relative to the euro. In essence, this comparison allows you to determine which security is outperforming the other. The implication is that you invest in the vehicle that is outperforming the other, be it the market, another commodity, or the CRB Index. RS steers you toward the outperformer and away from the underperformer and helps you to invest in, and stay with, that winner for as long as the RS chart suggests outperformance. One simply focuses his or her buying on those securities exemplifying the strongest RS, and either sell or sell short those vehicles that exhibit the weakest RS.

Calculating RS is quite easy. You simply take the price of one security and divide it by the other (the security you want to compare); then take the resulting number and plot it on a Point & Figure chart. The same basic chart rules apply for an RS chart, in keeping with the three-box reversal method, as they do with our trend charts. The scale and pattern per se are not important, but rather the signal and column on the RS chart.

RS CALCULATION EXAMPLE

A graphical explanation will make this concept easier to grasp. Below we have chosen to compare coffee to the CRB Spot Index, to pinpoint whether or not coffee has positive RS versus the broader commodity market, as measured by the CRB Spot Index. In this case, we have chosen to use the CRB as the yardstick, given that it is (at the time of this example) an equal-weighted commodity index. For RS comparisons after 2005, we would consider using the Continuous Commodity Index (UV/Y) as this is the "old" CRB Index, and remains equal weighted. Of course, the Goldman Sachs Commodity Index (GSCI) or Dow Jones–AIG Commodity Index (DJAIG) is equally useable for this exercise, depending on which index you prefer to use as a benchmark. For our example, we will use coffee, March 2005 (KC/H5):

$$\text{Commodity Price/CRB Spot Index (CR/Y) or other Index} \times 100$$
$$\text{Coffee March (KC/H5)/CR/Y} \times 100$$
$$91.36/268.34 \times 100 = 30.87 \text{ RS Reading}$$
$$92.87/270.11 \times 100 = 31.46 \text{ RS Reading}$$

In this example, while the price of March coffee has risen and the CRB Index has also risen, the RS calculation has actually moved higher. This means that coffee is performing better "relative" to the broad commodity market, as measured by the CRB Index. As mentioned above, this RS reading would then be taken and plotted using Point & Figure charting principles. The RS reading is calculated every day using closing prices. Exhibit 4.1 is the RS chart of coffee, March versus the CRB Spot Index (CR/Y), along with coffee's Point & Figure trend chart.

When interpreting an RS chart, there are two main points to determine—the most recent signal given on the chart and the current column. In other words, was the last signal given on the RS chart a buy signal (a previous top broken) or a sell signal (a previous bottom broken)? Also, is the chart currently in a column of X's or a column of O's? So go back to our discussion of chart patterns. We first want to ascertain if the RS chart is on a buy or sell signal. This will demonstrate the long-term implications for the underlying commodity. If that last signal on the RS chart was a double top, the relative strength is said to be "positive"; if the last signal on the RS chart was a double bottom, then relative strength is "negative." Positive RS

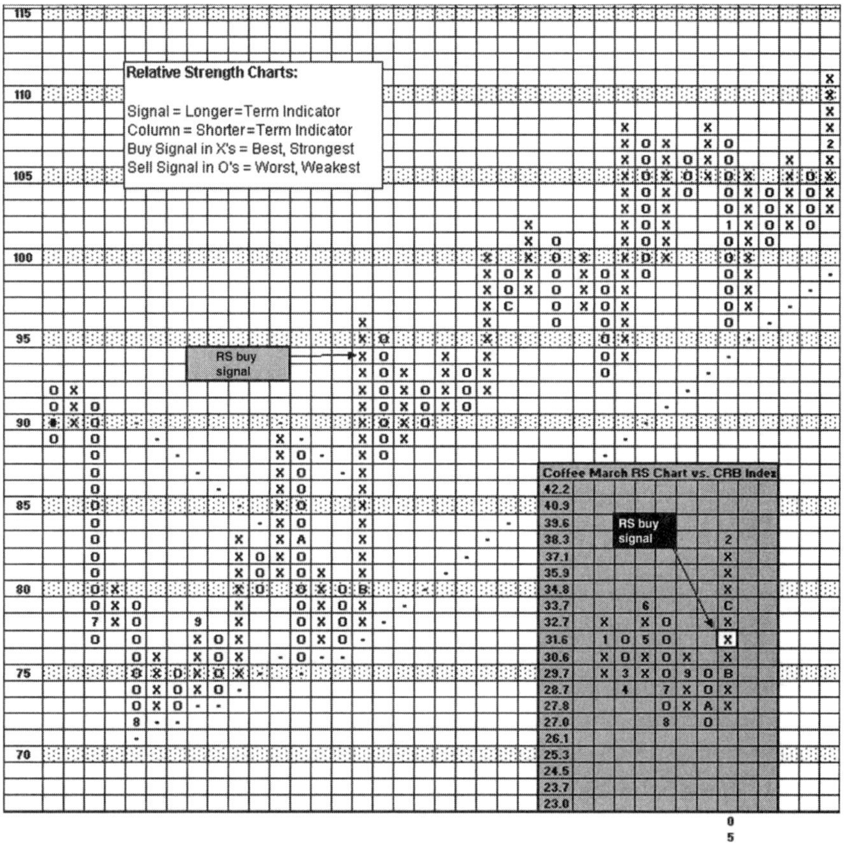

Relative Strength Charts:

Signal = Longer=Term Indicator
Column = Shorter=Term Indicator
Buy Signal in X's = Best, Strongest
Sell Signal in O's = Worst, Weakest

RS buy signal

Coffee March RS Chart vs. CRB Index

RS buy signal

EXHIBIT 4.1 Relative Strength Chart of Coffee vs. CRB Index.

implies outperformance, while negative RS suggests underperformance. In measuring RS on a shorter-term basis, we want to focus on which column the RS chart is in. If the current column is X's, the commodity is said to have "positive" RS on a short-term basis; if in O's, the short-term RS is "negative." Ideally, you want to focus your buying on those commodities exhibiting positive RS, while avoiding or shorting those commodities that are exhibiting negative RS. In sum, then, the strongest RS reading is one in which the most recent signal on the RS chart was a buy signal and the most recent column is in X's.

Let's take a look again at the March coffee RS chart shown in Exhibit 4.1. Notice how in November 2004 coffee reversed up into a column of X's, suggesting the commodity was starting to outperform the CRB on a near-term basis, yet the RS reading continued to improve and managed to break a previous top later in November. By breaking this previous top at 31.6, coffee gave an RS buy signal, moving from what had been an RS sell signal (underperformance) to a positive RS signal (outperformance). Coffee continued to put in more X's on its RS chart, exhibiting persistent positive RS. By consulting the RS chart, it would have suggested that you take a hard look at buying coffee, based on this outperformance. After March coffee's RS buy signal was given in November, the contract rose from 94.55 to a high of 112.60. At $375 per point for each coffee contract, that would equate to a $6,768.75 gain per contract.

But remember, the RS signal is typically a longer-term measurement of relative strength, while the most recent column is more indicative of the shorter-term RS of a given commodity. For trading purposes, you may find it more useful to rely on the column for your determination of RS, as mentioned above. In all, RS in and of itself is a very robust tool in technical analysis. But an important caveat to remember with RS is that the measurement is "relative." Positive RS does not mean the commodity has to rise in price, and negative RS doesn't guarantee a fall in price. It is a relative measurement to another index or commodity, and merely suggests outperformance or underperformance, as the case may be. *So it is paramount that you use relative strength in conjunction with other "absolute" Point & Figure measurements, such as overall trend and chart pattern analysis.*

Not only is relative strength useful when measuring a commodity versus a broad commodity index, such as coffee to the CRB, but it's also a viable tool to use for peer evaluation or for determining strength within a commodity group or sector. For example, an RS chart can be constructed for the U.S. dollar versus the euro, or against any other currency. In fact, you could create an RS matrix that itemizes exactly which foreign currency is performing the best versus all of its peers. We routinely do these calculations on our web site, www.dorseywright.com. Or you might do the same comparisons with the grains. Is it best to go long soybeans, on an RS basis, and short wheat? A simple RS chart can help with this determination. Clearly, this type of RS analysis can be very helpful when trading spreads—going long the grain that exhibits the strongest RS, and selling short the one with the poorest or weakest RS. Following are a few more applications of this RS concept. First, let's look at two more examples of specific RS charts—the U.S. dollar versus the euro; then the CRB Index compared to the GSCI. These two RS charts will serve to confirm what we have previously discussed with respect to the trend of the dollar and that of crude oil.

In looking at the relative strength chart of the U.S. Dollar Spot Index (DX/Y) versus the Euro Spot (EC/Y), you can see that the relative strength for the dollar has gotten weaker and weaker over the past handful of years. The dollar gave an RS sell signal (against the euro) in June 2002, suggesting

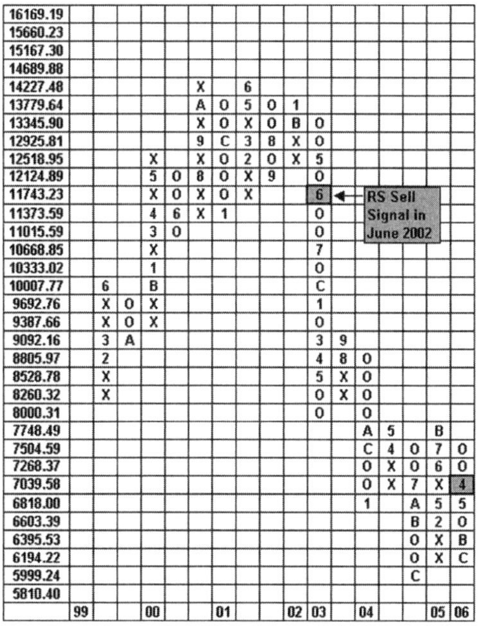

U.S. Dollar Spot vs. Euro FX Spot RS signals

US Dollar on RS	DX/Y	EC/Y
Buy signal		
1/27/00 - 6/6/02	7.52%	-4.35%
Sell signal		
6/6/02 - 1/30/07	-23.45%	37.24%

U.S. Dollar Spot vs. Euro FX Column Changes

US Dollar reversed	DX/Y G/L	EC/Y G/L
to O's 5/3/02	-13.16%	19.21%
Reversed to X's 8/21/2003	-4.83%	5.22%
Reversed to O's 9/22/2003	-4.28%	3.92%
Reversed to X's 4/13/2004	-2.99%	4.27%
Reversed to O's 7/16/2004	-2.85%	3.11%
Reversed to X's 2/7/2005	2.72%	-2.68%
Reversed to O's 4/25/2006	-2.60%	4.21%

Point-and-figure relative strength chart price scale (top to bottom): 16169.19, 15660.23, 15167.30, 14689.88, 14227.48, 13779.64, 13345.90, 12925.81, 12518.95, 12124.89, 11743.23, 11373.59, 11015.59, 10668.85, 10333.02, 10007.77, 9692.76, 9387.66, 9092.16, 8805.97, 8528.78, 8260.32, 8000.31, 7748.49, 7504.59, 7268.37, 7039.58, 6818.00, 6603.39, 6395.53, 6194.22, 5999.24, 5810.40. Year axis: 99, 00, 01, 02, 03, 04, 05, 06. Chart annotation: "RS Sell Signal in June 2002."

EXHIBIT 4.2 U.S. Dollar Spot vs. Euro FX Spot Relative Strength Chart.

the dollar would underperform the euro for some time to come. This is exactly what has transpired over the past few years—the euro has vastly outperformed the dollar, moving to new highs while the dollar fell to nine-year lows. Each time the U.S. dollar managed to reverse into a column of X's on its RS chart, albeit for very brief intervals—in August 2003, April 2004, and February 2005—the rallies off the bottom were muted and failed, while the longer-term RS sell signal remained in force. When you match this RS chart up with the trend chart of the spot dollar, it would have suggested that you cover your shorts once the RS briefly improved (to X's) and the trend chart suggested near-term strength. But since the longer-term RS sell signal remained, it suggested you monitor the trend chart for the next viable entry for shorts. This chart easily demonstrates the power of long-term relative strength. Since giving the RS sell signal in June 2002, the dollar has fallen 23.45 percent, while the euro has gained 37.24 percent. When you match this information up with the trend charts of the dollar and euro, you can see how the RS chart confirmed a trading posture of being short the dollar and/or long the euro (see Exhibit 4.2).

The RS chart in Exhibit 4.3, which compares the Goldman Sachs Spot Return Commodity Index (GN/X) to the CRB Spot Index (CR/Y), clearly depicts the effects crude oil has had on the GN/X. Notice how the GN/X

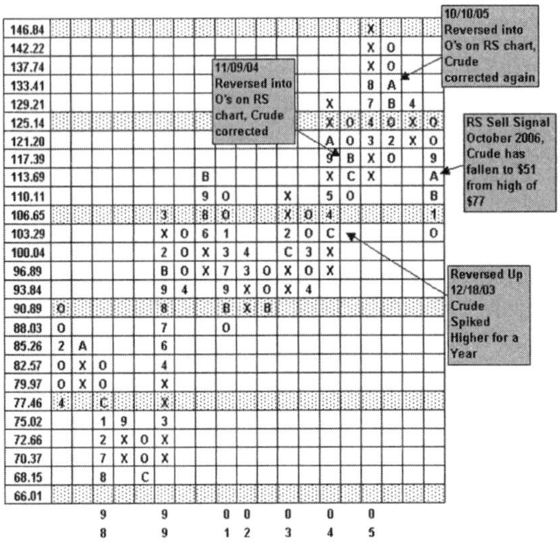

Point-and-figure relative strength chart with the following y-axis values (top to bottom): 146.84, 142.22, 137.74, 133.41, 129.21, 125.14, 121.20, 117.39, 113.69, 110.11, 106.65, 103.29, 100.04, 96.89, 93.84, 90.89, 88.03, 85.26, 82.57, 79.97, 77.46, 75.02, 72.66, 70.37, 68.15, 66.01.

Chart annotations:

- **10/10/05** Reversed into O's on RS chart, Crude corrected again
- **11/09/04** Reversed into O's on RS chart, Crude corrected
- **RS Sell Signal** October 2006, Crude has fallen to $51 from high of $77
- **Reversed Up 12/18/03** Crude Spiked Higher for a Year

GN/X	Gain / Loss	
RS Buy Signal	GN/X	CR/Y
From 3/18/99 to 11/6/01	15.12%	-1.51%
RS Buy Signal	GN/X	CR/Y
From 2/5/03 to 10/2/06	63.34%	49.48%
RS Sell Signal	GN/X	CR/Y
From 10/2/06 to 1/30/07	-3.58%	4.46%

** The return is based on the "old" CRB (UV/Y), which is now known as the Continuous Commodity Index; recall the index was changed in 2005

EXHIBIT 4.3 Goldman Sachs Spot Return Commodity Index (GN/X) vs. CRB Spot Index (CR/Y) Relative Strength Chart.

gave an RS buy signal in February 2003 versus the CRB Index (this calculation was based on the CRB as an equal-weighted index, prior to the 2005 changes, whose symbol is now UV/Y). The RS chart continued to move higher from there, putting in more X's, displaying increased, positive RS compared to the CRB. This RS chart would have helped confirm two things: that the energy complex was an area to consider for long positions; and secondly, if you wanted to gain commodity exposure via an index, the GN/X would have been the better play overall compared to the CRB. In other words, the vast weighting of energy in the GN/X greatly affected its returns and vaulted it into a condition of outperformance versus the equal-weighted CRB Index. Keep in mind, the CRB did go up in price, too; it's just that the GN/X went up "relatively" more. But in looking at Exhibit 4.3 further, you will notice that this condition of outperformance by the GN/X halted in October 2006 when an RS sell signal was given. This suggested that the equal-weighted CRB had moved into a posture of outperformance over the GN/X, and implied that there was likely weakness in the energy markets; which, of course, was the case. This type of RS chart can also be helpful if looking to purchase the "real asset"–based mutual funds and related exchange-traded funds. We will cover this in more detail in later chapters.

Another application of relative strength, as alluded to above, is in maintaining an RS matrix for a given group or sector of the commodity market. The goal here is to identify which commodity has the best relative strength compared to all others in its group; conversely the matrix will also clearly show which has the worst. For example, you could use this type of analysis on the grains, foreign currencies, or for the members of the livestock group; and for that matter, you could construct an RS matrix that included all commodities. This will allow you to pinpoint more precisely which commodity in a group deserves your attention on the long side, and which may be best for a short sale. Naturally, this concept would be very applicable for spread trading. To develop such a matrix, you would merely construct an RS chart on each commodity versus each other member in the group, and then record the signal and column for each resulting chart. In using the grains sector for this example, you would have an RS chart for soybeans versus wheat, another chart for soybeans versus oats, one for soybeans versus corn, and wheat versus corn, wheat versus rough rice, and so on (see Exhibit 4.4). You get the idea. After quantifying each RS chart, you will be able to see which grain has the most relative strength buy signals compared to its peers. Also, you will be able to see which grain has the weakest RS—the one that has the most RS charts on a sell signal and in O's. This type of data can help confirm your trading posture, and can aid in narrowing your choices if you are planning to trade only the best RS in the group. Or, as suggested, this analysis can be a great tool to help in spread trading. For example, in looking at the RS matrix in Exhibit 4.4, you would deduce that 2005 March oats has the best overall RS compared to all of its peers, while corn and wheat have the worst RS of all the grains. You could then take this information and narrow down, based on the underlying trend chart when to go long oats, and/or when to go short wheat or corn, with the overall trend being a major determinant. (Note that Exhibit 4.4 is based on RS data as of February 2005).

This same matrix concept can also be used on the entire commodity universe; the matrix in Exhibit 4.5 for example, is not group specific, and is comprised of 22 commodities, cutting across all the different groups. To construct the matrix, we literally create an RS chart of every commodity in the list against every other commodity. This allows us to identify the strongest commodities relative to the others. For example, corn would have 21 RS charts, one against wheat, crude oil, live cattle, and so on. In addition to the different commodities, we also include an RS chart versus the CRB Index (CR/Y) and the Continuous Commodity Index (UV/Y). All told, this commodity matrix, which is done nightly by our computers at Dorsey, Wright, allows us to know at any given point, on a relative basis, what are the best performing commodities.

The layout of this matrix is similar to the grains one shown in Exhibit 4.4, yet we made the grains one by hand in order to spell out more specifically the concept behind it. For all RS matrixes found in our database, they will be laid out similar to Exhibit 4.5. Within the matrix, the

Group RS Matrix Table Example: Grains

Commodity	Oats	Rough Rice	Bean Oil	Soybean Meal	Soybeans	heat	Corn
Oats		O/H5 vs RR/H5 Buy in X's	O/H5 vs BO/H5 Buy in X's	O/H5 vs SM/H5 Buy in X's	O/H5 vs S/H5 Buy in X's	O/H5 vs W/H5 Buy in X's	O/H5 vs C/H5 Buy in X's
Rough Rice	RR/H5 vs O/H5 Sell in O's		RR/H5 vs BO/H5 Buy in X's	RR/H5 vs SM/H5 Buy in O's	RR/H5 vs S/H5 Buy in O's	RR/H5 vs W/H5 Buy in O's	RR/H5 vs C/H5 Buy in O's
Bean Oil	BO/H5 vs O/H5 Sell in O's	BO/H5 vs RR/H5 Buy in O's		BO/H5 vs SM/H5 Sell in O's	BO/H5 vs S/H5 Buy in X's	BO/H5 vs W/H5 Buy in X's	BO/H5 vs C/H5 Buy in X's
Soybean Meal	SM/H5 vs O/H5 Sell in O's	SM/H5 vs RR/H5 Buy in X's	SM/H5 vs BO/H5 Buy in X's		SM/H5 vs S/H5 Buy in O's	SM/H5 vs W/H5 Sell in X's	SM/H5 vs C/H5 Buy in X's
Soybeans	S/H5 vs O/H5 Sell in O's	S/H5 vs RR/H5 Sell in X's	S/H5 vs BO/H5 Sell in O's	S/H5 vs SM/H5 Buy in X's		S/H5 vs W/H5 Sell in X's	S/H5 vs C/H5 Buy in X's
heat	W/H5 vs O/H5 Sell in O's	W/H5 vs RR/H5 Buy in X's	W/H5 vs BO/H5 Sell in O's	W/H5 vs SM/H5 Buy in O's	W/H5 vs S/H5 Buy in O's		W/H5 vs C/H5 Sell in X's
Corn	C/H5 vs O/H5 Sell in O's	C/H5 vs RR/H5 Sell in X's	C/H5 vs BO/H5 Sell in O's	C/H5 vs SM/H5 Sell in O's	C/H5 vs S/H5 Sell in O's	C/H5 vs W/H5 Buy in O's	

EXHIBIT 4.4 Group RS Matrix Table Example—Grains.

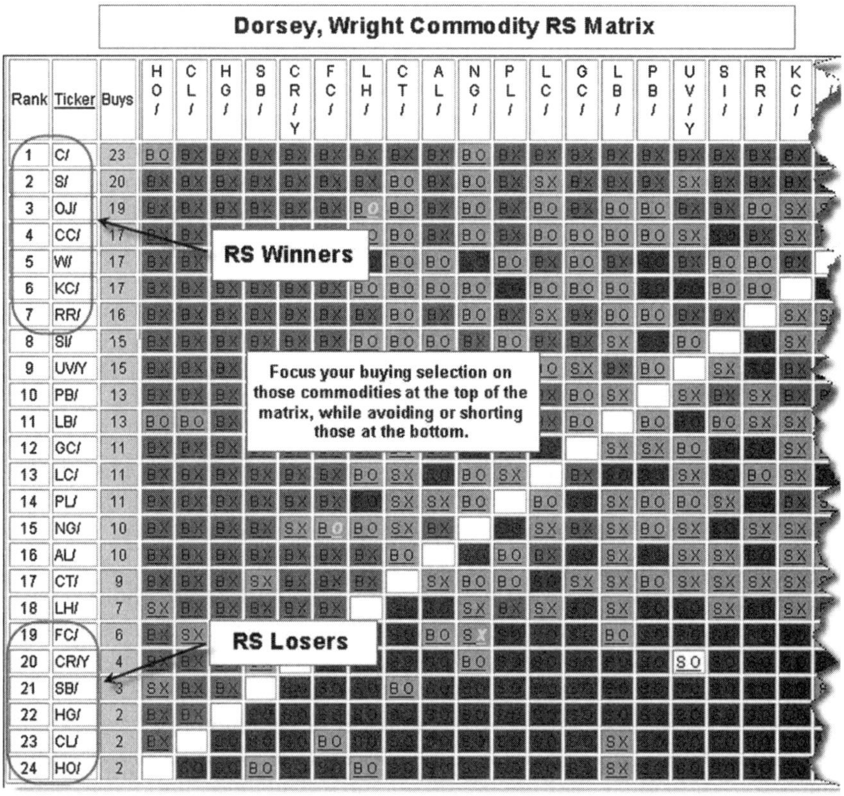

Dorsey, Wright Commodity RS Matrix

Rank	Ticker	Buys	HO/	CL/	HG/	SB/	CR/Y	FC/	LH/	CT/	AL/	NG/	PL/	LC/	GC/	LB/	PB/	UV/Y	SI/	RR/	KC/
1	C/	23	BO	BX	BX	BX	BX	BX	BX	BX	BO	BX	BX	BX	BX	BX	BX	BX	BX	BX	BX
2	S/	20	BX	BX	BX	BX	BX	BX	BX	BO	BX	BO	BX	SX	BX	BX	BX	SX	BX	BX	BX
3	OJ/	19	BX	BX	BX	BX	BX	BX	BO	BO	BX	BO	BX	BO	BX	BO	BO	BX	BX	BO	SX
4	CC/	17		BX					BO	BX	BO	BX	BO	BO	BO	BO	SX		BX	SX	
5	W/	17	BX	BX					BO	BO		BO	BX	BO	BX		BX	BO	BO	BX	
6	KC/	17	BX	BX	BX	BX	BX	BO	BO	BO	BO		BO	BO	BO			BO	BO		
7	RR/	16	BX	BX	BX	BX	BX	BX	BO	BX	BO	BX	SX	BX	BO	BO	BX	BX		SX	S
8	S/	15	BX	BX	BX	BX	BX	BO	BO	BO	BX	BO	BX	BX	SX		BO			SX	
9	UV/Y	15	BX	BX	BX							BO	SX	BX	BO		SX		BX	
10	PB/	13	BX	BX	BX							BX	BO	SX		SX	BX	SX	BX	
11	LB/	13	BO	BO	BX							BX	BO		BO		BO	SX	SX	
12	GC/	11	BX	BX	BX									SX	SX	BO			SX	
13	LC/	11	BX	BX	BX	BX	BX	BO	SX	BO	SX		BX			SX		BO	SX	
14	PL/	11	BX	BX	BX	BX	BX		SX	SX	BO		BO		SX	BO	BO	SX		
15	NG/	10	BX	BX	BX	BX	SX	BO	BO	SX	BX		SX	BX	SX	BO	SX		SX	SX
16	AL/	10	BX	BX	BX	BX	BX	BX	BO		BO	BX		SX		SX	SX		SX	
17	CT/	9	BX	BX	BX	SX	BX	BX		SX	BO	BO		SX	SX	BO	SX	SX	SX	SX
18	LH/	7	SX	BX	BX	BX	BX	BX		SX	BX	SX		SX		SX		SX		SX
19	FC/	6	BX	SX				BO	SX			BO								
20	CR/Y	4		BX				BO									SO			
21	SB/	3	SX	BX	BX			BO												
22	HG/	2	BX	BX				BO												
23	CL/	2	BX			BO								SX						
24	HO/	2			BO		BO							SX						

RS Winners

Focus your buying selection on those commodities at the top of the matrix, while avoiding or shorting those at the bottom.

RS Losers

EXHIBIT 4.5 Dorsey, Wright Commodity RS Matrix.

RS signal of each chart is represented by a "B" for buy signal, an "S" for sell signal, with the "X" and "O" representing the recent column reading of each RS chart. Likewise, a similar ranking system is used to tally all of this RS data. Again, it is based on the total number of RS charts that are on a buy signal for a given commodity, and the one that has the most is ranked as number 1 (corn in this example). For the commodity with the lowest number of buy signals, it is ranked last, and appears at the bottom of the matrix (heating oil). In the event of a tie, it is broken based on the ones that have the most RS charts in a column of X's. (Note that the date of Exhibit 4.5 is January 2007, explaining the change in position for corn compared to its position in Exhibit 4.4.)

When using such a matrix for individual commodity purchases, you undoubtedly want to focus your buying on those that are at the top of the matrix as they are the ones that are outperforming the other member commodities. This matrix shows you the sheer power of this Dorsey, Wright database feature, in that it is applicable to any universe you desire to evaluate on a relative strength basis—even commodities. All told, this is yet another way to help you analyze the commodity market and see where you should focus your longs, and where to look for shorts.

Before moving on, we want to present another very important use of relative strength with respect to commodities, and more generally speaking as it pertains to your overall asset allocation. So far, we have discussed using the Point & Figure methodology to aid in the purchase and sale of a particular commodity; or have learned how to consult the spot and continuous charts for long-term trend guidance. In doing so, we have assumed that you have already made the decision to invest in commodities. But let's step back a second to see how relative strength can help you to determine in a broad asset allocation respect whether or not commodities as an asset class deserves your investment dollars.

As a general rule, much attention is paid to asset allocation, with the greatest emphasis typically placed on the equity slice of the allocation pie, then fixed income; while many investors have a tendency to avoid or forget about allocating money to commodities. What many investors fail to realize though, is how commodities are negatively correlated to equities, and therefore can provide meaningful diversification to a portfolio. Most investors believe they are "diversified" by having exposure to growth, value, small cap, midcap, and large cap; but in fact, all of these equity styles are very highly correlated, and therefore don't offer significant diversification. Granted, fixed income exposure can offer some degree of noncorrelation, but not to the extent that commodities can offer due to this class being "negatively correlated." We will delve into this topic in more detail in Chapter 8, but before doing so we want to show you one simple relative strength chart that can aid you in knowing whether or not to overweight commodities with respect to equities.

Exhibit 4.6 succinctly summarizes this important asset allocation decision for you. This particular RS chart compares the CRB Index (CR/Y) to the venerable equity index benchmark—the S&P 500 Index (SPX). In this instance, when the RS chart is on a buy signal, as it was from October 2000 to June 2003, it implies that you should definitely have exposure to commodities as an asset class, as commodities are in a state of outperformance over equities. The numbers bear this out as commodities, measured by the CRB Index, gained 1.83 percent while the SPX fell −26.82 percent. But when the chart moves to an RS sell signal, as it did in 1995 and then again in 2003, it suggests that equities deserve your investment dollars to a greater degree, and that any exposure to commodities should be mitigated or lessened vis-à-vis equities. This type of RS chart clearly is something to use, in a broad-brushed application, to help you with important asset allocation decisions. This same type of RS evaluation is transferable to other

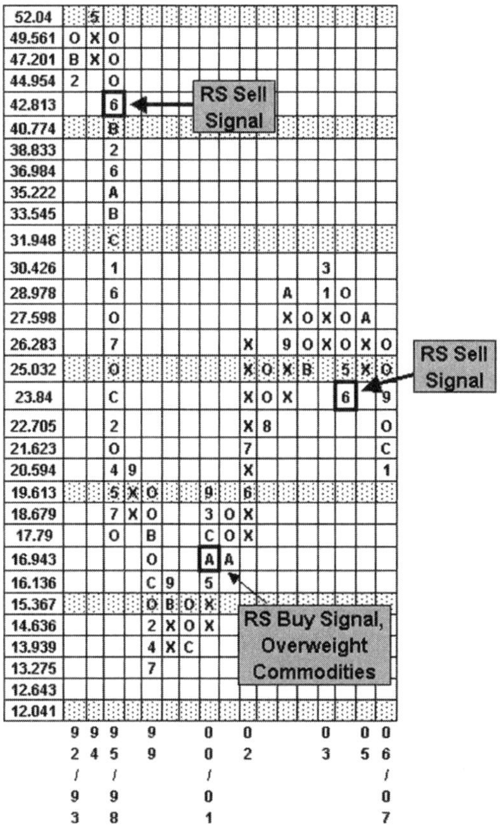

Price																
52.04		5														
49.561	O	X	O													
47.201	B	X	O													
44.954	2		O													
42.813			6	← **RS Sell Signal**												
40.774			B													
38.833			2													
36.984			6													
35.222			A													
33.545			B													
31.948			C													
30.426			1						3							
28.978			6					A	1	O						
27.598			O					X	O	X	O	A				
26.283			7				X		9	O	X	O	X	O	**RS Sell Signal**	
25.032			O				X	O	X	B		5	X	O		
23.84			C				X	O	X		6			9		
22.705			2				X	8						O		
21.623			O				7							C		
20.594			4	9			X							1		
19.613			5	X	O		9	6								
18.679			7	X	O		3	O	X							
17.79			O		B		C	O	X							
16.943					O		A	A								
16.136				C	9		5									
15.367				O	B	O	X		**RS Buy Signal, Overweight Commodities**							
14.636				2	X	O	X									
13.939				4	X	C										
13.275				7												
12.643																
12.041																

Bottom axis:
```
9 9 9   9      0   0        0    0 0
2 4 5   9      0   2        3    5 6
/ /     /                        /
9 9     0                        0
3 8     1                        7
```

CRB RS Signals	Gain / Loss	
RS Sell Signal	CR/Y	SPX
From 6/30/95 to 10/11/00	-0.46%	150.49%
RS Buy Signal	CR/Y	SPX
From 10/11/00 to 6/12/03	1.83%	-26.82%
RS Sell Signal	CR/Y	SPX
From 6/12/03 to 1/30/07	26.45%	43.10%

EXHIBIT 4.6 Relative Strength Chart of CRB Index vs. S&P 500 (SPX).

asset class comparisons, such as commodities to fixed income, or commodities to global equity. The ultimate goal of this process is to ascertain where best to place your money in order to position yourself to garner outperformance, while at the same time taking on less risk than the market if possible, and while also trying to mitigate volatility in your portfolio.

In summary, relative strength is yet another tool to use when determining your trading strategies in commodities. The trend charts can lead you to the same deduction, yet the RS chart simply quantifies which of the underlying commodities has the higher probability of outperforming; and broadly speaking, whether as an asset class it is positioned to outperform other assets. The key to more consistent success is to use chart patterns, trend lines, spot and continuous chart evaluation, and relative strength *together* to arrive at the best decisions for your commodity trading.

CHAPTER 5

Other Strategies and Tools

In the first several chapters we laid out the basic building blocks of Point & Figure charting as they pertain to the commodity markets. These previously discussed topics provide a solid framework for analyzing the commodity market on a more macro level. Now, we want to expand your knowledge even further, adding to your toolbox other techniques and strategies for you to use when trading in this marketplace. In this chapter, we focus on supplemental topics and indicators, ones that will aid in refining your entry and exit points—and basically give you tools that drill down a little deeper, to a more micro level of decision making with respect to initiating and managing the position.

SUPPORT AND RESISTANCE

When talking about support and resistance, and what these terms mean, we are referring back to the trend chart of a given commodity. (This will be the case with respect to several of the new topics we will be discussing in these next pages.) One of the keys to trading commodities on a technical basis is being able to properly analyze the technical condition of the underlying commodity.

Support is basically a level where the commodity stops moving lower in price. For whatever reason, selling pressure begins to wane as buying pressure begins to takes control at a given price. The commodity is in essence passing from weak hands to strong hands at this point. On a Point

& Figure chart we would begin to see some back and forth motion generally producing slightly higher bottoms and higher tops.

Conversely, resistance is a level at which a commodity stops rising in price. Again, for whatever the reason, demand becomes less significant than it previously was and supply begins to take control of the underlying commodity. This is the beginning of a decline in price where the chart will produce a series of lower tops and lower bottoms. The commodity is moving from strong hands to weak hands. Each time the commodity tries to rise it is met with supply. The reasons for this are unimportant; that it is happening is all that is important.

Being able to identify significant support and resistance on a chart can greatly improve your overall trading success. As a general rule of thumb, scale into purchases on pullbacks close to support; or scale into short sales on rallies to resistance, provided your macro analysis of trend, relative strength, and chart patterns has already been completed and corroborates your posture. Buying at support can oftentimes mitigate your risk to the stop loss point, while at the same time increase your upside potential. The same is true for shorts when selling near overhead resistance. As well, rallies up to key longer-term resistance can provide a profit-taking level for long positions, (or drops to significant long-term support for short sales). An example will probably make this explanation more clear-cut.

Exhibit 5.1 is a chart of corn, July 2005 (C/N5). On this chart, you can see definitive *support* had formed in August 2004 at the 246–248 range. This level was tested numerous times, and held, until the fifth attempt when support was unable to be held at that level. In other words, as corn declined to the 246–248 level, buyers were there to support corn. On the fifth retest of this support the buyers had exhausted all their demand, and corn slipped below that level. This created a spread quadruple bottom breakdown occurring on this drop in price to 244. This was considered a strong sell signal. Anyone long July corn should have stopped out on that breakdown. But with the trend clearly negative, any long positions would have been considered "bottom fishing" or aggressive in nature. Corn resumed its downward bias after the breakdown at 244, and subsequently formed *resistance*—first at 224, then more so at 232 (as the chart indicates). Rallies up to the 232 area in October–November 2004 presented shorting opportunities; and then in January 2005 shorts could have been initiated on rallies up toward the 224 level. A short position would then be covered on any break through this overhead resistance. Resistance is just as the name implies. The underlying commodity is resisting any further upside movement. The reason for this is simply that selling pressure, for whatever reason, overtakes demand at these levels and the price is forced down. It would be interesting to get into the minds of those who sell at resistance levels but that is impossible. The next best thing is a Point & Figure chart.

274	O																		274
272	O																		272
270	O																		270
268	O																		268
266	O																		266
264	O						•												264
262	O				X		X	•											262
260	O				X	O	X	O	•										260
258	O				X	O	9	O		•									258
256	O			X	X	O	X	O			•								256
254	O			X	O	X	O	X	O			•							254
252	O	X		8	O	X	O	X	O				•						252
250	O	X	O	X	O	X	O	X	O					•					250
248	O	X	O	X	O	X	O		O						•				248
246	O		O		O			O	← Support at 246 area				•						246
244								O	← Support broken at 244					•					244
242								O							•				242
240								O									•		240
238								O											238
236								O											236
234								O											234
232								O	X		X		X	← Resistance at 232					232
230								O	X	O	X	O	X	O					230
228								A	X	O	X	O	X	O					228
226								O	X	O	B	X	O						226
224								O	X		O	X	O	X		X	← Resistance		224
222								O			O	X	O	X	O		at 224		222
220											O	X	O	X	O				220
218											C		O	X	O				218
216			Can buy on pullbacks to								1		O						216
214			**support**, or can initiate shorts										O						214
212			on rallies to **resistance**.										O						212
210													O						210
208																			208
206																			206
	04										05								

EXHIBIT 5.1 Corn July 2005—Support and Resistance Example.

The soybean meal July 2005 chart, shown in Exhibit 5.2, is another good example of resistance and support. In particular, bean meal displays why you must recognize where significant resistance lies before embarking on a trade. Notice in early January 2005 that a triple top buy signal was given at 169. Technically speaking, you could have drawn a short-term bearish resistance line from the December peak at 172, so the move to 169 would have violated this downtrend line, suggesting you could have considered a long posture. But such a trade would not have been in your best interest. Here's why. Evaluating bean meal more closely, you would have seen that formidable overhead resistance resided at 172—a level that it retreated from three previous times. In addition, the longer-term bearish

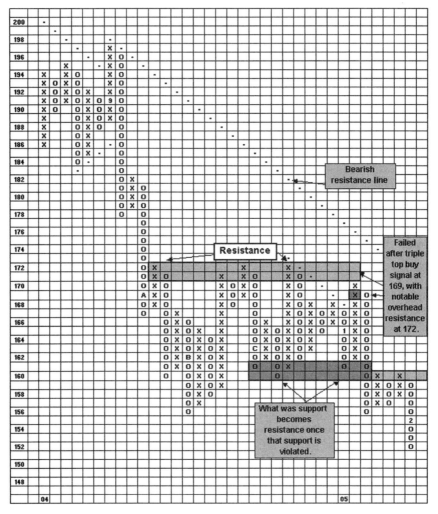

EXHIBIT 5.2 Soybean Meal, July 2005—Support and Resistance Example.

resistance line was hovering just above that 172 level. This serves to show that you can't be myopic about just the chart pattern itself—in this case a triple top buy signal, but instead need to inspect the chart with a broader view; by doing so, you would pick up on the key overhead resistance at 172, and no trade would be taken. It would be best to wait instead for a better set-up. Bean meal failed again, just shy of the 172 resistance, and promptly resumed its downward bias. Not only that, the support that had existed in the 160–161 area was penetrated, too.

This leads us to one last point we want to make on support and resistance. There is an old adage on Wall Street that says, "What was support becomes resistance; and what was resistance becomes support." Once a violation of major support occurs, that level will often become a level of key resistance. In looking at the July soybean meal chart once again, we noted that support in the 160–161 level was penetrated. Notice how on two rally attempts back up, the contract failed at the 160 level—what was support then became resistance for bean meal. Being aware of this phenomenon can also aid in the process of scaling in to new long or new short positions.

BIG BASE BREAKOUTS

The preceding commentary leads us to our next discussion on big base breakouts. For all intents and purposes, this topic is really a combination of two previously discussed points on support and resistance, along with the science of ballistics and the horizontal count. Over the years, with both stocks and commodities, we have found it useful to watch our charts for the formation of "big bases" of accumulation or distribution. In keeping with the horizontal count, the bigger the base, the larger the price objective; or said another way, the bigger the base, the bigger the move (or "bang for your buck") up out of the base. So it stands to reason that you should be looking out for such a pattern, with the action point for initiating a position being when the commodity breaks out of the base. Think back to our recent discussion on support and resistance; you would not want to be a buyer of a commodity when it has rallied up to resistance, but instead want to see it penetrate the key resistance. Think of resistance as a bunch of gremlins hanging around on that street corner with sell orders in hand. The only exception to this would be if you are merely trying to trade the "range" of a base—meaning you buy on the pullback to the bottom of the base (support), and sell on the rally to overhead resistance (or the top of the base); such a posture would be considered more of a short term trading tactic.

Exhibits 5.3 and 5.4 should help to clarify the "big base breakout." Sugar, July 2005 (SB/N5) had experienced a strong, orderly up move during the first part of 2004. But then starting in July, the contract went through a period of consolidation, working sideways for several months, and digesting its previous move up. As sugar worked sideways in a fairly tight range, support was formed in the 7.95–8.10 range; while noteworthy resistance was at 8.45. It wasn't until late September that sugar finally managed to breakout to the upside, after its fifth attempt at testing this resistance level at 8.45. The contract gave a spread quintuple top buy signal at 8.50, and from there saw a straight spike up to the 9.15 level. This is not an un-

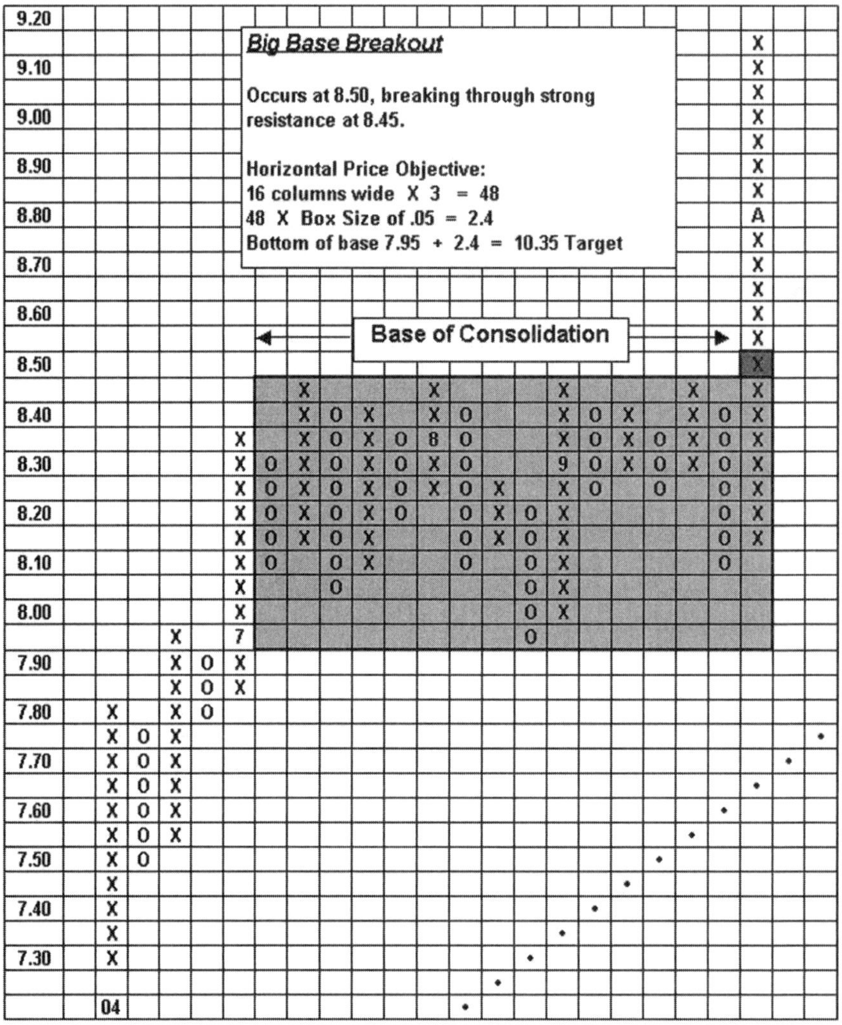

```
9.20 |                                                                    |   |
9.10 |        Big Base Breakout                                      | X |
9.00 |        Occurs at 8.50, breaking through strong resistance     | X |
     |        at 8.45.                                                | X |
8.90 |                                                                | X |
     |        Horizontal Price Objective:                            | X |
8.80 |        16 columns wide  X 3  = 48                             | A |
     |        48 X  Box Size of .05  =  2.4                           | X |
8.70 |        Bottom of base 7.95 + 2.4 = 10.35 Target               | X |
     |                                                                | X |
8.60 |   |----        Base of Consolidation        ----|             | X |
8.50 |                                                                | X |
     |         X         X         X         X           X
8.40 |         X O X     X O       X O X     X O X
     |     X   X O X O 8 O         X O X O   X O X
8.30 |     X O X O X O X O         9 O X O   X O X
     |     X O X O X O X O X       X O   O     O X
8.20 |     X O X O X O   O X O X           O X
     |     X O X O X     O X O X           O X
8.10 |     X O   O X     O   O X             O
     |     X     O           O X
8.00 |     X                 O X
     | X   7                 O
7.90 | X O X
     | X O X
7.80 | X   X O
     | X O X
7.70 | X O X                                                          •
     | X O X                                                        •
7.60 | X O X                                                      •
     | X O X                                                    •
7.50 | X O                                                    •
     | X                                                    •
7.40 | X                                                  •
     | X                                               •
7.30 | X                                             •
     |                                             •
     | 04                                        •
```

EXHIBIT 5.3 Sugar, July 2005—Big Base Breakout Example.

usual occurrence following the break out of a huge base. Again, remember the phrase, "the bigger the base, the bigger the move up out of that base." A horizontal price count yielded an objective of 10.35, given there was 16 columns in the base, and a box size of .05.

The eurodollars, March 2005 (ED/H5) chart, conversely, displays a commodity breaking down out of a base, following a period of distribution. Observe the base of distribution that March eurodollars formed during the

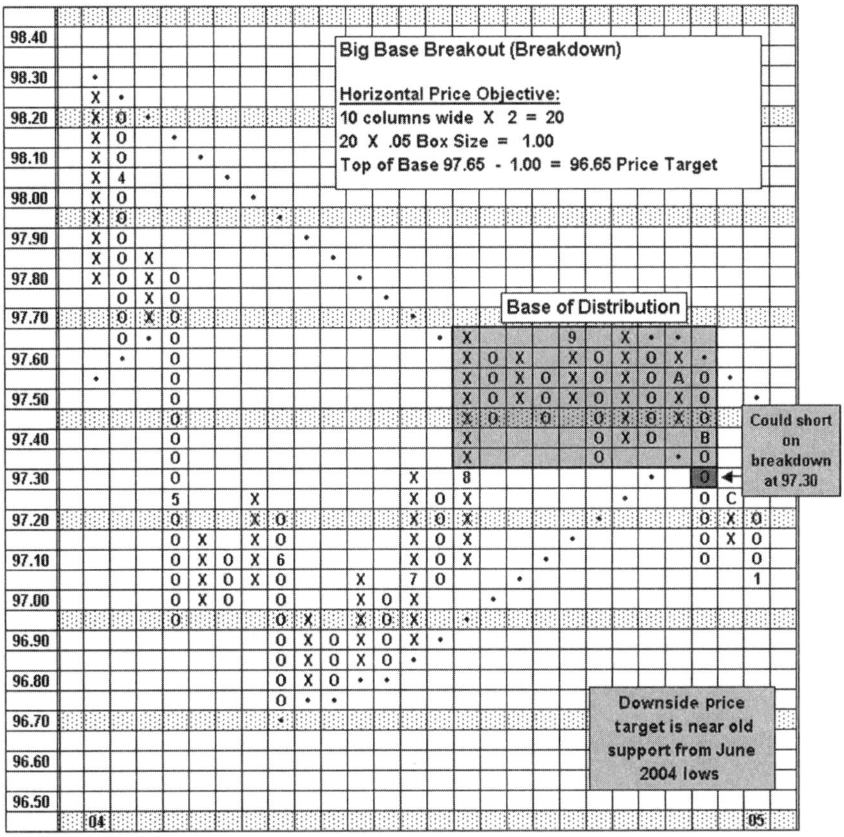

Big Base Breakout (Breakdown)

Horizontal Price Objective:
10 columns wide X 2 = 20
20 X .05 Box Size = 1.00
Top of Base 97.65 - 1.00 = 96.65 Price Target

Base of Distribution

Could short on breakdown at 97.30

Downside price target is near old support from June 2004 lows

EXHIBIT 5.4 Eurodollars, March 2005—Big Base Breakout Example.

second half of 2004. After a spike up to 97.65 by August, March eurodollars started to show signs of distribution, working sideways in a range between 97.35 and 97.65. After plenty of back-and-forth action on the chart, eurodollars resolved itself to the downside, breaking down out of the base at 97.30. With this breakdown also came a change in trend to negative, as the bullish support line was violated. At this juncture, short positions could have been considered with a downside price target of 96.65, based on the horizontal count, and a buy stop loss point of 97.70.

CHANGING BOX SIZE

When analyzing a commodity on a technical basis, your main tool is the actual trend chart of the commodity. As you have learned, the trend chart will show you important data such as the overall trend, where key support or resistance exists, and particular Point & Figure patterns. All told, it is this chart that depicts who is winning the battle of supply and demand for a given commodity. Often, the commodity chart will progress in a very orderly fashion, showing a series of higher tops and higher bottoms (if in an uptrend), or a consistent series of lower tops and lower bottoms (if in a downtrend). But there are times when a commodity will experience a straight spike up (or down) in price, resulting in an extended condition with no apparent support (or resistance) at hand. This can be troublesome for two reasons—no viable stop loss point is apparent, nor are any pullbacks shown to allow for new entries into the commodity.

This is where changing the box size can be used. When necessary, reducing the box size on the chart can be a very helpful method to employ to gain insight into levels of support and resistance, areas of consolidation, potential entry levels, and viable stop loss points. If the regular default chart shows a very discernible supply and demand picture, typically we would not arbitrarily reduce the box size to multiple lower sizes, as this can serve to only confuse you in your decision-making process. But when no nearer-term support or resistance levels are shown on the chart (or pullbacks), as was the case with the euro FX December 2004 (EC/Z4), then elect to take a look at the smaller box size. It can aid you both in your entry and exit.

The Euro FX, December 2004 contract (EC/Z4) broke out of a big base in mid-October at 1.245. This was a strong buy signal, and one that we actually took in our in-house commodity investment account. The euro quickly spiked straight up to 1.283 without a breather. Exhibit 5.5 obviously displayed an extended condition, with the contract well above any near-term support. At this point, new entries would have been tenuous given the lack of near-term support or a viable stop loss point. This is where bumping the box size down, cutting it in half from .005 per box to .0025 per box, could help with the management of trading the euro. By doing this, the chart exhibited a textbook shakeout pattern that wasn't apparent on the .005 per box chart. Therefore, had you consulted the smaller box size chart, you would have been afforded an entry point on the reversal up from the shakeout pattern. The smaller box size also gave you a slightly tighter stop loss point of 1.317 where it broke a double bottom following a lower top. As a result of bumping the box size down, you could have bought the December euro at 1.275 on the reversal up from the shakeout pattern. (Had you never looked at the smaller box size, no reasonable entry level would have presented itself.) In buying the December euro at 1.275 and selling at 1.317 resulted in a profit of $5,312.50 per contract, rather than totally missing out on the trade altogether.

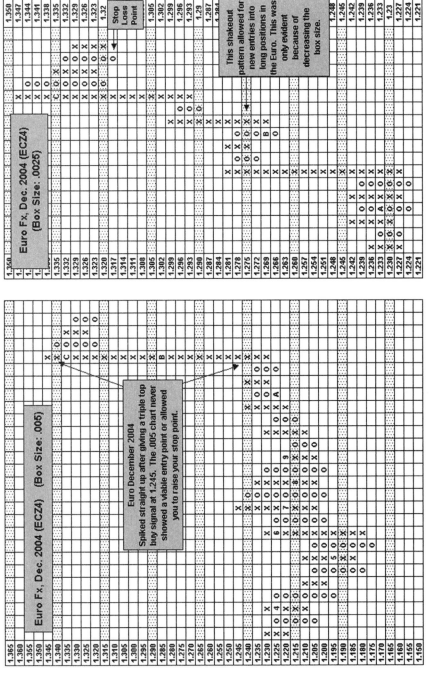

EXHIBIT 5.5 Euro FX, December 2004—Changing the Box Size.

Just as you can reduce the box size to gain shorter-term insight and help with trade management, the opposite can be done to allow for longer-term perspective. By increasing the box size, it permits you to see longer-term resistance and support levels, as well as longer term trends. An example of this can be seen with copper, March 2005 (HG/H5). This contract had been trending higher for several years, but during this time frame copper had been prone to wild swings in price; this was quite evident in the second half of 2004 and early 2005. Such erratic chart action can often times scare most investors away; yet copper actually offered some viable trading opportunities in the face of this volatile action, if only you had consulted the 1 point per box chart, rather than just looking at the default .50 per box chart. Take a look at the 1-point chart of copper in Exhibit 5.6, and you will see several instances where copper sold off hard after making new highs, only to correct down to (and hold) its bullish support line. These retreats to the uptrend line could have been used as tradable entry points for new long positions. One occasion in particular to zero in on is October 2004. Notice how copper had rallied to a new high of 139.50 early in the month. But then, as the saying goes, copper stepped on the proverbial banana peel and slipped quickly from 139.50 down to 120.50. This sell-off was violent as copper literally gave up all of its gains from September and October. Had you just looked at the default .50 per box chart (with fear in your eyes), you would have likely had nothing to do with this base metal contract. But the 1-point chart revealed a much different picture—a bona fide trading opportunity. The massive sell-off in copper basically just brought the contract right back to significant August-September support, and back to its bullish support line. Not only was March copper back at support, but a very affordable stop loss point of 118 was presented (which would have been a triple bottom sell signal and violation of the uptrend line). By increasing the box size, you were presented with an excellent entry point for new long positions while also preserving a very palatable stop loss point. Copper proceeded to rally 25 points from there, equating to $6,000 per contract. As an addendum, the price of copper is now quoted with the decimal two places to the left, so the above prices would now appear as 1.18, for example. Also, copper is a great example of how you must be willing to adapt the box size of your main default chart based on volatility. We currently use a .04 point per box chart (or what would be 4 points per box, based on the above example) for copper. It is important to be flexible with your box sizes in order to be provided with the most discernible and useable trend chart.

Generally speaking, by changing the box size, you can gain longer-term or shorter-term perspective on a commodity. This is useful for longer-term investment decisions, or for shorter-term trading plays; and for providing you viable entry points and stop loss points, when none other may be of-

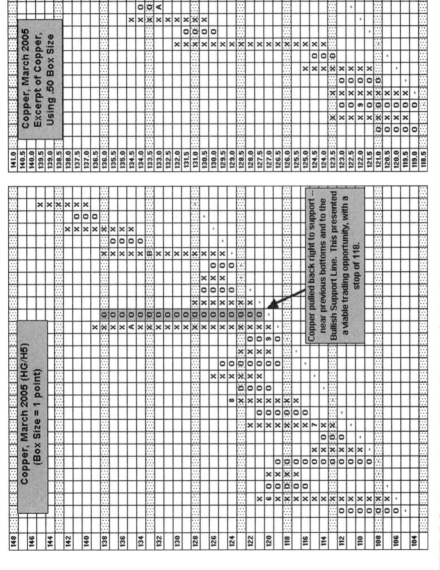

EXHIBIT 5.6 Copper, March 2005—Changing the Box Size.

fered. This is one more facet of Point & Figure analysis to add to your toolbox when trying to manage your commodity trading decisions.

USING PULLBACKS AND RALLIES TO IMPROVE RISK-REWARD

Risk-reward analysis is a very important component of both stock and commodity selection. Before initiating any trade, whether it be a long or a short, it is imperative that you go through this process. Overall success in investing, in large part, is a function of proper risk management—basically, you must strike a balance between focusing on gains, while not ignoring the risk of loss. Preservation of capital by keeping your losses small and maximizing the size of your winners will be a key to your commodity trading success. This is the essence of risk-reward analysis.

Risk-reward is just what the name implies. It is the process of evaluating how much risk you will take, compared to how much reward you can expect to have on any given trade. Or said another way, how many points could the commodity fall if the trade doesn't work out, versus how many points you could expect to gain if the commodity rises in your favor (assuming a long position); the opposite would be true for a short sale. Typically, when evaluating risk-reward, we like to see a two-to-one ratio, at a minimum. In other words, for every point (or dollar) at risk, we want to have 2 points (or $2) of potential reward. This suggests you need to be able to figure out what the expected reward is, and what the potential risk is. Let's examine how we might analyze the risk-reward before we take a trading position:

- Determine where significant resistance lies, or where the commodity would be overbought on its trading band. (One might use these price objectives in lieu of a vertical or horizontal count.)
- Determine where significant support lies. Remember, this support lies below the current price of the underlying commodity. Support levels are often times good areas to consider buying a commodity.
- Calculate the price objective for the commodity, using either the vertical or horizontal count. It's important to have an idea of what could happen if things go right.
- Determine your stop loss point—where the commodity will break a significant bottom or violate its trend line—basically, a point at which you no longer want to be long the commodity. You must be able to handle the worst-case scenario. The potential loss must be in keeping with your risk tolerance and the size of your account.

- Know the price you plan to purchase the commodity. The current market price or your limit price.

Let's go through an example of evaluating risk-reward using live cattle, April 2005 (LC/J5) in Exhibits 5.7 and 5.8.

Risk-Reward Analysis

Scenario One:

Live cattle, April (LC/J5) has broken out to the upside, having moved through all overhead resistance. The overall trend is positive, and the chart is currently on a bullish triangle pattern, after breaking a double top at 88.50; since that breakout Cattle has rallied to a high of 90.00. The vertical price objective is 93.50. Initial support for the contract exists at 86.00, while the stop loss point for long positions is 85.00. You could choose to use 85.50, which would break a double bottom, yet in this case given that the Uptrend line is right at that 85.50 level, we prefer to use 85.00 as the stop since that would be a violation of the bullish support line.

Risk-Reward Calculation:

Current Price = 90.00
Price Objective = 93.50
Stop Loss = 85.00
Reward = 93.5 (price objective) − 90.00 (current price) = 3.50
Risk = 90.00 (current price) − 85.00 (stop loss) = 5.00
Risk-Reward Ratio = 3.50 / 5.00 = .70 points of reward for every point of risk (unacceptable)

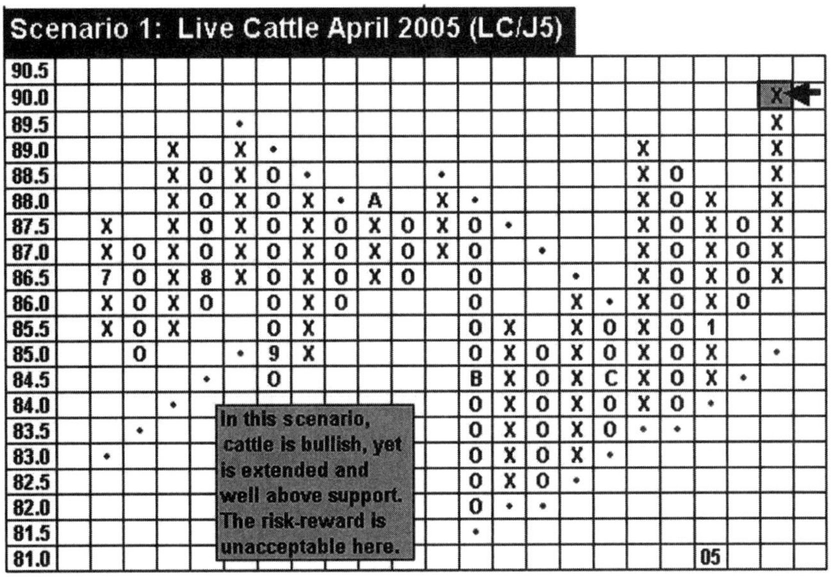

Scenario 1: Live Cattle April 2005 (LC/J5)

	1	2	3	4	5	6	7	8	9	10	11	12	13	14	15	16	17	18
90.5																		
90.0																		X◄
89.5				•														X
89.0		X		X	•								X					X
88.5		X	O	X	O	•			•				X	O				X
88.0		X	O	X	O	X	•	A	X	•			X	O	X			X
87.5	X	X	O	X	O	X	O	X	O	X	O	•	X	O	X	O	X	
87.0	X	O	X	O	X	O	X	O	X	O		•	X	O	X	O	X	
86.5	7	O	X	8	X	O	X	O	X	O	O	•	X	O	X	O	X	
86.0	X	O	X	O		O	X	O		O		X •	X	O	X	O		
85.5	X	O	X			O	X			O	X	X	O	X	O	1		
85.0		O			•	9	X			O	X	O	X	O	X	O	X	•
84.5					•	O				B	X	O	X	C	X	O	X	•
84.0				•						O	X	O	X	O	X	O	•	
83.5			•							O	X	O	X	O	•	•		
83.0		•								O	X	O	X	•				
82.5										O	X	O	•					
82.0										O	•	•						
81.5										•								
81.0														05				

In this scenario, cattle is bullish, yet is extended and well above support. The risk-reward is unacceptable here.

EXHIBIT 5.7 Live Cattle, April 2005—Risk-reward Analysis Example.

Risk-Reward Analysis

Scenario Two:

Live cattle, April (LC/J5) had broken out to the upside and moved through all overhead resistance, after completing a bullish triangle pattern. The overall trend is positive, too. The contract has since pulled back to 87.00, after reaching new highs of 90.00. The vertical price objective is 93.50. Initial support for the contract exists at 86.00, while the stop loss point for long positions is 85.00. You could choose to use 85.50, which would break a double bottom, yet in this case given that the Uptrend line is right at that 85.50 level, we prefer to use 85.00 as the stop since that would be a violation of the bullish support line.

Risk-Reward Calculation:

Current Price = 87.00
Price Objective = 93.50
Stop Loss = 85.00
Reward = 93.5 (price objective) – 87.00 (current price) = 6.50
Risk = 87.00 (current price) – 85.00 (stop loss) = 2.00
Risk-Reward Ratio = 6.50 / 2.00 = 3.25 points of reward for every point of risk (acceptable)

Scenario 2: Live Cattle April 2005 (LC/J5)

90.5																		
90.0																X		
89.5					•											X	O	
89.0			X		X	•								X		X	O	
88.5			X	O	X	O	•			•				X	O	X	O	
88.0			X	O	X	O	X	•	A	X	•			X	O	X	X	O
87.5	X		X	O	X	O	X	O	X	O	X	O	•	X	O	X	O	X	O
87.0	X	O	X	O	X	O	X	O	X	O	X	O	•	X	O	X	O	X	O	←
86.5	7	O	X	8	X	O	X	O	X	O		O	•	X	O	X	O	X
86.0	X	O	X	O		O	X	O		O		X	•	X	O	X	O
85.5	X	O	X		O	X			O	X		X	O	X	O	1
85.0		O		•	9	X			O	X	O	X	O	X	O	X	•
84.5			•		O		B	X	O	X	C	X	O	X	•
84.0		•			O	X	O	X	O	X	O	•
83.5		•		O	X	O	X	O	•	•
83.0	•			O	X	O	X	•
82.5			O	X	O	•
82.0			O	•	•
81.5		•
81.0																05

In this scenario, cattle has pulled back to 87.00, providing a more attractive risk-reward situation.

EXHIBIT 5.8   Live Cattle, April 2005—Risk-reward Analysis Example.

In summary, by waiting for a pullback in live cattle, you greatly improved your risk-reward situation. In scenario one, the risk was unacceptable, making only .70 points for every point of risk. But with cattle pulling back to the 87.00 level in scenario two, your potential reward increased while your risk was mitigated—at 3.25 points of reward for every point of risk. This is much more acceptable from a risk management perspective. When you are trying to determine which commodities to buy and which to short, be sure to take the time to determine your risk-reward ratio. There will be times when you don't necessarily have to wait for a "pullback" to initiate a position. In other words, you can go long on a breakout, as long as the risk-reward situation is still an acceptable two-to-one ratio (or better).

MOMENTUM

Momentum, along with trading bands discussed later, are two more tools to add to your "technical analysis toolbox." But in the hierarchy of importance, these two indicators have a secondary role. That is not to say they aren't extremely useful in refining your entry and exit points—they are, but you must remember that they are supplemental to the more important analysis of trend, pattern, relative strength, and risk-reward.

There are many different "momentum" indicators in the field of technical analysis, but all basically are applied in a similar fashion—being oscillators that are calculated from price data. At Dorsey, Wright we calculate three momentums—monthly, weekly and daily—which are proprietary. Weekly momentum is the indicator we mostly turn to for guidance, as it provides an intermediate-term indication of price direction. The monthly momentum provides a long-term indication of trend and price action, so it can be very useful in detecting a change in trend or turnaround situation, whereas daily momentum is a short-term tool to use for timing your entry (or exit) into a trade. With commodities, we typically rely most on the weekly and monthly momentums.

All three momentums are calculated the same, with the only difference being the time period. In the case of the weekly momentum, it is slow enough to prevent many whipsaws between positive and negative, and faster than the long-term monthly momentum, making it a useful trading tool. For this discussion, we focus on the weekly momentum, but the concept is the same when applied to the other momentum time frames. The calculation, in simplest terms, is an evaluation of two moving averages that are weighted and smoothed. These two averages are based on 1 and 5 data points. For example, the weekly momentum uses one-week and five-week moving averages that are weighted and smoothed. When the shorter-term average (one-week) is above the longer-term average (five-week), the momentum is "positive" and we would expect to see strength from the commodity (or at least a pause if in a downtrend). When the one-week moving average falls below the five-week moving average, it turns to "negative momentum," suggesting weakness in the commodity, or at least a breather if in a strong uptrend. Each week we calculate the averages and determine at what price the commodity will have to trade to cause the one-week average to cross the five-week average. We call this price the "cross point," which is helpful to know when trying to determine if the momentum is close to changing. Remember that these moving averages are weighted and smoothed to help prevent whipsaws compared to what you can find with simple averages. Typically, when a momentum changes from positive to negative, or vice versa, it will stay in that condition for 6 to 8 data points (weeks, days, or months). These time frames are just guidelines, so it is not uncommon to see momentum stay positive or negative for a much longer or shorter time period.

Momentum becomes most useful once you have established your overall posture on the commodity, as a function of trend, chart pattern, risk-reward, and so on. In other words, if you have determined that you want to buy a given commodity because of the above-mentioned technical criteria, then look to the momentum to help define if "now" is the best time to purchase it. If the weekly momentum has just turned back to positive after having been negative for numerous weeks, it is a good sign that now is the time to buy. Momentum will help to pinpoint the right time to enter, as well as exit or take profits. It gives you that extra bit of confidence to pull the trigger. A couple of examples, which we outline below, will likely help you to see the effectiveness of incorporating momentum into your timing of a trade. These can be found on the charts at www.dorseywright.com.

We have selected two particular momentum examples for you—one for weekly momentum using the U.S. dollar, December 2004 (DXZ4) contract; and the other using corn, March 2005 (C/H5), to show you the application of monthly momentum.

The U.S. dollar, December contract is a textbook illustration of weekly momentum. As a sidebar, from our experience we have found weekly momentum to be exceptionally effective as a timing tool with respect to currency and financial futures contracts. In the case of the December dollar contract, it should come as no surprise to you, based on our previous discussions, that the December 2004 dollar trended lower for several years, as the chart in Exhibit 5.9 confirms. When you couple this trend chart together with the weekly momentum signals, you come up with a winning hand. In Exhibit 5.9, we have overlaid the dollar's trend chart with its weekly momentum reading, doing so by shading the chart according to the weekly momentum reading, whether positive or negative. Notice how the weekly momentum had been negative from late May 2004 until late July, with the dollar selling off throughout this time. Then momentum turned to positive the week of July 30, suggesting a bounce in the dollar, or at least a pause in the precipitous decline. This was borne out over the next couple of months as the dollar chopped around with no clear direction. This "breather" for the dollar came to an abrupt end by the first of October as momentum again crossed back to negative, suggesting a resumption of its downward

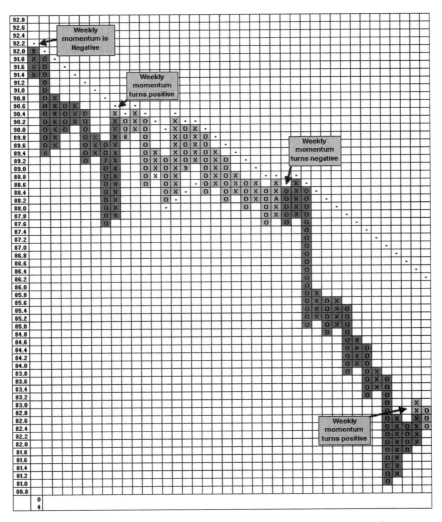

EXHIBIT 5.9 U.S. Dollar, December 2004—Weekly Momentum Example.

bias. The greenback's demise didn't come to a halt until it had dropped from 87.40, after a triple bottom sell signal, to a December low of 81.00. By mid-December, the dollar managed to not only find a bottom, but also broke out to the upside with a double top buy signal at 82.80. This came concurrently with a change back to positive weekly momentum, suggesting a bounce back up. This momentum change, coupled with the breakout to the upside, was a prime indication that shorts should be covered and profits locked in. In essence, the momentum served as a confirmation that

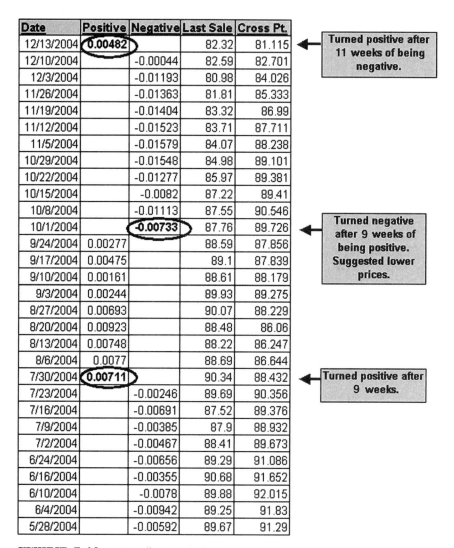

Date	Positive	Negative	Last Sale	Cross Pt.
12/13/2004	0.00482		82.32	81.115
12/10/2004		-0.00044	82.59	82.701
12/3/2004		-0.01193	80.98	84.026
11/26/2004		-0.01363	81.81	85.333
11/19/2004		-0.01404	83.32	86.99
11/12/2004		-0.01523	83.71	87.711
11/5/2004		-0.01579	84.07	88.238
10/29/2004		-0.01548	84.98	89.101
10/22/2004		-0.01277	85.97	89.381
10/15/2004		-0.0082	87.22	89.41
10/8/2004		-0.01113	87.55	90.546
10/1/2004		-0.00733	87.76	89.726
9/24/2004	0.00277		88.59	87.856
9/17/2004	0.00475		89.1	87.839
9/10/2004	0.00161		88.61	88.179
9/3/2004	0.00244		89.93	89.275
8/27/2004	0.00693		90.07	88.229
8/20/2004	0.00923		88.48	86.06
8/13/2004	0.00748		88.22	86.247
8/6/2004	0.0077		88.69	86.644
7/30/2004	0.00711		90.34	88.432
7/23/2004		-0.00246	89.69	90.356
7/16/2004		-0.00691	87.52	89.376
7/9/2004		-0.00385	87.9	88.932
7/2/2004		-0.00467	88.41	89.673
6/24/2004		-0.00656	89.29	91.086
6/16/2004		-0.00355	90.68	91.652
6/10/2004		-0.0078	89.88	92.015
6/4/2004		-0.00942	89.25	91.83
5/28/2004		-0.00592	89.67	91.29

Turned positive after 11 weeks of being negative.

Turned negative after 9 weeks of being positive. Suggested lower prices.

Turned positive after 9 weeks.

EXHIBIT 5.10   U.S. Dollar, December 2004—Weekly Momentum Table.

prices were likely to head higher (which they did). You can more easily see the actual weekly momentum changes in Exhibit 5.10, which shows the U.S. dollar December 2004's weekly momentum in a tabular format.

Our second example of momentum focuses on the viability of it as a longer-term indicator, using the monthly momentum. In this case, we turn our attention to March corn (C/H5). In Exhibit 5.11, we display a trend chart

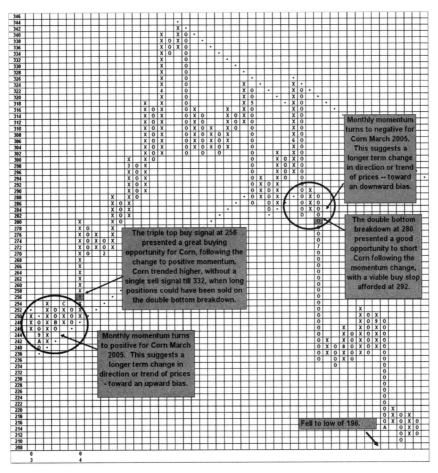

EXHIBIT 5.11 Corn, March 2005—Monthly Momentum Example.

of corn dating back to September 2003; in Exhibit 5.12 you can view its corresponding monthly momentum table. In glancing at the chart, you can see that corn bottomed in September–December 2003. At this same time (in October), the longer-term monthly momentum turned to positive, suggesting a trend change was at hand. This came to fruition as corn trended noticeably higher over the next few months. In fact, had you bought corn on the notable triple top buy signal given at 256, you would have been nicely rewarded as the contract rallied to 342, and did not break down until 332 (which would have been the stop loss point on the double bottom sell signal). This would have equated to a profit of $3,800 per contract. But just

Date	Positive	Negative	Last Sale	Cross Pt.
2/10/2005		-0.01216	198.25	206.43
1/31/2005		-0.05734	197.00	239.41
12/30/2004		-0.06929	204.75	258.06
11/30/2004		-0.12905	203.75	317.54
10/29/2004		-0.15826	213.00	364.11
9/30/2004		-0.17246	216.25	385.68
8/31/2004		-0.14483	245.25	382.66
7/30/2004		-0.11171	234.25	331.84
6/30/2004		(-0.01011)	273.75	281.94
5/28/2004	0.08229		301.50	239.09
4/30/2004	0.11676		319.75	231.73
3/31/2004	0.11092		318.75	235.41
2/27/2004	0.08661		296.75	233.04
1/30/2004	0.03905		277.50	248.21
12/31/2003	0.00613		253.25	248.65
11/28/2003	0.00351		251.50	248.87
10/31/2003	(0.00211)		254.00	252.42
9/30/2003		-0.00967	242.75	250.00

Monthly momentum turns negative during June when the price of corn crossed below 281.94. This longer term change in momentum suggested lower prices for corn.

Monthly momentum turns positive during October when the price of corn crossed above 252.42. This longer term change in momentum suggested higher prices for corn.

EXHIBIT 5.12   Corn, March 2005—Monthly Momentum Table.

as the monthly momentum was a harbinger of higher prices while positive, it was equally on the mark when it turned back to negative in June 2004. Corn was trading at roughly 282 when the monthly momentum flipped to negative. After doing so, the contract fell to a low of 196 with momentum staying negative throughout the decline; at $50 per point, that equated to a $4,300 gain per contract (if you shorted corn). As you can see, this longer-term supplemental tool can be very supportive in confirming changes in trend, giving you extra confidence to play both sides—both long and short.

TRADING BANDS

Trading bands are the second supplemental timing indicator we use when trying to refine our timing of the trade. The concept of trading bands relies on that law of nature called "regression to mean," and the oft-learned bell curve from Statistics 101 class. Given a set of data, we can construct a range that is depicted as a bell curve—this is the basis of our trading band indicators.

At Dorsey, Wright we calculate both daily and weekly distributions, which are also referred to as trading bands. These calculations are also proprietary; however, they are similar to a standard deviation calculation (bell curve). Another term for standard deviation is *volatility*. Ten data points are used to determine the trading bands—for the daily it is 10 days, and for the weekly it's 10 weeks. Obviously, the daily is short term in nature, while the weekly is longer term and slower to change. There are six standard deviations to a bell curve. The calculation evaluates the range between the high and low prices of the commodity for the 10 data points. A volatility variable is then applied to the data and it is smoothed to create the distribution or trading band. The calculation results in a 100 percent overbought value based on the 10 data points, as well as a 100 percent oversold value. From these values we calculate the midpoint or a "normal" position in the trading band. This is the center of the bell curve. The 100 percent overbought and oversold levels are displayed on the chart (on the right-hand side) using TOP and BOT respectively, while the middle of the distribution is marked MED. Three standard deviations to the left of the midpoint are also analogous to being 100 percent oversold, while three standard deviations to the right of the norm are considered 100 percent overbought. In keeping with the theory of a bell curve, stocks and commodities tend to stay just one standard deviation to either the left or right most of the time (68 percent). So when you have a circumstance when a commodity moves to either the top of the trading band or the bottom, it is an extreme instance, and suggests a "regression back to mean"—a movement back to a more normal condition on the trading band. This is where trading bands can be of use in timing your purchase or sale. Entries can be made on moves back toward the midpoint, or best at the 100 percent oversold level for longs or at the 100 percent overbought level for shorts. Profits can be locked in (on a long position) with rallies to the top of the trading band; or in the case of shorts, on a drop in price to the bottom of the band.

We find that strong, upward trending commodities typically trade in the upper half, overbought side, of their weekly band, therefore a pullback to the midrange is often a great entry point, provided the chart still shows a bullish technical picture. Technically weaker commodities that may be experiencing a short-term rally often make their way up to this weekly midpoint but have difficulty sustaining an overbought condition. This is a good scenario to consider shorts, provided the chart confirms such a position.

With respect to the shorter-term daily trading band, a commodity will often move into a more extreme overbought and oversold condition. This is not unusual given the fact that only 10 days of data are used. But such a scenario also aids in entry and exit, just in a more refined capacity. For example, if a bullish configured commodity has reached very oversold territory on its 10-day distribution, and while doing so has pulled back on its chart providing an attractive entry point for new long positions, we then consult the ten-day band, watching for what we call a "curl" back toward the midpoint. This "curl" or first day of lessening the oversold condition suggests to us that the pullback has ceased—the rubber band is no longer being stretched downward, but instead has been released—and the commodity is set to bounce back up in price from there. So by using the 10-day band, you can help pinpoint your entry (or exit) more efficiently. Of course, this concept can be applied to shorts on rallies to overbought territory, but can also be used for short-term profit taking. Examples of both the weekly and daily trading bands are shown below.

The S&P 500, March (SP/H5) is a classic example of using the 10-week trading band. As the chart in Exhibit 5.13 depicts, the S&P 500 has a bullish pattern, and is in an overall uptrend. So our general posture toward the commodity is a long position. SP/H5 had broken out to the upside, breaking a spread quadruple top at 1198. The contract rallied to 1206, into overbought territory, but then pulled back on the chart right to the middle of the trading band, at 1192. A quick glance at the chart shows this 1192 level to be MED. The contract ceased to pull back further, finding support in essence at this midpoint. This pullback provided an excellent chance to buy the SP/H5. The chart was bullish, trend positive, weekly momentum had been negative for nine weeks, and the pullback greatly improved the risk-reward situation. The SP/H5 contract quickly rallied right back up to 1210 level, resulting in a winning trade within days.

An application of the daily trading band is shown with April live cattle (LC/J5). Recall that we just viewed this contract in our lesson on risk-reward. In that exhibit we showed you how waiting for a pullback was advantageous and that by doing so, your risk-reward ratio was greatly improved. Now let's look at how the daily trading bands could have aided you in this process of timing your entry into a long position in cattle.

First let's take a look again at cattle after it had rallied up to 90.00 on its chart (shown in Exhibit 5.14). Not only do we know from our previous calculations that the risk-reward was unacceptable at that level, but when we consult the daily (10-day) trading band, we see that cattle was 76.1 percent overbought on January 10. The next day the 10-day band "curls" back down—this basically happens as a result of a drop in prices, and tends to suggest a waning in upward short-term momentum. This curl down suggests to us that the contract will pull back or regress back toward the mean. So this was a sign that you could be patient and wait for lower prices, and a better risk-reward, before buying cattle. As we know, cattle did in fact pull back from 90.00 down to 87.00. But how would you know that April live cattle was going to cease to pull back any further after retracing back down to the 87.00 level? Well, of course, you never know for sure that a pullback has exhausted itself, but the daily trading band can be a great secondary tool to rely on in suggesting the pullback is complete. Live cattle pulled back to 87.00, in doing so the daily distribution (10-day trading band) indicated the contract was now 67.6 percent oversold. At this point we watch for an indication that this pullback is complete—this is where we wait for the

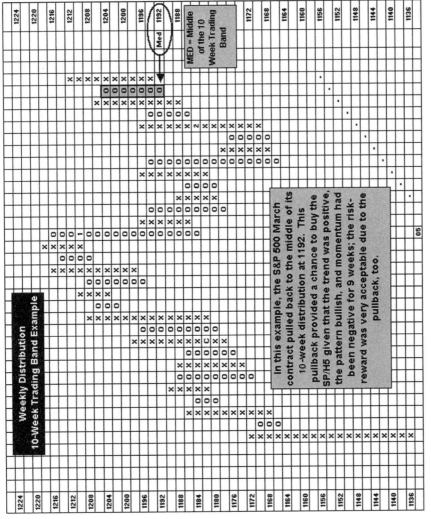

EXHIBIT 5.13 S&P 500, March 2005—10-week Trading Band Example.

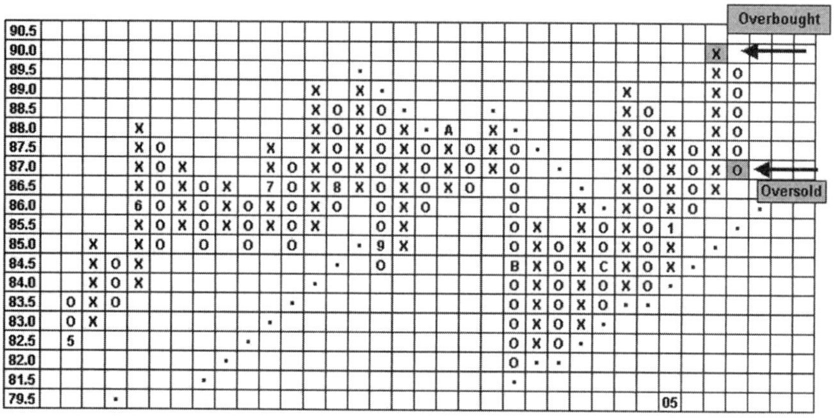

Live, Cattle April (LC/J5) Daily Distribution Table

Date	High	Mid	Low	Over Sold	Over Bought	OBOS	Price
1/28/2005	90.1644	87.9769	85.7894			-13.8	87.675
1/27/2005	90.2084	88.1209	86.0334			-22.6	87.650
1/26/2005	90.5343	88.3530	86.1718			-47.1	87.325
1/25/2005	90.9243	88.5180	86.1118	Curl		-41.3	87.525
1/24/2005	91.1300	88.6362	86.1425			-67.6	86.950
1/21/2005	91.1625	88.6625	86.1625			-30.5	87.900
1/20/2005	91.4068	88.5443	85.6818			-19.9	87.975
1/19/2005	91.5587	88.5024	85.4462			-18.1	87.950
1/18/2005	91.4257	88.4132	85.4007			33.6	89.425
1/14/2005	91.2138	88.1201	85.0263			33.3	89.150
1/13/2005	91.0776	87.7089	84.3401			53.9	89.525
1/12/2005	91.0909	87.4721	83.8534		Curl	64.3	89.800
1/11/2005	90.8451	87.3076	83.7701			76.1	90.000
1/10/2005	90.5152	87.1902	83.8652			53.7	88.975
1/7/2005	90.5103	87.1728	83.8353			17.3	87.750

Cattle had dropped to 86.95, becoming 67.6% oversold on its 10-day trading band.

Cattle had risen to 90.00, becoming 76.1% overbought on its 10-day trading band.

EXHIBIT 5.14 Live Cattle, April 2005—10-week Trading Band Example.

"curl" back up on the 10-day band; this occurred on January 25. This curl then suggests the pullback is complete and that cattle is ready to resume its upward bias. With an attractive risk-reward in place, and a curl up from oversold territory on the 10-day band, a long position can be established.

Remember, like momentum, trading bands play a secondary role in your technical analysis of a commodity. But they can be very helpful in making the final timing calls on your trade, once your primary analysis of trend, pattern, relative strength, and risk-reward has been completed.

There was a tremendous amount of information in this chapter. Get a cup of coffee, sit back, and think about it before you go on to the next chapter. You know what? Once you get the hang of it, it is pretty simple and becomes second nature. In fact, in the next chapter we will bring together everything that you have learned so far, with practical examples; this will likely bring you closer to "getting the hang of it."

CHAPTER 6

Putting It All Together

PART ONE: OLD FRIENDS WITH A NEW TREND

By this point in our journey we hope that at a minimum we agree on two things: (1) that simply having a set of rational tools at your disposal is quite helpful in deciphering the commodities markets, and (2), that none of these tools need be hoes, pitchforks, or McCormick's famous reaper. Rather, while remaining attentive to a few key ingredients, which pertain to any commodity, we can begin to train ourselves to find consistent opportunity in the futures market. Certainly, there are times that seemingly present great opportunity, a bumper crop if you will, and others that reflect a market wedged between trends; however, a trend-following system can be the biggest contributor to success in commodities. When trading with the trend it is as if the wind is at your back, filling your sails. Mistakes can still be made, but often it would take a series of mistakes to cause major damage as long as you stay with the prevailing trend. However, the process of forming a long-term top or a long-term bottom can be the most painstaking, and profit-killing, part of trading. This is the period where trends are changing, and most investors are either reluctant, or oblivious, in admitting this possibility.

This takes us back to what is simply the nature of trends. Like any natural process, a trend consists of a series of stages. Like infancy and

95

death, the birth and demise of market trends are typically the most difficult to endure. Think back to the top of the technology stock bubble in late 1999 and early 2000, a key inflection point that marked both the death of one trend and the infancy of another. This type of trend change is likely most confusing for some because the market was not topping for lack of optimism, as that was one commodity that was certainly not short of supply. Amazon.com's CEO Jeff Bezos was named *Time* magazine's "Person of the Year" in late 1999, and no other magazine cover seemed complete without an unswerving blessing being placed on some four-letter stock symbol. It was not a lack of demand that caused the tech bubble to reverse course out of a stern upward trend, it was a lack of *new* demand. It wasn't that there were no investors willing to jump on shares of Cisco Systems, or Lucent Technologies, or even Pets.com for that matter; it was just that practically everyone with the capacity (or margin) to do so already owned these stocks. If *Worth* magazine went to the presses with a bold cover featuring Cisco Systems CEO John Chambers and the statement "BUY HIS STOCK," which they did in 2000, the few investors that didn't already own CSCO shares likely dropped what they were doing and piled in like sheep. But, to do so, they had to first sell some Microsoft stock because in early 2000, not only were most investors fully invested, but likely on margin. So adding demand to one tech stock meant adding supply to another; the end result was no new demand being added to the market on a net basis—the kitchen pot is simply stirred but no heat is being added.

Bottoms in the market happen similarly, but with a lack of new supply able to be generated rather than a lack of new demand. A great example of this process taking place recently on a large scale is right here in the commodities market. As the technology bubble was bursting, those who escaped with their shirt still firmly on their backs (though I think everyone lost at least a few token cufflinks) hid assets in "safer" areas of the market. The massive move higher in market indexes during the late 1990s, much of which was propelled by a handful of technology stocks, meant that there was an unprecedented amount of capital in the stock market when the tech stocks began to fold their hand. Investing had become mainstream you might recall, and everyone was tied to the market—or "married to the market," as a memorable cover of *Newsweek* magazine quoted at the time. At any rate, some (we should say *many*) of those assets never made it past the stage of "unrealized" returns, but those that did began flowing into other areas of the market, creating bull markets in sectors like health care, energy, and real estate. This was also the beginning of a trend of outperformance of small-cap value stocks over the floundering large-cap tech behemoths. The rampant inflation ceased with the tech bubble, sparking a massive bull market in bonds that has outlasted most any pundits' original estimations. So, while those living on Planet Technology felt as if an asteroid had just hit and wiped out life as they knew it, another door opened to many other forms of life in the markets. And in some cases, it was a chance at a second life for some stodgy old assets like commodities. This "chance" was available to anyone who was willing to be open-minded about the possibility that trends were a-changin'. Those that weren't watching for trend changes went down with whatever ship.com they were on at the time.

Earlier in the book you saw the very same charts that we saw developing from mid-1999 to mid-2001. These were commodity indexes finding bottoms and beginning to show very clear indications of just what the technology stocks were lacking over on the NASDAQ—new demand! Charts of gold, copper, crude oil, and many other assets placed distinct bottoms throughout the years of 1999 through 2001, and it happened in many cases because so many investors simply threw in the towel and gave up on the idea of making money in these assets. Crude oil was at $11 per barrel in 1999, hardly a precious commodity at that price, and *The Economist* magazine even ran a cover with the title, "Drowning in Oil." Meanwhile, gold stocks had long since become the stepchildren of Wall Street by 2001. The shares of gold-mining companies still traded (occasionally), but those who traded them were treated with about the same esteem as those "New Economy" supporters were at the top of the dot-com bubble. There were roughly 20 gold and silver stocks that traded on the major exchanges when gold began to bottom, and in an act that perhaps personified the level of disdain that Wall Street held for this band of misfits, the great wirehouses on Wall Street actually began to halt fundamental coverage on the sector. If that isn't a sign of a bottom forming, I don't know what is.

While it wasn't one particular event that drew our attention toward the commodity market during this time, it was the culmination of these many developments that caused an almost unconscious fascination with this changing environment; indeed, it was the weight of the evidence presented by the commodities market that drew our gaze. In fact, for years we had held a small corporate commodity account open with REFCO in New York, and this account was essentially forgotten until tax time every year. The changes we began seeing in the commodities market in 1999, however, were decisive enough for us to dust off the trading hats and begin actively investing that account in early 2000. At the time, this account carried a balance of only $18,891 into the year 2000, but as you will see that is a suitable stake to begin diversifying into the commodities market.

Our Approach

Now, as a form of disclosure, we should mention here that we have not withdrawn any money from this account, nor have we contributed any new money, since becoming active with it in 2000. While there may have been instances along the way where margin was employed, this would be very rare indeed and the account by and large maintained a very low-risk approach toward commodities trading with typically only a few positions on at any given point in time. We weren't overly active with the trading—after all, we each had day jobs—but when we found opportunities where the weight of the evidence suggested we play it, we did so. We carried no emotional attachment, which you will find is a discipline far easier to employ with commodities than with stocks. We played the market both long and short, but making certain that just about every trade was with the prevailing trend at the time. We always placed stop loss orders on our trades and very rarely risked any more than $1,000 on any given trade. The results of this portfolio over the last five years are what we would expect from a disciplined trend-following application of the Point & Figure methodology, simply applying the tools we have discussed in previous chapters (see Exhibit 6.1).

In the end, the Dorsey, Wright & Associates (DWA) account essentially serves as an example that there are always opportunities to be found in the markets, if one is willing to look where others can't or won't. This willingness can have an extremely positive impact on one's portfolio over time. With relatively little activity, and little, if any, margin employed over the past five years, that account had grown to a value of $89,156 at the end of 2004. Not every trade worked and not every year was positive, but risk was always managed and the vast majority of trades were "with the trend." The result was nice performance during a stretch when equities were not nearly as buoyant as their long-term historical returns. There is always an open door somewhere, and while many investors continued to ram their head into the closed door of technology stocks, commodities were an area of tremendous opportunity. If nothing else, it has served to do just what the common perception of commodities loves to contradict—it has smoothed out returns from a more volatile stock market!

True Diversification—You Don't Have to Go Far to Find It

There are many sound reasons for adding commodities to your investment process, not the least of which being a time-tested lack of correlation between stocks and commodities. This will be discussed in more depth later in this book, but suffice it to say this lack of correlation gives investors a valid way to diversify assets by using the commodities market. The more common approach toward diversification is to allocate funds toward large-cap stocks, small-cap stocks, international stocks, and so on, to achieve an overall portfolio allocation that doesn't simply swing harmoniously with the ups and downs of the Standard & Poor's (S&P) 500. However, this

Returns of Various Assets Since 12/31/1999

Year	Lehman 20 Year + Treasury Bond Fund TLT	S&P 500 Index SPX	Goldmand Sachs Commodity Index GNX	DWA Corporate Account DWA
2000	21.48%	-10.12%	49.74%	111.00%
2001	3.64%	-13.05%	-31.94%	-31.80%
2002	14.67%	-23.37%	32.07%	142.80%
2003	-3.42%	26.38%	20.72%	14.80%
2004	3.46%	8.99%	17.28%	17.60%
Total Return	44.26%	-17.51%	90.56%	371.70%

Growth of $10,000 Since 12/31/1999

Year	Lehman 20 Year + Treasury Bond Fund	S&P 500 Index	Goldman Sachs Commodity Index	DWA Corporate Account
Initial	$ 10,000.00	$ 10,000.00	$ 10,000.00	$ 10,000.00
2000	$ 12,148.00	$ 8,988.00	$ 14,974.00	$ 21,100.00
2001	$ 12,590.19	$ 7,815.07	$ 10,191.30	$ 14,390.20
2002	$ 14,437.17	$ 5,988.69	$ 13,459.66	$ 34,939.41
2003	$ 13,943.42	$ 7,568.50	$ 16,248.50	$ 40,110.44
2004	$ 14,425.86	$ 8,248.91	$ 19,056.24	$ 47,169.87

A Few Investment Options

Based on portfolios being annually rebalanced

Year	Stocks Only 100%	Stocks/Bonds 70/30	Stocks/Bonds/Commodities 60/20/20	Stocks/Bonds/DWA 60/20/20
Initial	$ 10,000.00	$ 10,000.00	$ 10,000.00	$ 10,000.00
2000	$ 8,988.00	$ 9,936.00	$ 10,817.20	$ 12,042.40
2001	$ 7,815.07	$ 9,136.85	$ 9,357.96	$ 10,421.25
2002	$ 5,988.69	$ 8,044.26	$ 8,920.57	$ 12,242.05
2003	$ 7,568.50	$ 9,447.18	$ 10,641.17	$ 14,458.35
2004	$ 8,248.91	$ 10,139.76	$ 11,656.55	$ 15,847.22

EXHIBIT 6.1 Reducing Volatility with Commodities?

is a task much easier explained than implemented, as many "diversified" investors found out the hard way in 2002, when nearly every area of the equities market finished solidly in the red. It was particularly obvious in that year that simply spreading money around different regions or style boxes is not true diversification, but that was because everyone was losing money. The truth is that it is simply a fallacy of composition to assume that foreign stocks are not correlated to U.S. stocks, or that small-cap stocks are in no way correlated to large-cap stocks. As we see in Exhibit 6.2, a "diversified" portfolio of some of the largest, most widely held mutual funds in existence can still fall prey to a deceivingly high correlation with the S&P 500.

A tremendous benefit that commodities can provide to an account is true diversification, that is, diversification by means of a noncorrelated asset. There are naturally times when commodities should play a larger role in an investor's portfolio, and times when their weighting should be muted. As Jim Rogers explains in his book *Hot Commodities* (New York: Random House, 2004), the commodities markets have tended to trend in roughly 20-year cycles; meaning a generally strong 20-year period has historically been followed by a generally weak stretch of similar duration. This is why changes in trend are so important, and also why you are reading this book now and not 10 years ago, when commodities were still entrenched in a long-term negative trend. You've seen the tools, and you've seen the results of these tools being put to use in a disciplined fashion—let's now put it all together and walk through some of the trades we implemented in recent history. Not all of them worked, but they never all will.

Putting It All Together

For those of you already familiar with Point & Figure analysis, what you have read thus far should help make it readily apparent that many of the tools we use to analyze stocks, mutual funds and market indexes are the very same that we apply toward a commodities account. Point & Figure is a trend-following approach first and foremost, and within that broad stroke we apply other tools that help us to time entry points and exit points to better manage risk. Whether you choose to actively use Point & Figure within your own personal investment game plan or not, hopefully the tools discussed in this book will at least decloak some of the many myths regarding technical analysis and the general complexity of markets. The most basic laws of supply and demand that are taught early on in any economics curriculum are indeed the same which govern price movement in futures markets. Just as this approach has provided many investors and professionals the skill and confidence to manage assets in the stock market successfully, it can do the same for those interested in adding another investment option to their process—commodities. We've certainly been very

Correlation to the S&P 500 for 2005 3-Year Range

	Value	SPX Correlation	Blend	SPX Correlation	Growth	SPX Correlation
Large	Amer Funds Washington Mutual Inv	0.96	Vanguard 500	1	Amer Funds Growth Fund of America	0.97
	Dodge & Cox Stock	0.93	Fidelity Magellan	0.99	Fidelity Capital Appreciation	0.95
Mid	T. Rowe Price Mid-Cap Value	0.91	Fidelity Mid-Cap Stock	0.91	Fidelity Aggressive Growth	0.9
	Goldman Sachs Mid-Cap Value	0.83	Vanguard Extended Market	0.88	T. Rowe Price New Horizon	0.88
Small	Scudder Dreman Small-Cap Value	0.73	Amer Funds Small-Cap World	0.83	Van Kampen Small-Cap Growth	0.72
	Vanguard Small-Cap Value Index	0.77	Fidelity Low-Priced Stock	0.84	Aim Opportunities	0.81
Global			Amer Funds New Perspective	0.96		
			Dodge & Cox International	0.87		
Bonds			Pimco Total Return Bond	-0.24		
			Federated Bond	0.08		

Equal Weighted Port Avg Equity Correlation	0.8783

Strategic EQ Weighted Port	%
	100
Large	60
Mid	7.5
Small	7.5
Global	25
Estimated EQ Weighted Correlation	0.9335

EXHIBIT 6.2 How Diversified Are You?

pleased with the returns we've seen in the commodities account over the last five years, but it is also quite humbling in the sense that it is very clearly just the system at work. Many of the trades haven't been big winners, plenty of the trades resulted in stops being hit, but there were a good number of trades that were huge successes, and no trades that were crippling losses. We attribute this to our trend-following system, managing risk with stop loss points, and using the tools we have to time entry and exit points. For those who may be struggling with tying the loose ends of those concepts together, hopefully the following examples will help you "put it all together."

PART TWO: INITIATING AND MANAGING A POSITION

Before we actually go through specific examples of "putting it all together," we want to address a few topics germane to initiating and managing positions in the futures market. In a nutshell, we want to delve into the topic of risk management, as it is a key component to success in investing, be it in stocks or commodities. It is interesting that at the 2006 Winter Olympics in Torino, Italy, Bode Miller, an American downhill skier, said this about the downhill race: "It's all about risk management. You have to know when the risk-reward ratio was right to either attack the course or lay back." And so it is with investing. Now, as we just discussed, diversification into non-correlated assets—commodities in this case—can itself provide enhanced performance and in a sense mitigate risk; but in the following discussion, we want to deal with risk management as it pertains to taking individual positions in the commodities market.

Risk Management

Risk is basically the amount and probability or possibility of incurring a loss (of capital), or series of losses. There are several types of risk inherent to trading commodities:

- *Avoidable risk* is risk that can be reduced or eliminated without any reduction or compromise in reward (see Robert Rotella, *The Elements of Successful Trading*, Englewood Cliffs, N.J.: New York Institute of Finance, 1992). A couple of examples of this type of risk would be trading an illiquid market, and not properly diversifying your commodity portfolio. Illiquid markets can provide a great deal of slippage and bad fills on trades. Diversification typically will serve to reduce risk.

- *Unavoidable risk* is risk that cannot be reduced or eliminated. In other words, there will always be some risk involved in trading commodities, stocks, or any investment, for that matter, given that there is an expected return or profit.
- *Controllable risk* is risk that can be reduced or mitigated as a function of your entry and exit points. This will be dealt with in more detail below in our discussion on stop loss points, and risk-reward.

As mentioned, with any investments, and in this case with commodity trading, there is risk involved. To a large extent, you can reduce or mitigate your risk with smart risk management techniques. Truly, over the long haul, it is proper risk management that will be the key to your success in commodity trading. You must always be aware of the risk you are taking on any given trade – the risk of loss. *Bottom line:* Never get consumed with the potential "reward." This was all too much the case with technology stocks back in 2000. Everyone thought those stocks would go up forever. Many never bothered to evaluate the risk of owning those stocks, but instead were overly consumed with profits. "What, me lose money on Cisco? Never!" As a result of this lack of respect for "risk," many people still own a plethora of "fallen tech angels," with hopes of one day just getting back to even.

The good news is that through the use of the Point & Figure method, risk can be controlled (and probabilities of success increased). Over the course of this book, you have learned about many tools that can help in this reduction of risk. Now you must take these tools and make them work for you because they are just that—tools—concepts and methods for analyzing the commodity market, but not a "black box." These tools can have a "starring" role in your commodity research, or you may choose to augment Point & Figure with other forms of analysis, such as adding fundamental research to your decision-making process. The larger goal is to develop your own system, or working set of rules, for managing commodities exposure.

Diversification   Overall investment diversification is achieved via asset classes that are not highly correlated, as we discussed earlier in this chapter. But diversification is something to consider within your "commodity" asset class, as it can reduce "avoidable risk." One way to provide diversification in your commodity account is to trade different markets. For example, having exposure in livestock, softs, grains, energy, and so on should tend to reduce your risk. Ideally, your goal here is to trade markets that have a low correlation to the others. Typically speaking, the price of orange juice is not going to be highly correlated to the price of live cattle, unless you are talking about your breakfast plate of steak and eggs with some juice!

The question then becomes, how many markets should be traded to gain proper diversification? According to Robert Rotella, "diversification increases with more markets but at a decreasing rate," as shown in Exhibit 6.3. Rotella displays in this graph that risk is dramatically reduced with just a few different markets, but is only "marginally reduced as more markets are added." So, again, how many markets are needed? He states that "diversifying with greater than 8 commodities does not provide any substantial difference in reducing risk." Rotella goes on to explain that "different theoretical studies suggest as few as 3, or as many as 15, unrelated markets are enough for a well diversified portfolio" (Rotella, *The Elements of Successful Trading*). The key phrase is *unrelated markets*. What do we mean more specifically? We mean you are not going to gain proper diversification by being long crude oil, natural gas, and heating oil, or being long soybeans, corn, and wheat. A better example of being diversified in your account would be to have exposure in, let's say, soybeans, live cattle, crude oil, sugar, copper, gold, Treasury bonds, and the British pound. Also notice in this example that we have representation by all the major markets in commodities—eight groups or commodity market sectors therefore eight positions. Another important consideration is liquidity. You want to be wary of trying to gain diversification in markets that are less liquid, as this can actually increase risk. For example, a distant-month lumber contract or the New Zealand dollar may not be the best choice for increasing your diversification, while trying to decrease your avoidable risk. So you will want to be sure to consult the open interest and volume figures on any given contract you are considering to ensure proper liquidity.

This leads us to another point we want to make. You can gain proper diversification by having representation with one commodity per commodity market group—such as being in live cattle for your livestock position. But the other benefit that can be harnessed is in the simplification of commodity research. In other words, if you are just starting out investing in commodities, you may find it helpful to narrow the playing field. Given that corn, soybeans, and wheat will tend to move similarly, why not follow only soybeans for your grain representation. Basically, you could merely follow eight different commodities, doing analysis on each of those, rather than being inundated with 25 or 30 charts. This is something to consider if just starting out in the commodities markets, but without sacrificing proper diversification.

Before we leave this discussion on diversification, we wanted to make one last point. Of course, an easy way to gain diversification is merely through the use of the commodity index futures contracts (discussed in Chapter 3), using the Commodity Research Bureau Index (CRB), Goldman

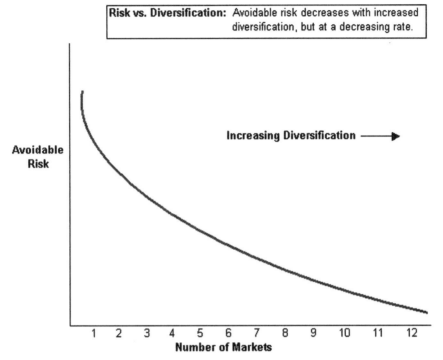

| Risk vs. Diversification: | Avoidable risk decreases with increased diversification, but at a decreasing rate. |

EXHIBIT 6.3 Decreasing Benefit of Increased Diversification.
Source: Robert Rotella, *The Elements of Successful Trading*, Englewood Cliffs, N.J.: New York Institute of Finance, 1992.

Sachs Commodity Index (GSCI), or the Dow Jones–AIG Commodity Index (DJAIG). The only thing to remember here is that the weighting of each index is different.

Stop Loss Points   Stop loss points are another way of saying risk control. Recall our definition of risk: the probability of significant loss of capital. One of the best ways to provide a control mechanism on risk is through the use of a stop loss. That is why we always determine where we are getting out before we even get in (to a trade). So to determine if the risk is acceptable on any given trade, you must know "where you are getting out"! At DWA we must deem the risk to the stop (the potential loss) acceptable before we place the trade. But then once that trade is executed, a stop order is placed good-until-canceled (GTC). This serves a pair of purposes: (1) you don't have to constantly watch each tick of trading for fear of missing your exit point, and (2) it removes the emotion from the trade. Having a predetermined exit strategy (a GTC stop) can protect you from large losses because you can't procrastinate or rationalize staying in a losing trade that has negated your reasons for entering. Avoidance of severe losses, truly, is the key to success in any trading. Using a stop loss point reduces this possibility of a severe loss. In fact, there has been plenty of research conducted on this subject, with the results showing that the key to a successful trading program is the size of your winners versus the size of your losers, not the number of winning trades versus the number of losing trades. So cutting your losses short, while letting your winners run is really what it's all about. This is why a trend-following system based on Point & Figure analysis can be so helpful in achieving this goal.

To that end, how do you know where to stop out using Point & Figure? If the *entry point* is where risk is low and the potential reward high, then the *exit point* (stop loss) is where the risk is high and the potential reward low or uncertain. So, where would risk be high and potential reward uncertain? Turning to the Point & Figure chart, it would be where the commodity will break a significant bottom or violate its trend line—basically, a point at which the chart suggests supply has won the battle, not necessarily the war but the battle, and therefore suggests you no longer want to be long the commodity. In Exhibit 6.4 we provide you with two such stop loss examples. The main point to remember is that you should always have an exit strategy for each and every trade you enter. The beauty of using the Point & Figure chart is the ease with which you can determine this exit point, or stop. Also, the Point & Figure chart allows you to raise (or lower) the stop as the chart unfolds. This serves to reduce risk further and, as price continues to rise, allows you to protect a profitable trade, ensuring a gain.

Risk-Reward   To a great extent, risk on any given trade, the potential for loss of capital, is a function of both your entry point and exit point. You will recall that we dealt with this subject in Chapter 3 when we taught you how to calculate a risk-reward ratio. In looking at entry points and exit points more closely, they can, for the most part, be classified into two categories. With respect to the entry point for long positions (or exit for shorts), you are either buying on strength after an upside breakout through resistance; or you are buying on weakness into support—a pullback. Conversely, when determining the exit point for longs (or entry for shorts), you are selling on weakness after support has been broken—a breakdown or trend line violation—or you are selling on strength into resistance. The point depends on the risk-reward scenario; there will be times when you will want to initiate a position on a breakout, yet other times when a pullback is ideal for entering a trade. Some of the factors that go into this decision have already been discussed, such as distance to the stop, where support resides, the chart pattern, momentum, where overhead resistance lies, or where the contract is on its trading band. All of these factors go

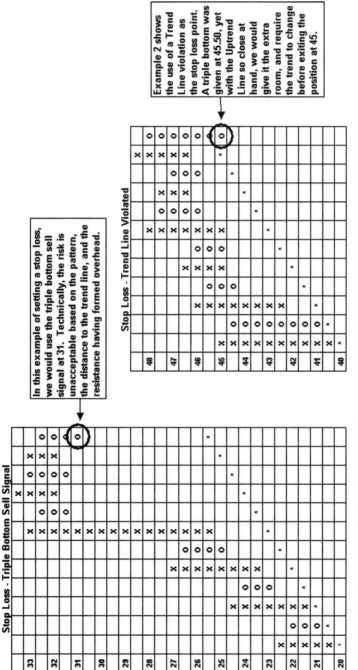

EXHIBIT 6.4 Examples of Selling Stop Loss Points.

into making a sound decision as to where you enter and where you exit a trade. In the end, you must look at the weight of the evidence, and stack the odds of success in your favor. An example may clarify this for you; see Exhibit 6.5.

Another issue with risk-reward is the percentage of total funds allocated to a given trade. Awareness of this detail can increase your longer-term probability of success in trading commodities. Basically what we mean by this is the amount of funds at risk on any given trade, as a percentage of the total equity of the account. We recommend that you limit the maximum risk on any trade to 3 percent or less of the total equity. So, for smaller-sized accounts, this limit requires that you restrict your trading to less volatile markets, mini-contracts, and therefore suggests that you may often have to buy on a pullback. So if you have $30,000 in total equity in your commodity account, it implies that you risk no more than $900 per trade. This will serve to dictate which trades you can take and when. For example, natural gas may not be the best choice for a smaller account, given its volatile swings in prices and dollar value per point move ($1,000 per .10 move). As a sidebar, our broker at Man Securities warned me one time when I was considering trading natural gas in my own account, "You know on the floor they call natural gas the widow maker!" Instead, I chose to buy the mini crude oil contract. I am happily married. This issue of risk-to-equity suggests that you may not necessarily, depending on the size of your account, be able to have positions, for example, in Treasury bonds, several foreign currencies, coffee, and crude oil all at the same time, given the dollar value per point for each of those commodities. Now, if the account grows, much like our DWA in-house account has from $18,000 to $89,000, the dollar amount you can risk on each trade increases to whatever the 3 percent benchmark becomes. When we started out, our risk per trade was limited to $540, but by the end of 2004 our risk per trade was $2,670. In all, by restricting your risk per trade to 3 percent, you live to play another day.

The maximum risk per trade can also be used to determine the number of contracts that can be initiated with a trade. For example, if the maximum risk per trade is 3 percent of total equity and the account size is $50,000, then the risk you are willing to take on the trade is $1,500. If you want to buy soybeans with a triple bottom sell signal as your stop loss point, which is 10 cents away from your entry, then you could buy three contracts.

$$\text{10 cents/bushel risk to stop} \times \$5,000 \text{ value per } \$1 \text{ move (or } \$50/\text{penny)}$$
$$= \$500 \text{ risk per contract}$$

This same math can be applied when considering adding contracts to existing positions—pyramiding—as the trade works in your favor. The

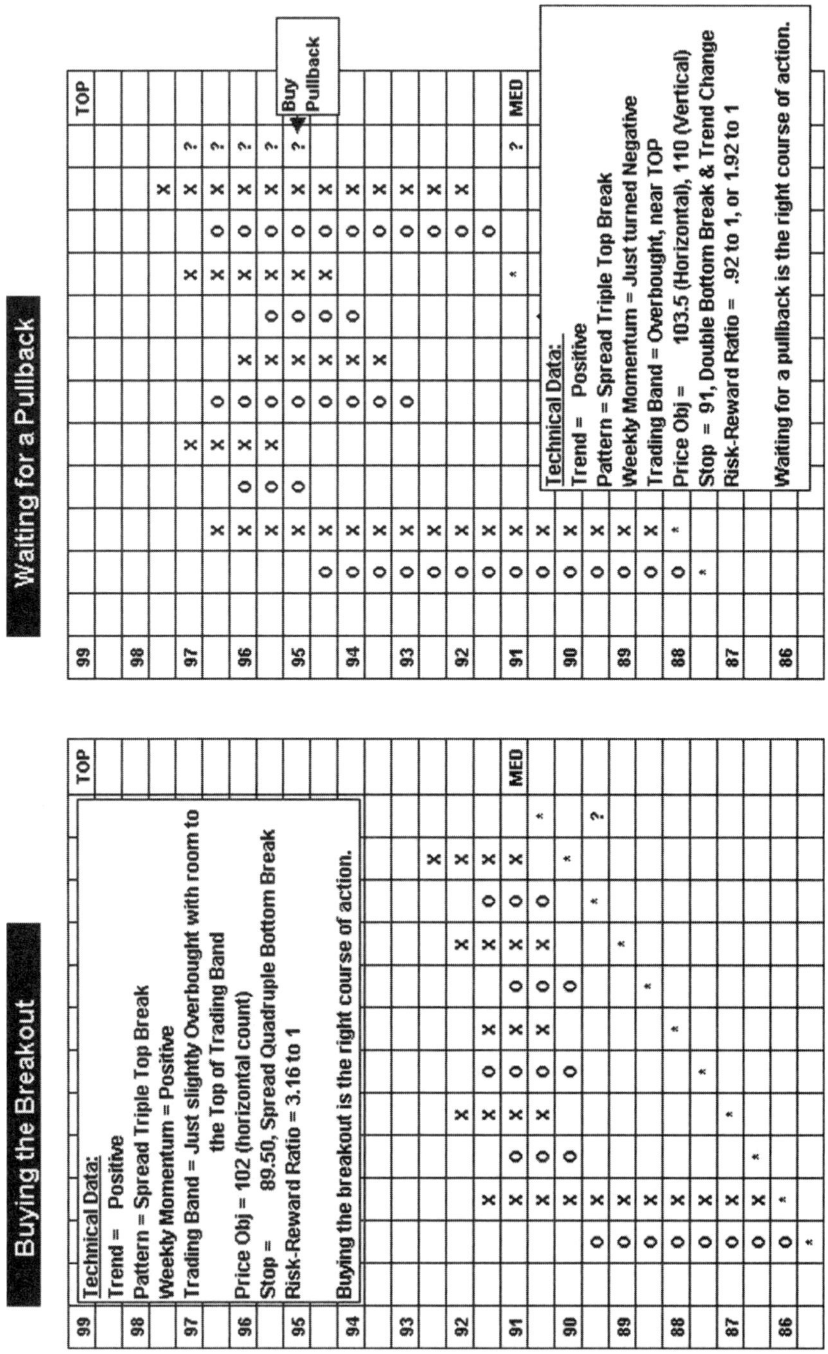
Buying the Breakout
Technical Data:
Trend = Positive
Pattern = Spread Triple Top Break
Weekly Momentum = Positive
Trading Band = Just slightly Overbought with room to the Top of Trading Band
Price Obj = 102 (horizontal count)
Stop = 89.50, Spread Quadruple Bottom Break
Risk-Reward Ratio = 3.16 to 1
Buying the breakout is the right course of action.
Waiting for a Pullback
Buy Pullback
Technical Data:
Trend = Positive
Pattern = Spread Triple Top Break
Weekly Momentum = Just turned Negative
Trading Band = Overbought, near TOP
Price Obj = 103.5 (Horizontal), 110 (Vertical)
Stop = 91, Double Bottom Break & Trend Change
Risk-Reward Ratio = .92 to 1, or 1.92 to 1
Waiting for a pullback is the right course of action.
TOP
MED

EXHIBIT 6.5 Taking that Breakout or Waiting for a Pullback?

main point to glean from this is the importance of evaluating risk on each and every trade. There will be times that you will have to pass on a specific trade because of unacceptable risk, but as we like to say, we would rather lose opportunity than lose money.

Putting It All Together: Specific Trading Examples

In the examples that follow, we are dealing with applying the tools to the purchase and sale of individual commodities. But as you will see in the ensuing chapters, you can parlay your commodity research, using it to invest in alternative, commodities-related instruments.

In selecting trades for this case study section of the book, we tried to choose examples that comprise multiple facets of applying the Point & Figure method to commodity trading. Our hope is that this "practical" exercise will serve to solidify the concepts you have learned in previous chapters, and will provide you with the confidence to "do it yourself."

Let's start this discussion by looking at the euro FX. Recall in Chapter 3 how we laid out the technical picture for the U.S. dollar and the euro by looking at the longer-term spot charts. That analysis showed how the dollar topped out in early 2002, changing its overall trend to negative by April. At the same time, the euro was making a bottom, having stopped its precipitous decline. The euro began trending upward and this trip north persisted, and as a result any trades in the euro were focused on the long side. That posture was continually reaffirmed by consulting the relative strength (RS) chart of the dollar versus the euro. The U.S. dollar RS sell signal given in June 2002 remained in force (until May 2005), acting as further confirmation of a short dollar, long euro stance. Given the overriding long-term trend of the euro and the positive RS versus the dollar, we chose to repeatedly play the euro long in our DWA account.

Trade Recap: Euro FX December 2004 (EC/Z4)

Technical Data

This trade was initiated on August 5, 2004. Given the overall trend and RS of the euro versus the dollar, our trading bias was to be long the euro.

Initial Entry: Using the September 2004 contract, we bought the euro on a pullback to support at 1.2045.

Stop Loss: 1.1850, violation of uptrend line, this stop would be raised to a triple bottom break at 1.195.

Price Obj: 1.3450 using a vertical count. A horizontal count could have been used in September, yielding a count of 1.3350.

Trend: Positive, turned so in May (longer-term spot trend was also positive).

Pattern: A spread quintuple top buy signal given in July at 1.2350.

Momentum: Daily just turned positive, weekly was negative for several weeks, monthly negative, but getting less so.

Trade Band: 10-day trading band was at midpoint; 10-week trading band showed a slightly oversold condition.

Resistance: Minor resistance at 1.24650, then more notable at 1.2750.

Support: 1.200, close to entry point.

Risk-Reward: Very attractive at 7.21 points of reward for 1 point of risk; even using resistance at 1.2750, the risk-reward ratio is 3.62 to 1.

After having bought the euro in early August, very little transpired over the course of the next few weeks; the euro worked sideways, staying in a fairly tight trading range. The technical picture of the September contract had not changed—the buy signal and trend remained positive. But as with all currencies and financial contracts, the expiration months are on the March calendar cycle. So, with our long position remaining when we flipped the calendar to September, we chose to roll out to the next contract—December 2004. By selling the September contract and buying the December contract we maintained the exposure while the technical scenario suggested this was the proper course. The base-building consolidation phase eventually gave way to an upside breakout in early October, as shown in Exhibit 6.6, allowing the patience of this trade to yield fruit. The euro December broke out of a big base at 1.2450, giving a triple top buy signal at that level. From there it was like a Roman candle heading upward into the July 4th night sky. The 1.2750–1.280 area proved to be the first resistance and with the contract extended, and 90 percent overbought on its 10-week trading band; we chose to lock in profits. No stop point was at hand, risk had thus increased, while the reward was largely realized after the quick move up. We locked in profits of $8,950 for one contract, having exited at 1.2786.

But the euro didn't stop its ascent until 1.3450. Hmm, remember that number—it was the vertical price objective! In hindsight, it was no coincidence that this happened. First, a big base had been broken, which as you learned can often elicit a big move up out of the base. Second, in analyzing this trade, we noticed that the weekly momentum turned back to positive

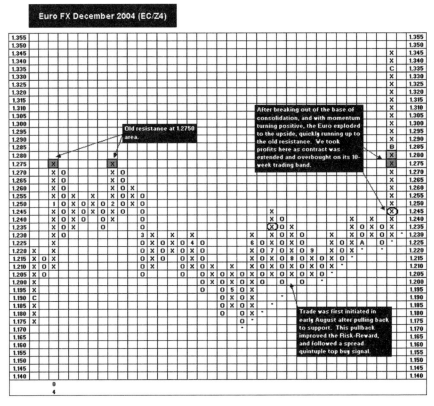

EXHIBIT 6.6 Example Trade—Euro FX.

the first week of October after having been negative for 10 weeks! Recall our earlier point of how the currencies and financials tend to perform coincidentally with their weekly momentum readings. That weekly momentum stayed positive for the next 11 weeks, until early December when the contract topped out and subsequently broke down at 1.3170 (on the .0025 box chart). Also not surprising is the fact that the euro had become 122 percent overbought on its 10-week trading band by early December, about the same time the momentum was waning and the contract was meeting its bullish price objective.

Now you may recall in our conversation on "changing the box size," that we used the euro for example purposes. Although exiting the euro when we did had merit, where we failed was not going back to the well again—reentering on the shakeout pattern on the .0025 per box chart. This would have allowed us to capture another sizeable gain.

Lessons and Points to Make

1. Buying on a pullback to support greatly improves your risk-reward situation.
2. Trend and RS are two overriding considerations when determining trading posture, and such factors can allow you to stay with a position and let it develop.
3. Overhead resistance can be an exit point, but you must watch for a penetration of that resistance as an indication to reestablish your position.
4. It is okay to stay with a trade as long as the technical picture suggests so.
5. Trading bands, and their inherent oversold and overbought indications, can offer a secondary confirmation of when to enter and when to exit a trade.
6. Momentum, especially weekly, is something to pay great attention to, especially when a historical benefit exists, and when coupled with a breakout (of a big base).
7. Contracts can be added when technicals improve, as they did for the euro in early October 2004. This can be considered only if the risk to total equity is in line with the 3 percent rule of thumb.
8. It is okay to tie up capital in a position, such as this trade in the euro, as long as the capital cannot be used for a more timely trade and the account is sufficiently funded.
9. When presented with a circumstance of a straight spike up, and therefore no apparent, viable stop loss point, consult a smaller box size chart for further insight.

While we are on the subject of currencies, let's turn our attention once again to the U.S. dollar. We have spoken numerous times about the greenback throughout this book, yet there are further points to make and practical lessons to learn. The dollar is a prime example of how a commodity can trend relentlessly lower—more specifically, we speak of the downtrend beginning in mid-2002. So just as our trading bias henceforth from 2002 has been long the euro, it has required a bearish posture with respect to the dollar. We specifically want to now examine the U.S. dollar, December 2004 contract, yet before doing so, realize that we traded the dollar many times over the course of the past several years. For that reason, we are going to refrain from itemizing particular trade entries and exits, but nonetheless wanted to make some key points through the use of the December dollar.

Chart Examination: U.S. Dollar December 2004 (DX/Z4)

Technical Data

Trend: Clearly bearish with a negative trend in place. Strictly speaking, the shorter-term trend changed to negative in early September 2004 and stayed that way until expiration.

Pattern: Consistent series of lower tops and lower bottoms. In October, a significant triple bottom sell signal was given at 87.4 after failing again at notable resistance at 88.6.

Momentum: Weekly momentum turned negative the first of October after having been positive for nine weeks. The momentum stayed negative for the next 11 weeks, until mid-December.

Support: On a long-term spot dollar chart, there was support at 85.00, dating back to January 2004. After forming this support at 85.00, following a massive decline in late 2003, the dollar experienced a contra-trend rally. That rally failed at the downtrend line, and the dollar resumed its downward bias.

Resistance: Initial resistance kept being formed at lower levels, as lower tops were repeatedly made.

Stop Loss: Initially at 90.20 if shorted in September, then consistently adjusted downward as each new lower top was made. Or if shorted in October, a quadruple top buy signal at 88.80 could have been used as the buy stop.

So, what is there to glean from this practical example of the U.S. dollar position? It once again displays the importance of staying with the overall trend, but like the euro trade shown earlier in this chapter, it also shows how weekly momentum can be of great use. Notice how the decline really got into full gear once the weekly momentum turned negative in early October. The downward spiral persisted for close to three months, until momentum turned to positive in mid-December; culminating with a contra-trend bounce off the bottom. Perhaps the most important point we want to make with this example pertains to setting stop loss points on a trade, and finding multiple opportunities to reenter positions.

In dealing with the issue of stop loss points, notice again the series of lower tops and bottoms. Each time a lower top was recorded, the stop loss point could be adjusted. This serves to reduce your risk in the position, and as the chart unfolds, puts you in a position to protect what has then become

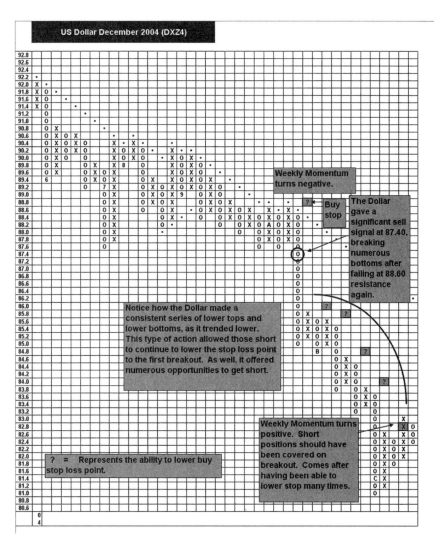

EXHIBIT 6.7 Adjusting Stop Loss Points.

a profitable trade. The only way this happens is by regular review of your open positions—analyzing the chart patterns each and every day—to evaluate if the technical picture has changed. As seen in Exhibit 6.7, if you had been short the dollar even since October 2004 when the weekly momentum turned negative and the triple bottom sell signal was given, you could have initiated with a buy stop of 88.80, but then lowered it to 86.00, then 85.80, to 84.80, then 84.00, and finally to 82.80; where you covered your short on the double top buy signal off the bottom (which also came in concert with the weekly momentum turning back to positive).

This trade also shows how a chart will often give you many chances to get in. There was ample opportunity to short the dollar. Starting back in September 2004, but obviously the breakdown in October was noteworthy in that it brought a violation of key initial support, but also penetrated the July bottom. From there, it was a quick drop to where? The 85.00 level—remember the support from January 2004? But here is the interesting thing: The dollar continued to give you opportunities to short it thereafter, with an orderly series of lower tops and bottoms. A lesson to take away from this is how a trend can become reinvigorated (in this case to the downside) once old standing support is penetrated. So in early November when the 85.00 longstanding support level was violated, it should have been a sign to grab a seat on the "dollar short bandwagon" if you weren't already on it! As from there, the U.S. Dollar proceeded to fall off a cliff. Also, by adding to positions as the chart allows, like the dollar did, you provide the account with another form of diversification—that of different time frames of entry.

Lessons and Points to Make

1. Let the trend be your friend.
2. Be cognizant of chart patterns forming—be able to identify significant breakdowns.
3. Weekly momentum can provide a great confirmation to a chart signal, especially when there is historic precedent of its effectiveness.
4. Constant review of open positions is a necessity as this will provide you will new entry possibilities, but will allow you to lower your buy stop point.
5. By adjusting your stop loss point as the chart affords, you reduce your risk in the position, and move toward protecting what has then become a profitable trade.
6. Being aware of key longer-term support (and violations of it) can provide yet another reason to enter a position.

Although we will be touching upon the topic of stop loss points again in this next case study, there are other lessons to learn, too. The goal, ultimately, is to show you different applications of the same tools—for you to see that trading commodities doesn't have to be a mysterious, dangerous, and highly complex task. Instead, it can be relatively straightforward if operating out of the right toolbox. Let's now direct our attention to gold. For this discussion, we turn to gold, December 2003 and December 2004. Gold is another commodity that has enjoyed a bull market after putting in a definitive bottom back in 2001 at $256 (per the London P.M. Gold chart). Given the persistent bullish trend in gold, we traded gold successfully and frequently on the long side. One such trade occurred in October 2003, when we traded the gold, December 2003 contract.

Trade Recap: Gold December 2003 (GC/Z3)

Technical Data

Initial Entry: At 350.80 on August 5, 2003, on pullback to support.

Stop Loss: Initially at 342, a triple bottom sell signal and violation of the trend line. Ultimately was raised to 374.

Price Obj: 418, using a vertical count.

Risk-Reward: Very attractive, at 7.6 points reward for every 1 point of risk.

Trend: Bullish—both the December 2003 contract, and the London gold spot.

Pattern: On double top buy signal given at 352. Spot chart broke out of bullish triangle pattern.

Momentum: Weekly momentum just turned back to positive for gold spot after having been negative for six weeks. Monthly momentum for spot on verge of turning positive.

Trade Band: Spot gold was 21 percent oversold on its 10-week trading band.

Support: The December contract had notable support at 344.

Resistance: No significant overhead resistance, but May peak was 376.

This trade is yet another example of the importance of longer-term trend analysis. In addition, it provides another illustration as to the benefit of buying on a pullback, serving to greatly enhance the risk-reward characteristics of the trade. At the same time, it displays how you can couple your research on the spot commodity with the near-month contract. In this case, gold spot suggested a renewed upward push was in the making for this metal. A triangle pattern had been completed, a slightly oversold condition existed, and momentum had turned to positive. December gold, shown in Exhibit 6.8, lifted as the technical data suggested, rallying in an orderly fashion to $384 per ounce before pausing. Throughout this run, we were able to raise our stop loss point several times during the trade. It wasn't until the breakdown at 374 that we exited the trade. All told, a handsome profit was recorded—$2,320 per contract (23.2 points × $100 per point).

Lessons and Points to Make

1. Long-term trend analysis of the underlying spot commodity can provide you opportunities to frequently trade the near-month contract. You can keep going back, trading the near-month chart pattern as it affords a viable entry.
2. Buying on a deep pullback to support greatly enhances your risk-reward characteristics, mitigating the "controllable risk."
3. Momentum and trading bands provide that extra incentive to place a trade when confirming the underlying trend and chart pattern agree.
4. Raising the stop loss point serves to control risk while eventually maximizing profit. By waiting for the breakdown to occur, you are able to catch the bulk of the up move, allowing your winners the chance to run, but not with unlimited risk to the trader.

Before we leave our discussion on gold, we want to take a brief moment to analyze the gold, December 2004 chart. There really is only one important point we want to make here, and it deals with setting, and adjusting, your stop loss point. Notice in Exhibit 6.9 how gold trended higher the latter part of 2004, generally showing a series of higher tops and higher bottoms, repeatedly holding its bullish support line. But take a closer look and you will see that gold, while able to hold its uptrend line, also gave brief double bottom sell signals along the way. At no time did the contract string together more than one sell signal at a time and, following each sell signal, gold was able to regroup and rally to a new high. So what's the point? In this example, you can see how setting your stop loss point requires a discriminating eye and an adaptive approach that provides logical options to the trader. Merely stating that you must exclusively take the first sell signal as your stop point doesn't necessarily make sense in certain circumstances. Gold, December 2004 illustrates how sometimes using a violation of the trend line can be more logical, especially when it is close at hand, so long as the risk is palatable for the trader. The point we want to make is simple: Your stop loss point needs to "make sense." Closely examine the chart and

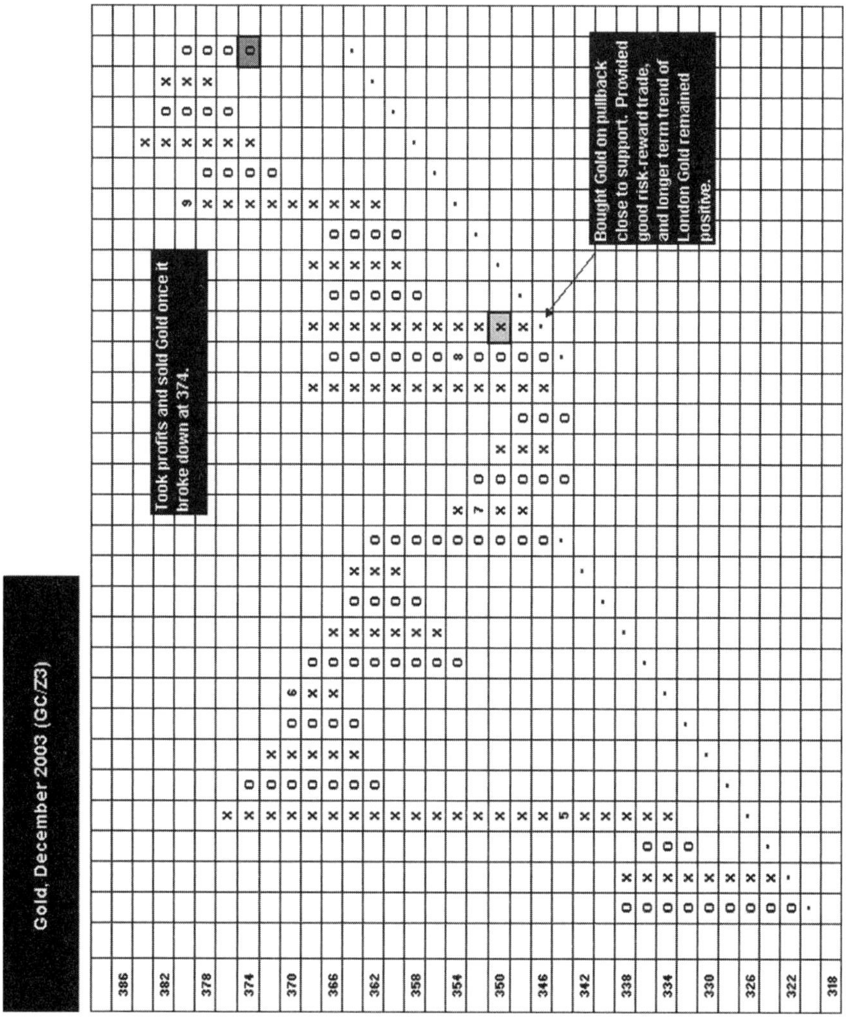

Gold, December 2003 (GC/Z3)

Took profits and sold Gold once it broke down at 374.

Bought Gold on pullback close to support. Provided good risk-reward trade, and longer term trend of London Gold remained positive.

EXHIBIT 6.8 Example Trade—Gold, December 2003.

apply your best judgment to the situation. While a trend line–based stop loss point would have kept the trade alive for a prolonged move higher, a tighter stop loss strategy may well have caused much higher turnover and subpar returns.

Before leaving the issue of stop loss points in a practical application, let's take a glance at the Swiss franc, March 2005 contract. It will probably come as no surprise that the longer-term trend of the Swiss franc was positive coming into 2005, as it is measured as a function of the U.S. dollar, which declined precipitously for the three years prior. In this instance, we actually shorted the franc based on the technical picture of the March contract as it developed. Let's explain the scenario.

Trade Recap: Swiss Franc March 2005 (SF/H5)

Technical Data

Initial Entry: .8411 on January 25, 2005, after a rally up to initial resistance and another lower top.

Stop Loss: .8525, a double top buy signal and a breakout to reverse the series of lower tops.

Price Obj: .8000, using a vertical count.

Risk-Reward: Very attractive, at 3.6 points of reward for each point of risk.

Trend: For the March contract, it just changed to negative with the bullish support line violated at .8425. The longer-term trend remained positive, as indicated by the spot chart.

Pattern: Several double bottom sell signals given, and lower tops and bottoms.

Momentum: Weekly momentum negative, monthly momentum positive, but less so.

Support: For the March contract, some support existed at .8300, while the spot chart could see support at the .8200 level, the previous breakout from a big base.

Resistance: At .8500.

The reasons to short the franc are evident in Exhibit 6.10. Probably the most glaring of these details is the change in trend to negative upon the violation of the bullish support line. Add to that the negative chart pattern established with multiple sell signals, while the risk-reward ratio

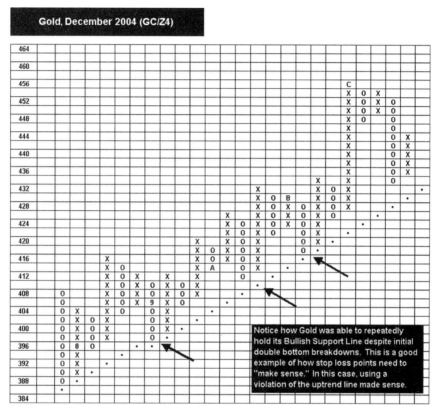

EXHIBIT 6.9 Another Glance at Gold.

was extremely conducive to placing a short position, and there is sufficient data there to make the case for a play to the short side. Pretty standard stuff in keeping with what you have learned throughout this book. But where this trade takes a different kind of twist is in the exit strategy.

For all intents and purposes, this short position was in conflict with the longer-term trend of the underlying franc spot chart, shown in Exhibit 6.11. Given the right conditions, contra-trend trades can be taken, yet that fact came into play when considering where to exit the trade. As Exhibits 6.10 and 6.11 show, the March franc (and franc spot) sold off quickly. Witnessing this unraveling, we could see the franc becoming statistically oversold. No direct support on the March chart was evident, yet by consulting the franc spot chart (Exhibit 6.11), we could see the likelihood for support around .8200. Why was this considered support? Well, this was the level at which the spot chart had broken out of a big base. Remember our discussion on this from Chapter 3, and the statement, "What was resis-

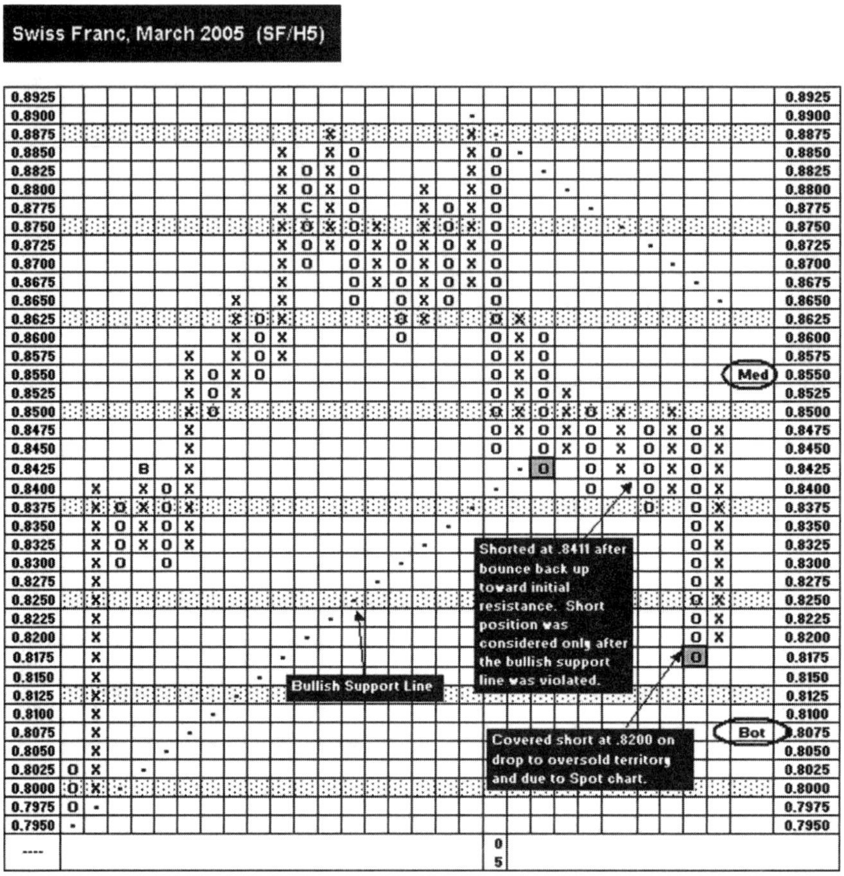

Swiss Franc, March 2005 (SF/H5)

Annotations within the chart:

- Med
- Bot
- Bullish Support Line
- Shorted at .8411 after bounce back up toward initial resistance. Short position was considered only after the bullish support line was violated.
- Covered short at .8200 on drop to oversold territory and due to Spot chart.

Price scale (both left and right axes): 0.8925, 0.8900, 0.8875, 0.8850, 0.8825, 0.8800, 0.8775, 0.8750, 0.8725, 0.8700, 0.8675, 0.8650, 0.8625, 0.8600, 0.8575, 0.8550, 0.8525, 0.8500, 0.8475, 0.8450, 0.8425, 0.8400, 0.8375, 0.8350, 0.8325, 0.8300, 0.8275, 0.8250, 0.8225, 0.8200, 0.8175, 0.8150, 0.8125, 0.8100, 0.8075, 0.8050, 0.8025, 0.8000, 0.7975, 0.7950

EXHIBIT 6.10   Example Trade—Swiss Franc.

tance becomes support." It was our opinion that the franc would likely garner support around this .8200 level, we chose to place a buy stop at .8200,
under the current market price at the time. In other words, we were willing to lock in our profits should the franc drop to .8200 and this is in fact
what eventually transpired. We closed the position, recording a profit of
$2,637.50 per contract. From there, the franc rallied straight back up from
what was a 100 percent oversold condition on its 10-day trading band, and
86 percent oversold reading on its 10-week band, which would have erased
a significant portion of the gains established. This is yet another example of
how to be flexible with your exit point, and given the prevailing conditions
(spot in overall uptrend), taking profits on the dramatic short-term moves
is acceptable.

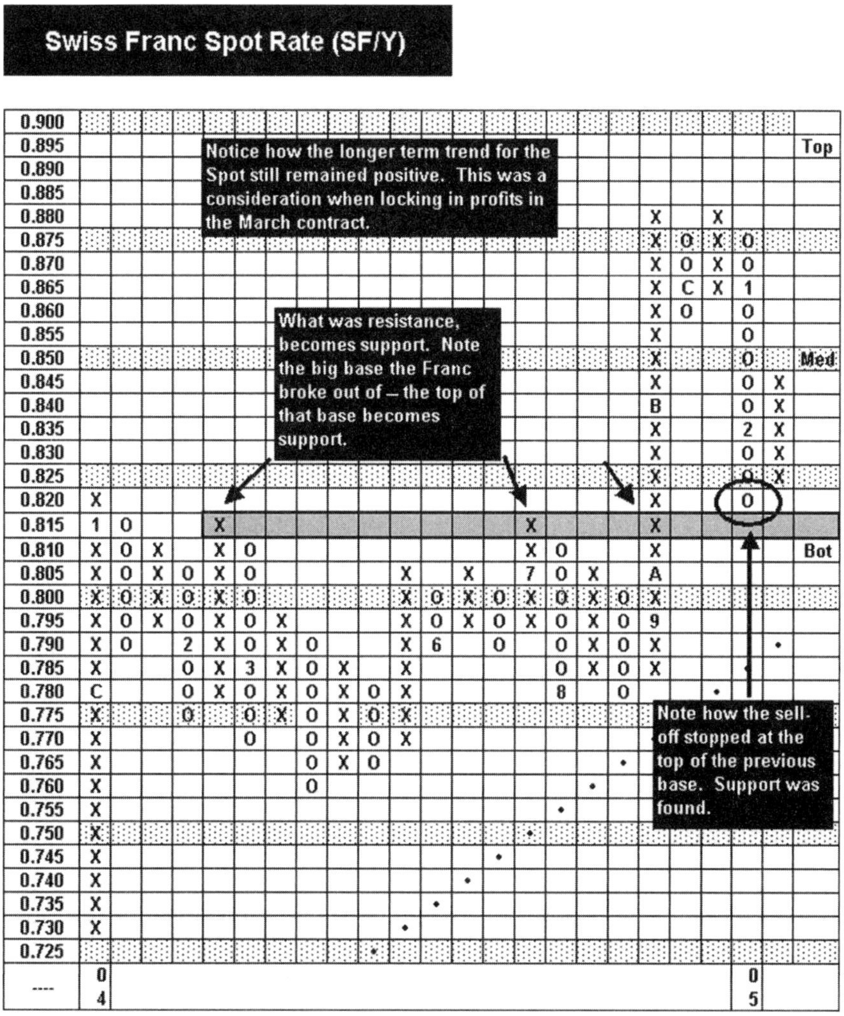

Swiss Franc Spot Rate (SF/Y)

0.900																	
0.895																	Top
0.890																	
0.885																	
0.880														X		X	
0.875														X	O	X	O
0.870														X	O	X	O
0.865														X	C	X	1
0.860														X	O		O
0.855														X			O
0.850														X		O		Med
0.845														X		O	X
0.840														B		O	X
0.835														X		2	X
0.830														X		O	X
0.825														X		O	X
0.820	X													X		O
0.815	1	0		X						X				X		
0.810	X	0	X	X	0				X	0				X			Bot
0.805	X	0	X	0	X	0		X	7	0	X			A
0.800	X	0	X	0	X	0		X	0	X	0	X	0	X
0.795	X	0	X	0	X	0	X	X	0	X	0	X	0	9
0.790	X	0		2	X	0	X	0	X	6		0		0	X	0	X
0.785	X		0	X	3	X	0	X	X		0	X	0	X
0.780	C		0	X	0	X	0	X	0	X	8		0
0.775	X		0		0	X	0	X	0	X
0.770	X				0		0	X	0	X
0.765	X						0	X	0					•
0.760	X						0						•
0.755	X											•
0.750	X										•
0.745	X									•
0.740	X								•
0.735	X							•
0.730	X						•
0.725						•
----	0 4																0 5

Text within chart:

"Notice how the longer term trend for the Spot still remained positive. This was a consideration when locking in profits in the March contract."

"What was resistance, becomes support. Note the big base the Franc broke out of — the top of that base becomes support."

"Note how the sell-off stopped at the top of the previous base. Support was found."

EXHIBIT 6.11 Long-Term Spot—Swiss Franc.

Lessons and Points to Make

1. It is important to watch for changes in trend, a spot or continuous chart can be highly effective in evaluating long-term price trends.
2. Rallies back up to resistance can provide attractive entry points for shorts.

3. Lower tops and bottoms are an indication that supply is taking over and winning the technical battle.
4. Taking profits on a sell-off toward a key support level is a viable exit strategy, especially when the short-term and long-term trends are not congruent, and the chart is extended.
5. Trading bands can also be of use when deciding to exit, especially when an extreme oversold condition matches up with visible support.

Now let's finish up our "putting it all together" section by revisiting the copper, December 2004 (HG/Z4) example. You may recall that we have mentioned copper numerous times along the way, pertaining to its correlation with the CRB Index, its notable multiyear uptrend, and in connection with changing the box size in Chapter 3. As has been the case with many commodities, playing copper from the long side over the past few years has primarily been the right course of action, or at least the more profitable. One trade in particular that we wanted to review was initiated in mid-September 2004.

Trade Recap: Copper December 2004 (HG/Z4)

Technical Data

Initial Entry: 126.50 on September 14, 2004, on pullback after spread triple top buy signal was given at 129.00.

Stop Loss: 124.00, a double bottom sell signal. Those longer term in nature could have chosen to use 121.50, a spread triple bottom sell signal. We stopped out of the position at 147.60 on October 8, 2004.

Price Obj: 138.50, using a vertical count.

Risk-Reward: 4.8 points reward for each point of risk (using 124 stop); using a 121.50 trading stop still affords 2.4 points reward for each point for risk.

Trend: Positive, and copper continuous chart is concurrently bullish.

Pattern: On spread triple top buy signal.

Momentum: Daily momentum just turned positive on September 14, weekly momentum was negative but becoming less so, and monthly momentum just turned positive.

Trade Band: The midpoint for copper on September 14 was 127.03; we entered on the pullback to the middle of the 10-week trading band.

Support: At 124.50, then more so at 122.00.

Resistance: 131.50—132.50 area.

As Exhibit 6.12 shows, we were the beneficiaries of a windfall rally in copper that didn't take long to materialize. But that is why when you "buy right," you can feel comfortable with the trade and the money at risk, and set yourself up to catch these kinds of trades that can make the difference in your returns for the year. As the technical data supports, we did in fact buy copper "right." The pullback after the spread triple top buy signal offered an attractive entry point, with a very palatable risk-reward situation. We were trading with the trend, which was also confirmed by the long-term continuous chart. Momentum was supportive in our decision, as was the trading band. Again, it is just a process of stacking the odds in our favor, making a decision based on the weight of the evidence. Based on the technical picture, the decision to buy copper was fairly straightforward. After a swift rally, we came upon the best kind of problem to have in our business—what to do about the massive short-term profits.

Copper quickly vaulted up to a new chart high of 148.00, moving through all overhead resistance. This then presented a very tenuous situation—the risk-reward had quickly become very unattractive by this point—recall that our price objective was 138.50, after all. We had substantial unrealized gains, but the chart showed an extended condition, well above any support with no viable stop loss point visible. The contract was more than 100 percent overbought on its 10-day trading band, and was actually 100 percent overbought on its longer-term 10-week trading band as well. Given this new technical data at our fingertips, the evidence suggested that we take profits or somehow protect these gains. As susceptible as the chart looked to a rally only a few weeks prior, it now appeared equally as likely to pull back from that overbought condition. There was too much risk in holding this position from our perspective, with too much reward on the table. We sold copper at 147.60, just barely off the top tick. In doing so, we recorded a profit of $5,275.00 per contract.

Lessons and Points to Make

1. Trend, once again, is all-important when selecting which side of the fence to play.

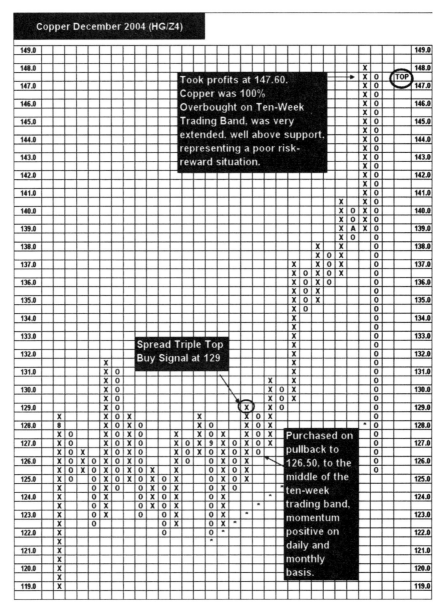

EXHIBIT 6.12 Copper December 2004 Trade.

2. A pullback to the middle of the 10-week trading band can offer an attractive entry point. As well, the pullback improves the risk-reward ratio.

3. When you use the tools properly, "buy right," then you allow yourself to stay with a trade and catch the big winners.
4. When risk (to the downside) greatly outweighs the benefits of staying with a trade, then profits can be taken, especially when supported by trading bands.

That finishes up our practical exercises of applying the Point & Figure method to specific commodity trades. Hopefully, this case study approach has served to solidify the concepts you have learned in previous chapters, and has provided you the confidence to "do it yourself." You can clearly see that the overriding theme in these example trades was adherence to the overall trend. When going against the trend (Swiss franc), we expect a lower probability of success and thus are more willing to take quick profits when we see them. However, just think about gold, crude oil, copper, the U.S. dollar, and the euro—all have had very definitive trends in place for years, presenting massive opportunity to commodity traders. This knowledge played a part in each trading decision, be it entry or exit. So remember, the key to your success over the long haul will be in the identification of trend, and then playing the direction of the trend for as long as it stays in force.

That said, over the years as you trade commodities or commodity-related products, you will likely catch a handful of long-lasting trends. There will also be times when the trends will not be so clear-cut, where trading ranges are more the norm, rather than the exception. We saw such an environment in the equity markets in 2004. It is not to say that money can't be made in such a condition, it is just tougher to do, but faith in a logical disciplined system will help you ride out such stretches with confidence. Your horizons typically have to be more "trading oriented," creating a reliance on such tools as momentum and trading bands, key resistance, and support. Either way, you have been armed with a Point & Figure toolbox that provides a solid foundation and will help you to build a sound commodity "house," regardless of the prevailing market conditions.

CHAPTER 7

Exchange-Traded Funds (ETFs) and Commodity Markets

TIMING IS EVERYTHING

The exchange-traded fund (ETF) market has been the most important innovation in the equity markets in the last 30 years. The ETF market started slowly but over the last couple of years has virtually exploded. In 2006 alone there were more than 150 ETFs added, and 2007 looks like it is going to rival that. It appears that the time has finally come for the commodity-based ETF too as we experienced a flood in this area. Prior to 2006, the only commodity-based ETF was gold related. There are now ETFs based on precious metals, the energy markets, the agriculture markets, currencies, and more. But before we get to the specifics on evaluating commodity based ETFs, let's talk about this important market and structure of product. For those of you who have read my book, *Point & Figure Charting*, 3rd edition, this story about the beginning of the ETF market and my involvement might be familiar, but this product is such an important evolution on Wall Street that it deserves considerable treatment in this book as well.

It is said that timing is everything. In my life I certainly have found this to be true. I remember my early Navy days and how just four short months changed my life. I joined the Navy with the express purpose of entering underwater demolition (UDT) and then moving on to SEAL Team I. Out of boot camp I was told I had to first go to my duty station, Naval Air

Squadron VP31, and then apply for underwater demolition. I did so and was accepted. Fortunately for me, I was stationed just down the road from the UDT training school while I waited for the next class to start. Since I was a Red Cross Water Safety Instructor, the squadron personnel department placed me in Air-Crew Training. They had been waiting for a water safety instructor to come through for months by then. I was immediately placed in the deep sea survival instructors group. My duties included teaching pilots who were heading to Vietnam how to survive in the ocean if they had to abandon their plane over the ocean.

As an enlisted man, the position as a deep water survival instructor was as good as it could get. So, when my underwater demolition class was about to begin, I decided to postpone the class for the second half of my enlistment if the squadron would allow me to stay in my survival instructor position. The squadron was perfectly happy to have me stay on, so the die was cast. I simply put on hold my desire to become a Navy SEAL until my last two years of enlistment. Well, all good things must come to an end, and my first two years of shore duty were rapidly expiring. I had a choice—go to sea or go back to underwater demolition class. I chose UDT/SEAL training.

I was accepted to class again after spending three months getting in shape for the entrance test a second time. I ran into a little administrative wrinkle though. Since I waited for the second half of my enlistment to attend class, the Navy required that I extend my enlistment by four months to qualify for having two full years of naval duty following the end of training. Since I had made a commitment to go back to college at the end of my enlistment, I decided not to extend. As I look back in retrospect, this was a major turning point in my life. I was transferred to Vietnam on an aircraft carrier already steaming in the South China Sea. In fact, they flew me out to the ship on a mail plane. Experiencing an arrested landing on an aircraft carrier under full steam in the middle of an ocean is an experience I'll never forget.

I spent the next two years both at sea and on shore in San Diego. When I was honorably discharged from the Navy, I immediately went back to college. I'm sure, had I chosen UDT, I would not have gone back to college and would more than likely own a dive shop in some remote part of the world. It's interesting how life is full of choices. I made the right choice for me and went back to college. Soon after graduation and a short stint as a production supervisor at a winery, I found employment on Wall Street as a stockbroker at Merrill Lynch. One decision, not to extend my enlistment for four months, profoundly affected how my life turned out. Timing is everything.

Interestingly enough, during World War II the United States was cut off from rubber produced in Southeast Asia just as demand for the rubber was increasing significantly. Do you know what happened? We made synthetic rubber through a large national effort to both increase the output and quality of this rubber. Here is the clincher, though: After the war, we went right back to natural rubber even though we had weaned ourselves off it by creating high-quality, synthetic rubber. Why would we do that? It doesn't make sense. We had already broken away from the addiction to Southeast Asian rubber, but we went right back. The reason is simple: We just weren't ready as a society for synthetic rubber. Many years later we gravitated back to synthetic rubber, but only when we were ready as a society to accept it. The war accelerated the process of substitution beyond what was natural. After the war we settled back to the natural curve.

It's a classic example of the technology gap. New technologies emerge while we fight tooth and nail to hold onto the old guard. I remember that my company had to drag me away from WordPerfect to begin using Microsoft Word when the quality of Word was already superior to WordPerfect. I wanted the old technology I was used to. Look at the resistance that electricity met when Thomas Edison first developed it. People cried about the demise of the candle industry, not the acceptance of this new source of light. And so it is with financial products. They have a time and a place and until the time is right, substitution for the new will be slow coming.

HISTORY OF EXCHANGE-TRADED FUNDS

I remember my first thoughts on securitizing a basket of stocks came from working with the Philadelphia Stock Exchange (PHLX) Gold and Silver Index. I knew early on, before ETFs hit the market, their viability, as an investment vehicle, was undeniable. I remember vividly my conversations at the time with Joseph Rizzello, head of product development and marketing at the PHLX. The PHLX is one of the most progressive and forward-thinking exchanges in America. In 1983, the PHLX had just come out with options trading on indexes. It was truly a revolutionary idea developed by Joseph Rizzello. Much like the first commodity-based ETF is in gold, the first index options traded were on the PHLX Gold and Silver Index (XAU). This was the first product of its kind where an investor could simply make an investment in an option on an index of stocks in a particular sector, rather than having to focus on one stock itself.

At the time, the index was priced around the $600 level, and the options were naturally very expensive as well. It hit me one day that the real product was not the options that traded on this index, but rather the ability to buy the index itself. Having been a stockbroker in the past, I knew exactly what would have made the greatest difference in my business, and it would have been the ability to buy the index, a basket of stocks with a common theme, instead of the options on the index. What the PHLX needed to do was split the XAU 10-for-1, making it a $60 per share index and then securitize it. In other words, trade the XAU as a $60 stock, a stand-alone product. Then, add the options for those who were so inclined.

I knew in my heart that this had to be a fantastically successful product. It was as clear as a bell to me. I went to Joseph Rizzello, who was a close friend of mine, and he concurred. It would be a huge undertaking to create a product like that. It would be expensive to accomplish and it was very forward thinking—maybe, in fact, too forward thinking for the time.

Nothing happened with that idea for the XAU. But, Joseph Rizzello and the PHLX did come out with a product called Cash Index Participation (CIP) units, on the S&P 500 (SNP) and Dow Jones (BIG). These were theoretical baskets of stocks that acted like an index portfolio. You owned the unit in perpetuity and had a cash-out provision once a quarter. If the cash-out provision was drifting away from the net asset value, those long the unit could ask for the net asset value of the unit. This prevented short sellers from manipulating the value of the unit. Because you owned the unit, when any components went ex-dividend, you would collect the dividend by debiting the short sellers and crediting those long the unit. The CIP unit could also be margined.

It was a fantastic product, but doomed from the start. I traveled all over the country with the PHLX holding seminars to packed houses. I mean packed houses of 500 to 600 brokers and professionals. The investment world wanted this product. But it was doomed because the futures exchanges decided to sue for the product. They suggested that the product was a futures contract and should come under their purview. This lawsuit resulted in a famous ruling called the Easterbrook Decision. The judge ruled in favor of the futures exchanges. While this instrument had all the elements of a security, it also had an element of futurity. Therefore, the courts ruled in favor of the futures exchanges. The futures exchanges, after winning the lawsuit, simply took the product and shelved it—"dead on arrival."

That decision spurred the workings of the ETF that we now have in our arsenal of trading tools, but it came from an unlikely source. The Toronto Stock Exchange came to the PHLX to learn how the CIP was created. The Toronto Stock Exchange created the first ETF called TIPs (Toronto Index Participation Units), which traded on the Toronto Stock Exchange. Following the debut of the TIPS, the AMEX created the S&P 500 SPDRs (SPY), and now we have numerous vehicles to invest in that have the same characteristics as the CIP we first traveled the country marketing. Once again, timing was everything—this time society was ready and willing.

TODAY'S COMMODITY/CURRENCY ETF MARKET

The first ETFs to come to the market were based upon the equity markets. In fact, some of the first ETFs were the SPDRs and the QQQs, representing the S&P 500 and the NASDAQ 100; respectively. Other ETF providers came onto the scene starting in 2000 with Barclays introducing the iShares line-up. Other providers have since come onto the scene. The first commodity-based ETF was introduced by State Street Global Advisors (SSGA) and it was the StreetTRACKS Gold Shares (GLD). At this writing, there are 16 commodity-based ETFs ranging from contract specific ETFs to a basket of commodities, 9 different currency-based ETFs, and fixed income ETFs. In this chapter we deal specifically with commodity- and currency-based ETFs. We'll leave the fixed income ETFs for another book, but you'll learn the tools and strategies that you can easily apply to the fixed income ETFs.

Before we get into the ins and outs of using technical analysis to trade and invest in ETFs, let's start out with some basics about ETFs. There are a couple of different types of structures to the ETFs, but the basic premise is that this vehicle allows us to mimic an underlying index, like gold, oil, or the Goldman Sachs Commodity Index (GSCI). ETFs are different from mutual funds and commodity futures in a couple of ways. ETFs differ from mutual funds because ETFs do not trade at net asset value. However, traders on the floor will arbitrage the commodities or stocks underlying the ETF if a price disparity develops. They are also different from mutual funds because they trade throughout the day. You can buy and sell anytime during the day using stop loss orders and limits just like you would with a commodity or a stock. ETFs are also transparent. That is, most mutual funds do not list their current holdings and weightings (there are a couple of exceptions to that including the Rydex Family of Funds). On any day, one could go to the web site of the ETF in question, and find the current holdings and the weighting. This is very important in the evaluation of the ETF as you will learn a little later in this chapter.

The first difference between ETFs and commodity contracts is the leverage. At this time, commodity ETFs are not leveraged products and no commodity ETFs trade options and that could be one way to increase leverage. ETFs can be margined, but still not to the extent that you are leveraged when you have a commodity contract. For instance, let's say that you believe gold is likely to rise 10 percent in price from $600 an ounce to $660 per ounce. If you were to buy the StreetTRACKS GLD, for each share you purchase, you are essentially buying one tenth of an ounce of gold or you'd be paying $60 for the GLD. On the futures side of things, each gold contract represents 100 ounces of gold. So let's say that you wanted to invest in 100 ounces of gold, as you believe it is going to rise in price. You could purchase one gold contract, which would require that you put up $2,500 (margin requirement). Or you could purchase 1,000 shares of the GLD (.1 ounce per share × 1000 shares = 100 ounces of gold). That would cost you $60,000. Should gold rise to $660 per ounce, you've made 10 percent on your $60,000 investment in the GLD ($66,000 less initial investment of $60,000). If you had purchased the commodity contract, though, you would have also made $6,000 ($60 rise in gold price × 100 ounces per contract = $6,000). However, instead of that $6,000 representing a 10 percent gain, you've made 140 percent gain on your initial investment of $2,500.

While you may not be able to get the same leverage as having a commodity account, the commodity ETFs bring the accessibility of the commodity markets to a much wider investing audience. Because you don't have the leverage, you don't have to pass the financial requirements to open a commodity account. As well, accounts like an individual retirement account (IRA) now have the ability to gain exposure to an asset class with low correlation to the equity markets, where they would traditionally be invested. On the note of accessibility, one other difference between commodities and the commodity ETFs is the trading hours. For instance, commodity ETFs trade on the stock exchange trading days and hours, 9:30 A.M. to 4:00 P.M. Eastern Standard Time. Many commodity and currency contracts differ from that, with many having fewer hours of trading. For instance, if you were to purchase a sugar contract, it would have to be between the hours of nine and noon—and they talk about bankers having good hours! However, I could purchase the PowerShares DB Agriculture Fund (DBA), which has exposure to sugar, anytime between 9:30 A.M. and 4:00 P.M. Also like commodities, ETFs can be sold short if you believe that commodity or currency is poised to move lower in price.

In Exhibit 7.1 we have listed some web sites you will find helpful in learning more about ETF structures and what's available as you begin to use this product in your investments and trading as well as all of the currently available commodity or currency based ETFs. Those with an asterisk represent those ETF providers offering commodity- or currency-based ETFs at the time of this writing. In Exhibit 7.2 you will find a listing of the current commodity- and currency-based ETFs available at the time this book was written.

ETF Providers

www.ssgafunds.com *
www.ishares.com *
www.ipathetn.com *
www.powershares.com *
www.currencyshares.com *
www.claymore.com *
www.vaneck.com
www.holdrs.com
www.ftportfolios.com
www.rydexfunds.com
www.proshares.com
www.vanguard.com
www.wisdomtree.com

*Denotes ETF providers with
commodity or currency ETFs.*

EXHIBIT 7.1   ETF providers.

Commodity ETFs

Name	Symbol
PowerShares DB Agriculture Fund	DBA
PowerShares DB Base Metals Fund	DBB
PowerShares DB Commodity Index Tracking	DBC
PowerShares DB Energy Fund	DBE
PowerShares DB Oil Fund	DBO
PowerShares DB Precious Metal Fund	DBP
PowerShares DB DB Silver Fund	DBS
Claymore MacroShares Oil Up	UCR
Claymore MacroShares Oil Down	DCR
PowerShares DB Gold Fund	DGL
iPATH Dow Jones-AIG Commodity Index ETN	DJP
streetTRACKS Gold Trust	GLD
iShares GSCI Commodity	GSG
iShares COMEX Gold Trust	IAU
iPATH Goldman Sachs Crude Oil ETN	OIL
iShares Silver Trust	SLV
United States Oil Fund	USO

As of February 2007.

Currency ETFs

Name	Symbol
PowerShares DB G10 Currency Harvest Fund	DBV
CurrencyShares^{SM} Australian Dollar Trust	FXA
CurrencyShares^{SM} British Pound Sterling Trust	FXB
CurrencyShares^{SM} Canadian Dollar Trust	FXC
CurrencyShares^{SM} Euro Trust	FXE
CurrencyShares^{SM} Swiss Franc	FXF
CurrencyShares^{SM} Japanese Yen Trust	FXY
CurrencyShares^{SM} Mexican Peso Trust	FXM
CurrencyShares^{SM} Swedish Krona Trust	FXS

As of February 2007.

EXHIBIT 7.2   Commodity and Currency ETFs.

EVALUATING THE POINT & FIGURE CHART OF COMMODITY ETFs

The introduction of the first ETF based on a commodity came in November 2004 with the StreetTRACKS gold shares under the symbol GLD. This ETF is priced as one tenth the price of gold with an expense ratio of generally .40 percent. Instead of stock backing the ETF, actual gold is held in vaults. As this is being written, the GLD price is tracking greater than 99.9 percent to gold for the past 30 days, so you can see it is tracking the way it was designed to track.

The next commodity-based ETF was introduced by Barclays Global Investors, the iShares COMEX Gold Trust under the symbol IAU, in January 2005. According to Barclays, the IAU seeks to correspond generally, to the day-to-day movement of the price of gold bullion. The objective of the Trust is for the value to reflect, at any given time, the price of gold owned by the Trust at that time, less the expenses and liabilities of the Trust. Remember from our discussion above, gold ETFs are intrinsically different from trading gold commodities because they are not leveraged.

With any ETF, the most important consideration when determining whether to buy or sell, and how to manage a position, is to examine the ETF chart you are purchasing or selling. When you go to our web site at www.dorseywright.com, you will find that what we have done for most ETFs is extrapolate backwards the theoretical price movement of the ETF based on the underlying index, or commodity index. This makes it easier for the user to just pull up the ETF in question and evaluate it. With respect to the GLD or IAU, we would use the underlying price of gold. And let's say that gold was up 1 percent on any given day, then we would assume that the ETF was also up 1 percent that day. By doing this, we can create a long-term trend chart as well as relative strength charts for commodity- and currency-based ETFs. Let's take a minute and go through some of the technical analysis we apply to commodity ETFs using the StreetTRACKS GLD. We should note here that for box sizes on commodity ETFs, we will typically use our standard ETF pricing, which is slightly different from stock pricing and shown in Exhibit 7.3.

In any Point & Figure evaluation, the first thing we want to do is get a handle on the longer-term trend. Is gold trading on I-95 North and above the bullish support line or is it trading on I-95 South and below the bearish resistance line. Once we know the longer-term trend, we can then formulate appropriate strategies. In the case of the GLD, at www.dorseywright.com we have a chart that has been extrapolated back years based on the underlying price of London gold. Over the past 10 years there have been only

Point & Figure Box Sizes for ETFs	
ETF Price	**Value Per Box**
Less than $20	.25 Per Box
Between $20 and $50	.50 Per Box
Between $50 and $100	1 Per Box
Between $100 and $200	2 Per Box

EXHIBIT 7.3 Point & figure box sizes for ETFs.

Dates	Trend	Return
January 1997–February 2002	Negative	-8.57%
February 2002–Current (Jan. 07)	Positive	103.13%

EXHIBIT 7.4 Trends in StreetTRACKS Gold Shares (GLD).

two trend changes in this chart. As discussed previously, trend changes are very important for an investor in gold, and any trend line change should be taken seriously. With only two trend changes in the last 10 years you can see that we are talking about trends that stay intact for years at a time. We'll get to some trading techniques in a minute, but let's first focus on the longer-term gold signals from the Point & Figure methodology.

In Exhibit 7.4 we see that in the past 10 years, there have only been two trend changes for the GLD, so you can see that the trend of gold can remain intact for several years and help you to identify longer-term themes in the metal. During the course of these years, there are certainly corrections during uptrends and rallies during downtrends, but this chart, shown in Exhibit 7.5, gives us a terrific guideline for the overall trend of gold. Keep in mind that it is this trend that helps us determine the type of strategies we want to employ.

In addition to the trend of the Point & Figure chart, we can also look for specific patterns developing as opportunities to enter new positions or add to existing positions. In addition, we can combine that with other technical tools we use, like monthly momentum. Momentum calculations are simply a comparison between two moving averages we developed many years ago. One is a short term and one is a long term moving average. We watch for crosses in the short-term weighted moving average over the longer-term average. Crosses of the short-term average to above the long-term average is said to create positive momentum. Conversely, crosses in the short-term average to below the long-term average is said to create negative momen-

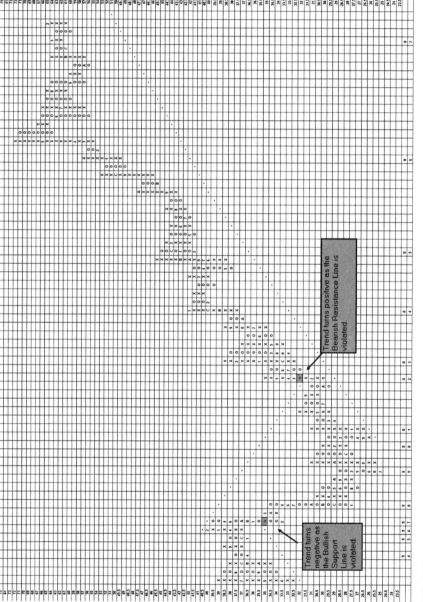

EXHIBIT 7.5 Point & Figure Chart of StreetTracks Gold Shares (GLD)—1997–2007.

tum. We developed these momentum indexes back in the late 1970s when I was head of option strategy at Wheat First Securities. We used them to help us time option trades. They worked well back then, so we simply began to use them on all equities we followed. They are simply an addition to the Point & Figure chart.

In Exhibit 7.6 you will see a monthly momentum table along with the Point & Figure trend chart of StreetTRACKS GLD in September 2005. Notice that the GLD was breaking a spread triple top at 45. This is typically a good pattern because the commodity has been going through a period of consolidation, and that consolidation creates a base from which it can move higher. If we combine that with the fact the monthly momentum turned positive for GLD in September 2005, it increases our probabilities that gold is ready for another upward move after about seven months of consolidation. In fact, during the time that the monthly momentum was positive, GLD rallied from 45 to 65, a gain of 44 percent in nine months. Then, the monthly momentum turned negative for the GLD and during the next nine months that the monthly momentum has been negative, the GLD has not made any net headway on its chart, still trading in the mid-60s. What's interesting is that now after nine months of negative monthly momentum, GLD has just broken a triple top on its chart, has maintained is long-term positive trend, and now momentum is very close to turning positive. Whether it plays out as well as last time or not is anyone's guess, but all we can do for any trade is stack as many odds in our favor as possible.

The patterns in commodity-based ETFs are all about the irrefutable law of supply and demand. I learned in my economics education that if there are more buyers than sellers willing to sell, the price must rise. Conversely, if there are more sellers than buyers willing to buy, then the price must go down. If buying and selling are equal, then the price must remain the same. This is as true for a stock, commodity, ETF, or cabbage. Again, for more information on trading strategies using currencies and commodities, we encourage you to revisit Chapters 4 and 5, as these same principles are applied to ETFs.

RELATIVE STRENGTH COMPARISONS

As you have gathered by now, relative strength (RS) is a very important tool in our work. It tells us where we should be and when we should be there. It smooths out the rough edges of the buy and sell signals and allows us to step back and see the big picture. When I think about relative strength, I recall the Zen story of an old man who accidentally falls into the river rapids leading to a high and dangerous waterfall. Onlookers feared

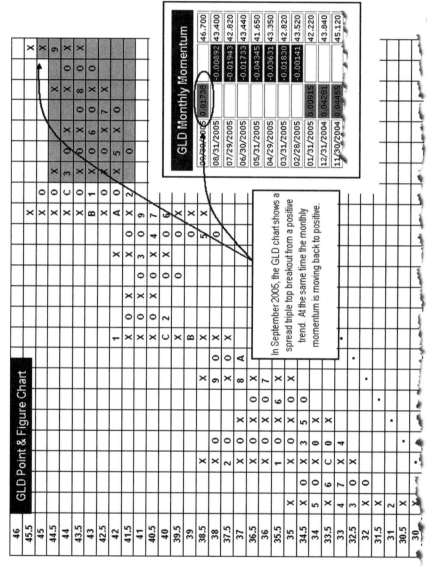

EXHIBIT 7.6 Combining Trend, Patterns, and Momentum.

for his life. Miraculously, he came out alive and unharmed downstream at the bottom of the falls. People were amazed he had lived and asked him how he managed to survive. The old man replied, "I accommodated myself to the water, not the water to me. Without thinking, I allowed myself to be shaped by it. Plunging into the swirl, I came out with the swirl. This is how I survived."

If we just let the market tell us what it is doing and we adapt ourselves, we'll come out fine. When we try to make the market accommodate us, that's when the trouble begins. This is probably where the old Wall Street adage, "The market can remain irrational much longer than we can remain solvent" comes from. Thinking back to 2000 in the equity markets, large-cap stocks were all the rage. It's where all the money flowing into funds was going. But those well versed in reading the tides and currents of the river, that is, understanding the Point & Figure work, knew that in February 2000 the small-cap stocks moved back in favor. Instead of trying to fight the current, go with it and change where you are investing. Since that change, to the end of 2006, the S&P Smallcap 600 (SML) is up 90 percent, while the S&P 500 (SPX) is up only 2 percent.

Or if you had wanted to buy large-cap stocks, it was best to purchase the S&P 500 on an equal-weighted basis instead of a cap-weighted basis. Again, the relative strength chart alerted us to this switch in May 2000. That move has meant the difference between being profitable and basically breakeven from May 2000 to December 2006 in large-cap stocks. The S&P 500 Equal Weighted Index is up 65 percent, while the S&P 500 Cap Weighted Index is up only 3 percent. Trying to fight the water would make it much more difficult to survive the turbulence. You must accommodate yourself to the markets, not the other way around.

The same RS calculations that we perform on indices can be applied to the commodity markets, helping us to determine when the tide is coming in and when it is going out. For instance, as you read in Chapter 4, using an RS comparison of a broad commodity index versus an equity index like the S&P 500 can tell us where to be more heavily weighted in the portfolio. We can continue to get more specific with our RS calculations to determine, within a specific area, what is the best vehicle to use.

Let's take a look at a couple of different ways we could apply the RS tool in commodity- and currency-based ETFs. One simple comparison would be to compare something like the GLD to the PowerShares DB Commodity Index (DBC). Essentially, what we are trying to do with this RS chart is tell us whether we are better off to be concentrated in gold investments or should we be in a broader array of commodities with the DBC. You can see this relative strength chart in Exhibit 7.7. In this RS chart, a buy signal would suggest an investment in the GLD over the DBC. Conversely, a sell signal would signal an investment in the DBC over the GLD.

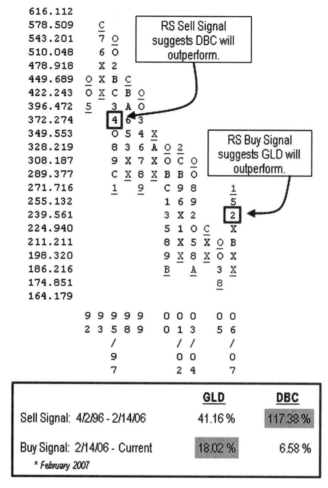

EXHIBIT 7.7 StreetTRACKS Gold Shares (GLD) versus Powershares DB Commodity Index (DBC) Relative Strength Chart.

Since 1996, there have only been two relative strength changes—yet another example of how RS tends to be longer term in nature. In this RS chart we see that the first signal was a sell (suggesting buying the DBC over the GLD), from April 2, 1996, to February 14, 2006. During this 10-year time frame, the DBC was up 117.38 percent compared to 41.16 percent for the GLD. Then the RS chart flipped to a buy signal, suggesting the GLD over the DBC. During the time frame that this signal has been in effect, the GLD is up 18.02 percent, almost three times the DBC, which is up 6.58 percent. With any RS chart, not every signal will work this well. However, what you will find is that you are still standing and able to fight another day, after the signals that don't work, because the chart will adapt and admit defeat, and that is all we can ask for any losing trade because no matter how many i's we dot and t's we cross, there will always be trades that don't work out. The key is to make sure your system is logical and then stick with your system, on each and every signal. So all in all, following the RS signals from this GLD versus DBC chart has kept you on the right side of the coin.

A couple of months prior to writing this book, CurrencyShares[SM] introduced eight ETFs allowing investors to gain exposure similar to that of holding a foreign currency. For the first time, investors have the ability to easily diversify holdings away from the U.S. dollar. This is especially attractive as we go beyond just being global; today, we are truly neighbors with other countries around the globe, and the sooner you get use to international investing, I think, the better off investors are going to be. One easy place to start is with the foreign currency market, which is the largest and most liquid financial market in the world. With the Point & Figure methodology's robust, adaptive nature, you will be armed with the tools you need to evaluate any ETFs on the market. Imagine, now you can hold your assets in your IRA in the euro instead of dollars should you choose. And, just like an equity, you can establish stop loss points. The possibilities that this opens are tremendous to the average investor.

Let's start off with an example alluded to above: Should I have cash in my accounts in U.S. dollars or the euro? To hold my cash in dollars I would just leave the money in a traditional money market account. However, I could choose to instead hold those monies in euros. But how would I know which one? The tool I like to use to answer that question is an RS chart. As you read about in Chapter 4, one can easily create an RS chart of the U.S. dollar to the euro. This same chart is shown again in Exhibit 7.8. As you can see in this figure, since 2002, the RS comparison has suggested that one be invested, longer term, in euros rather than the U.S. dollar. With the introduction in December 2005 of the Euro Currency Trust (FXE), this is easy to accomplish. The FXE is designed to track the price of the euro, net of Trust expenses, which will be taken from interest earned on the deposited euro. The Trust will not hold or trade in any currency swaps, options, futures, or other currency derivative products, or engage in any foreign exchange market transactions. The sole assets of the Trust are the euro deposited into the deposit account upon the creation of baskets and the euro earned as interest on the deposit account. The FXE is priced at 100 times the price of the euro.

But what if you wanted to drill deeper into the currency markets than just a comparison of the U.S. dollar to the euro? Here, the matrix concept also discussed in Chapter 4 can play an integral role. For instance, a DWA relative strength matrix between currencies could be created. You

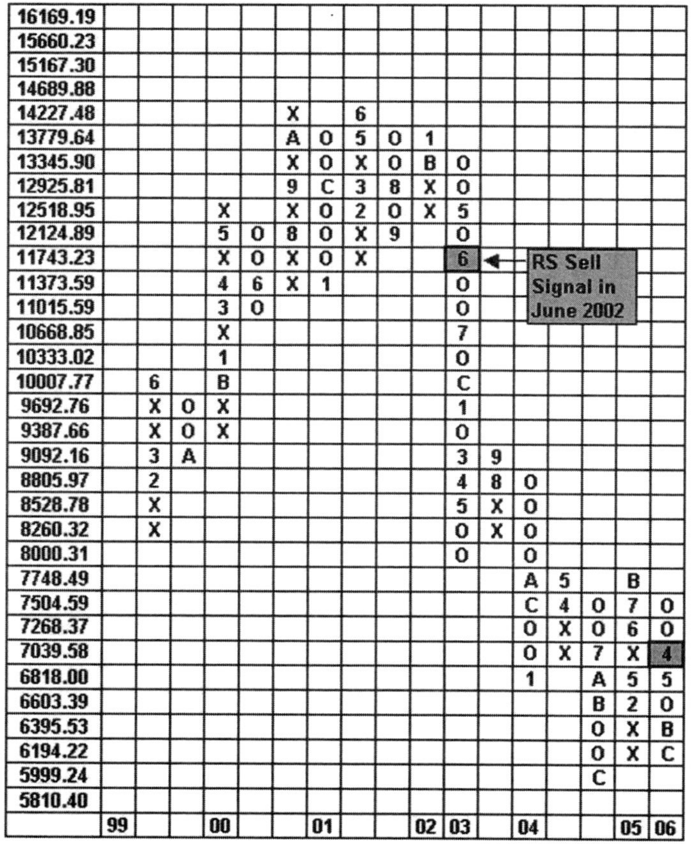

U.S. Dollar Spot vs. Euro FX Spot RS signals

US Dollar on RS	DXY	ECY
Buy signal 1/27/00 - 6/6/02	7.52%	-4.35%
Sell signal 6/6/02 - 1/30/07	-23.45%	37.24%

U.S. Dollar Spot vs. Euro FX Column Changes

US Dollar reversed	DXY G/L	ECY G/L
to O's 5/3/02	-13.16%	19.21%
Reversed to X's 8/21/2003	-4.83%	5.22%
Reversed to O's 9/22/2003	-4.28%	3.92%
Reversed to X's 4/13/2004	-2.99%	4.27%
Reversed to O's 7/16/2004	-2.85%	3.11%
Reversed to X's 2/7/2005	2.72%	-2.68%
Reversed to O's 4/25/2006	-2.60%	4.21%

RS Sell Signal in June 2002

EXHIBIT 7.8 U.S. Dollar versus Euro Relative Strength Chart.

Rank	Ticker	Buys	X's	FXY	FXC	DX/Y	FXM	FXF	FXA	FXE	FXS	FXB
1	FXB	7	6	BX	BX	BO	BO	BX	BX	BX	SX	
2	FXS	7	5	BX	BX	BO	BO	BX	BX	SX		BO
3	FXE	7	3	BX	BX	BO	BO	BX	BO		BO	SO
4	FXA	6	5	BO	BX	BO	BX	BX		BX	SX	SO
5	FXF	4	2	BX	BX	BO	BO		SO	SO	SO	SO
6	FXM	2	6	SX	BX	BO		SX	SX	SX	SX	SO
7	DX/Y	1	8	SX	BX		SX	SX	SX	SX	SX	SX
8	FXC	1	1	BX		SO	SO	SO	SO	SO	SO	SO
9	FXY	1	1		SX	BO	SO	SO	SO	SO	SO	SO

Legend:

FXB CurrencySharesSM British Pound Sterling Trust
FXS CurrencySharesSM Swedish Krona Trust
FXE CurrencySharesSM Euro Trust
FXA CurrencySharesSM Australian Dollar Trust
FXF CurrencySharesSM Swiss Franc
FXM CurrencySharesSM Mexican Peso Trust
DX/Y NYCE U.S. Dollar Index Spot
FXC CurrencySharesSM Canadian Dollar Trust
FXY CurrencySharesSM Japanese Yen Trust

EXHIBIT 7.9 DWA Currency Relative Strength Matrix.

will find such a matrix in Exhibit 7.9. Recall that the DWA matrix is merely a compilation of RS charts. This graphic is a simplified way of showing how the Mexican peso, for instance, stacks up against all other currencies. The more RS buy signals it has versus others, the higher its ranking will be. In our example, the CurrencyShares British Pound Sterling Trust (FXB), CurrencyShares Swedish Krona Trust (FXS), and the CurrencyShares Euro Trust (FXE) all have seven RS buy signals, and that puts them at the top of the matrix (the number of X's, a measure of short-term RS, breaks the "tie"). Conversely, the NYCE U.S. Dollar Index Spot (DX/Y), the CurrencyShares Canadian Dollar Trust (FXC) and the CurrencyShares Japanese Yen Trust (FXY) all have only one buy signal, which places them at the bottom of the matrix.

Using this DWA matrix as a guideline, it would tell you where to hold your cash assets. At DWA, we always have numerous interns working with us. These interns are the brightest young people out there, and whenever we can, we try to work with international students. One thing we have always found interesting is the international students' understanding of currency risk. For many international students, currency exchange rate news is common dinnertime banter, but most American students have never thought about holding their cash in any other currency than the U.S. dollar. A tool like this matrix provides a snapshot picture of the strongest currencies and the weakest. It will serve you well to get more familiar with the international landscape.

The primary benefit of RS over time is to provide an effective entry point into areas of the market most likely to provide outperformance, and to then provide a tool that will stay with that area so long as it continues to generally outperform. RS has proven its merit within many different markets, and its application within the confines of a matrix format takes the RS concept to another level. From this RS concept, DWA has created a currency ETF allocation portfolio for our professional clients to utilize. Again, the basis for allocations within the portfolio will be made based on RS. Two levels of comparisons are made, the first of which determines whether the broad focus for a cash allocation should be domestic or foreign, and the second comparison being which foreign currency offers the best combination of near-term and long-term RS. The portfolio remains fully invested at all times but will always remain 50 percent invested in domestic currency (U.S. dollars) when the dollar is exhibiting strong RS against the average foreign currency. Conversely, if the domestic currency is not exhibiting positive RS versus the average foreign currency product, there will be no exposure to the U.S. dollar.

RS is a trend-following tool that naturally performs best in trending markets. Choppy markets, or periods of time when long-term RS signals are in the process of changing, typically present tough stretches for any RS-based portfolio. But the long-term benefits suggest that riding out these stretches of congestion more than fairly compensate the investor as the next market trend unveils itself. Exhibit 7.10 shows the annual returns of nine major currencies dating back to January 1999, as well as returns of an equal-weighted foreign currency index (DWAFXI) constituted by those nine currencies less the U.S. Dollar Index, and the hypothetical returns of the DWA Currency Model.

When I look at the returns of different currencies after an eight-year period, one of the most interesting things I notice is that the U.S. dollar is either at the top or at the bottom. There really isn't any in-between ground. Because of this, some type of tactical approach is necessary to determine when I want to hold assets in dollars and when I want to hold them in foreign currencies. Utilizing a tactical model like our RS tools, a hypothetical back-tested portfolio constructed as we outlined above has kept our returns at the top of the comparison each year, and this consistent performance has put it as the number one performing entity over this eight-year stretch. (Note that none of these returns reflect interest.)

DWA ETF CURRENCY MODEL BACKTESTED RETURNS (NAV ONLY)

1999	2000	2001	2002	2003	2004	2005	2006	1999-2006
Tactical Portfolio 12.77%	DXY 7.31%	DXY 6.75%	SEK 20.61%	AUD 33.90%	CHF 8.66%	DXY 12.70%	SEK 16.13%	**Tactical Portfolio 45.60%**
JPY 10.12%	MXN -1.22%	MXN 5.08%	CHF 20.00%	CAD 21.19%	SEK 8.01%	MXN 4.82%	GBP 14.05%	CAD 42.40%
DXY 7.74	CHF -1.27%	**Tactical Portfolio 1.56%**	EUR 17.95%	SEK 20.88%	CAD 7.91%	CAD 3.43%	EUR 11.66%	AUD 26.39%
AUD 4.52%	**Tactical Portfolio -1.78%**	GBP -2.57%	**Tactical Portfolio 12.80%**	EUR 20.04%	EUR 7.61%	AUD -6.09%	AUD 8.37%	GBP 18.67%
CAD 4.52%	CAD -3.54%	CHF -2.96%	JPY 10.83%	**Tactical Portfolio 18.07%**	GBP 7.41%	**Tactical Portfolio -5.76%**	CHF 7.87%	SEK 16.15%
MXN 2.76%	EUR -6.31%	DWAFXI -5.33%	GBP 10.68%	DWAFXI 14.93%	DWAFXI 6.27%	DWAFXI -7.99%	DWAFXI 6.93%	DWAFXI 14.61%
DWAFXI -1.65%	DWAFXI -6.65%	EUR -5.64%	AUD 10.23%	CHF 11.66%	JPY 4.47%	GBP -10.17%	**Tactical Portfolio 3.19%**	CHF 14.36%
GBP -2.27%	GBP -7.74%	CAD -5.89%	DWAFXI 9.75%	GBP 10.92%	AUD 3.76%	EUR -12.58%	CAD -0.11%	EUR 13.79%
SEK -6.77%	SEK -9.55	AUD -8.81%	CAD 1.35%	JPY 10.79%	**Tactical Portfolio -0.06%**	JPY -12.84%	MXN -1.03%	JPY -5.18%
CHF -12.47%	JPY -10.40%	SEK -10.16%	MXN -11.69%	MXN -7.65%	MXN 0.73%	CHF -13.18%	JPY -1.09%	MXN -9.10%
EUR -13.47%	AUD -14.92%	JPY -13.10%	DXY -12.71%	DXY -14.66%	DXY -6.98%	SEK -16.16%	DXY -8.19%	DXY 11.50%

** Returns above are based upon changes in Net Asset Value only, and does not include any relevant interest, fees or commissions. Time period of study includes Jan 1999 - June 2007.

Prior to inception date of CurrencyShare ETFs, returns are based upon Currency Spot Index prices.

EXHIBIT 7.10 DWA Currency Relative Strength Matrix.

KNOW WHAT IS INSIDE

There are a number of different ways that ETFs can weight their components. As a quick review, with equity-based ETFs, one method is to price weight. In price weighting, the higher the price of the stock, the more weight it carries. This is the way the Dow Jones Industrial Average is priced. Another way to weight an index is by capitalization. That is, the larger capitalized the stock (shares outstanding times price), the more influence it has on the index. This is the most common way to weight indices and ETFs. With this type of weighting, just a handful of stocks can control the vast majority of an index's move. One can also weight an index equally. That is, each stock gets an equal vote. This is the way the DWA sector indicators and bullish percents are constructed, and we are seeing more and more ETFs constructed this way.

To be successful in playing ETFs, you must learn to look under the hood when evaluating the investment merits of any ETF. This is also the case with respect to commodity based ETFs. There are a number of different structures to ETFs and there is no better example than the energy or crude oil market. With the current line-up of almost 20 commodity-based ETFs and almost a dozen currency-based funds, there are at least five distinctly different fund structures that can have a very meaningful impact on how the fund reacts to different markets. To explain the differences within the various exchange-traded vehicles we will use the crude oil market as an example, as there are now four differently structured ways to gain access to the oil market through an exchange-traded medium.

In 2006 one of the new additions to the fund world was the iPath Exchange Traded Note (ETN) lineup of commodity-based products, one of which is the iPath Goldman Sachs Crude Oil Total Return Index (OIL) that began trading on the New York Stock Exchange (NYSE). OIL shares provide exposure to crude oil, but do so in a very different manner than the first crude oil–based product that was launched, the U.S. Oil Fund (USO). Barclays created OIL as a vehicle that tracks the Goldman Sachs Crude Oil Total Return Index through a note-linked security. This is different than the commodity pool ETF that trades under the symbol USO. Both are based on the price of crude oil, but the "tracking risk" falls upon the investor in the USO, while it falls upon Barclays with the OIL product. The difference between the two is important to understand if you plan on using these funds. The USO began trading at an opening price of $68.25 on the American Stock Exchange. The price this ETF began trading was certainly not arbitrary—it was the same price at which May 2006 crude oil futures contracts had closed the previous day on the New York Mercantile Exchange. The stated objective of this fund is to track the spot price of West Texas Intermediate light, sweet crude by investing in oil futures contracts traded on the New York Mercantile Exchange, or other U.S. and foreign exchanges if necessary. Investors in the fund have their money pooled together, and a manager allocates the fund across futures contracts, cash-settled options, and other cashlike vehicles in order to provide exposure similar to the price of oil.

The way that the USO is constructed is actually very different than the manner in which the previous commodity-based ETFs are created.

The USO is created through the use of futures contracts, while the Gold & Silver ETFs (IAU, GLD, and SLV) are actually backed with the raw material in physical form, and the more recent ETN additions are created using note-linked securities. The assets of the Gold & Silver Bullion–related ETF's consist of stacks of gold or silver bars in a vault somewhere. A share of these ETFs represents actual ownership in bullion, rather than a futures contract. There is no such vault with barrels upon barrels of crude oil that represent units of the USO ETF. Rather, the managers of the oil fund essentially maintain a balance of crude oil futures contracts and cash, which together replicate the price of crude oil. The periodic problem with this construction, as many investors have seen in the early going of the fund, is the potential for tracking error due to contango or backwardation. *Contango*, specifically, is a term familiar to commodities traders that describes the occurrence of forward contracts being more expensive than near-month futures contracts on expiration. This means that commodity traders rolling out of October crude oil, and into November crude oil, for instance, have to somehow make up for the $0.95 difference in price between the two. Without going into a long dissertation on the subject, simply look at the tracking error of the USO for the first few months after it began trading in April 2006. This was a time when crude oil futures were in "contango" the entire time, the source of considerable tracking error from the spot crude market.

Con-tangled Up

USO Holdings on 4/10/06

96 contracts—June NYMEX Crude Oil (CL/M6)
4/10/06 Px of CL/M6: $68.25
$6,793,000 cash
USO Px: $68.25

USO Holdings on 8/21/06

5,051 contracts—October NYMEX Crude Oil (CL/V6)
8/21/06 Px of CL/V6: $73.30
$386,416,785 cash
USO Px: $67.42

Notice that USO began trading at a price of 68.25 back in April and has actually fallen in price to 67.42 by August. During that same time the "near-month" crude oil futures contracts have risen in price from 68.25 in April, to 73.30 by August 21, 2006. The October crude oil futures have rallied from

70.26 to 73.30. The issue, in other words, is that the fund has to pay more for the same amount of exposure every month, and this has caused a significant tracking error for the fund, such that the fund is down 1 percent while crude oil was actually up about 4 percent based on the October contracts. Shareholders of USO maintain tracking error risk as a function of contango, as well as slippage since the manager of the fund is literally turning over the fund's entire inventory of oil contracts every month.

The iPath Goldman Sachs Crude Oil Total Return Index (OIL) began trading on the NYSE in 2006 as an ETN, which is constructed quite differently, essentially transferring a large portion of the tracking risk to the fund provider (Barclays) and away from the investor. Clearly, buying OIL is not without risk, it just carries different risks. One risk is obviously that crude oil may actually go down in price, adversely affecting the price of something tied to the price of crude oil. Another risk specific to the iPath Oil Fund is that Barclays could file chapter 11. However, the tracking risk is a bit different with an ETN. This index measures the performance of a simple investment in oil futures, and that performance includes the change in the price of the futures contracts, the "roll yield" (positive if in backwardation, or negative if in contango), and the Treasury bill rate of interest that could be earned on collateral funds. The benefit on that front when compared to the USO shares is that there is no "slippage" in actually transacting a move from one contract to the next, eliminating some of the tracking error risk. But, because the GSCI Total Return Index does not finesse the "roll" of the futures contracts to maximize profits (contracts are simply rolled from the expiring month to the next month), the index may also lag other strategies when the oil markets remain in contango.

And then came yet another structure for commodity-based ETFs, primarily as a result of the exploited tracking error risk in the earlier funds. Early in 2007 PowerShares launched a number of commodity-based products, one of which being the PowerShares DB Oil Fund (DBO), based on the Deutsche Bank Liquid Commodity Crude Oil Index. The similarity to the other funds is that it is composed of futures contracts on light, sweet crude oil (WTI) and is intended to reflect the performance of crude oil. The primarily difference is that the index it tracks uses an "optimum yield" strategy that employs a rules-based method of selecting which contracts to "roll" to each month. The fund is structured such that it may look out up to 13 months to try and minimize the effects of contango, and maximize any backwardation that may be present within the oil markets. This fund actually invests in crude oil futures contracts like the U.S. Oil Fund, but applies a very different strategy in managing the fund over time.

The latest evolution within the world of commodity-based ETFs has come with the proliferation of MACRO Securities (MACROs), a joint venture between Claymore Advisors and MacroMarkets. MACROs are exchange-traded securities that are issued together, trade separately, and respectively track the upward or downward movement of an index or benchmark price. The first MACROs were launched in late 2006, paired across the value of spot crude oil. Based on the manner in which the MACROs are constructed, there are two exchange-traded vehicles that comprise the set, – an "up" MACRO for crude oil (UCR) and a "down" MACRO for crude oil (DCR). The two securities function as a zero-sum entity, if one rises in value, it does so at the expense of the other. For instance, as the value of crude oil rises, the value of the "up" MACRO rises in kind, and the value of the "down" MACRO falls accordingly. Contrarily, if crude oil falls, the reverse happens.

These funds are structured in a unique fashion as the assets of each fund are wholly invested in Treasuries, with the two MACROs simply trading assets back and forth based on the value of the underlying benchmark. The income generated from the treasuries is used to cover expenses, and excess income is distributed to shareholders each quarter. There are circuit breakers, of sorts, for the crude oil MACROs. If crude falls to $9.00, or rises above $111.0, for three consecutive days the MACROs will cease trading. The expenses are currently higher than those of other commodity products, but while the OIL and USO are highly susceptible to negative "roll yields," caused by contango, the crude oil MACROs are based on the spot price for crude oil and do not include any similar roll yield. In markets where the "roll yield" is positive for crude, UCR should underperform, while in markets with negative roll yields (such as 2006) UCR offers an exchange-traded solution that will likely hold up much better than other products.

In the end, there are now a number of different oil-related exchanged-traded products, and while the details are a bit voluminous, hopefully you now have a better understanding of what distinguishes one fund from the next. Essentially, we have five types of commodity-based ETFs today; they are roughly categorized in Exhibit 7.11.

WHAT DOES THE FUTURE HOLD?

What is the future of commodity- and currency-based ETFs? I can't see how the horizon looks any different than the ETF landscape as a whole and that is to expand. We will continue to see the philosophies behind these ETFs develop. For instance, the PowerShares DB G10 Currency Harvest Fund (DBV), according to the web site www.dbfunds.com, "seeks to track the Deutsche Bank G10 Currency Future Harvest Index^{TM} by (1) entering into long futures contracts on the three G10 currencies associated with the highest interest rates, (2) entering into short futures contracts on the three

MACRO-Style Funds	
Name	Symbol
Claymore MacroShares Oil Up	UCR
Claymore MacroShares Oil Down	DCR

Bullion-Based Funds	
Name	Symbol
PowerShares DB G10 Currency Harvest Fund	DBV
CurrencyShares™ Australian Dollar Trust	FXA

Futures-Based Funds	
Name	Symbol
iShares GSCI Commodity	GSG
United States Oil Fund	USO

Exchange-Traded Notes	
Name	Symbol
iPATH Dow Jones-AIG Commodity Fund	DJP
iPATH Goldman Sachs Crude Oil Fund	OIL

Optimum Yield Futures-Based Funds	
Name	Symbol
PowerShares DB Agriculture Fund	DBA
PowerShares DB Base Metals Fund	DBB
PowerShares DB Commodity Index Fund	DBC
PowerShares DB Energy Fund	DBE
PowerShares DB Oil Fund	DBO
PowerShares DB Precious Metals Fund	DBP
PowerShares DB Silver Fund	DBS
PowerShares DB Gold Fund	DGL

EXHIBIT 7.11 Commodity ETF Structures.

G10 currencies associated with the lowest interest rates, and (3) collateralizing the futures contracts with United States 3-month Treasury bills." A mere three years ago this type of strategy would have been available only through a hedge fund format. Now, we are seeing these types of formats expanding their reach through the ETF format.

With the Point & Figure methodology's robust, adaptive nature, you will be armed with the tools you need to evaluate any ETFs on the market though. In this extensive chapter we hope to have provided you with a better understanding of the ETF landscape. This includes both the development and the current expansion, as well as learning about the differences in ETF structures and the similarities between trading currency and commodity ETFs versus their counterparts in the futures world. And we hope that you have been able to see that the principles you learned about the Point & Figure methodology from *Point & Figure Charting*, 3rd edition, can be applied to the commodity and currency ETF market with ease since the irrefutable law of supply and demand drives all prices.

CHAPTER 8

Mutual Funds and the Evolution of the Commodity Markets

FROM FRUIT BASKETS TO BASKETS OF FRUIT

The old truism that "the more things change, the more they stay the same" is as accurate for the commodities market as it is for nearly anything. In fact, having the perspective of how the commodities market began may provide the greatest appreciation for the current market vehicles available for the investor today. In much the same way that I'm quite certain Dr. James Naismith would be astounded to see not only the game of basketball today, but the industry surrounding it, so too would the early users of McCormick's reaper be impressed with the efficiencies that wheat is exchanged in today's markets. In both instances, however, the "game" maintains many of the same nuances, but packaged in such a way that would at first seem unrecognizable to the initial purveyors of the craft.

After all, it was in the 1840s that Chicago became a commercial center where farmers and dealers could meet to deal in "spot" grain. At the time it was simple to exchange cash for immediate delivery of wheat. This was the point in time when railroads, telegraphs, and the McCormick reaper provided a confluence of both supply and widespread demand. The reaper led to exponentially greater wheat production, while the railroads and telegraph allows farmers of the Midwest to sell their wheat to dealers who then shipped it 'all over the country. Where previously the farmer was at the mercy of a city with very few storage facilities for such a supply of wheat and the limited availability of dealers (demand) standing ready to purchase his crop, the technology of the time allowed for both supply and demand to establish a more liquid equilibrium.

This liquidity allowed the futures contract to evolve toward essentially what we know it to be today—farmers (supply) and dealers (demand) committing to future exchanges of grain for cash. Then, as today, a farmer can agree with the dealer on a price to deliver to him 5,000 bushels of wheat at a point in the future—the end of December, for example. The arrangement suits both parties. The farmer knows how much he would be paid for his future wheat production and the dealer knows his costs in advance of taking delivery of the wheat. This becomes a written contract, with a small amount of money, the initial margin requirement, representing a "good faith deposit," much like a down payment on a house. As these contracts became more commonly used, and accepted as a means for business, they also began to change hands before the actual delivery date. So if the dealer decided for whatever reason that he didn't want the wheat, or didn't want the wheat at that price, he could sell the contract to someone who did. Similarly, the farmer who decided that he either couldn't or didn't want to deliver his wheat at the specified price could then pass his obligation on to another farmer so inclined. As with any free and open market, the price goes up and down depending on the supply/demand relationship of wheat, which could be influenced by any combination of weather, soil conditions, or the number of consumers suddenly adopting the "Atkins diet" as a lifestyle of choice.

This market—if not the influences on it—is mirrored in the futures markets of live cattle, soybeans, and even the very currencies that are used to buy and sell the contracts thereof. Today, these markets are just as populated by those who have no intention of ever producing, or taking delivery of, a commodity such as wheat. Rather, they are speculating on the future price action of the futures contract, hoping to either buy low and sell high or sell high and buy low, but unwittingly helping to create a more liquid market for everyone involved in the process. It all relates to the "Invisible Hand" concept made popular by the father of economics, Adam Smith. So, just as Michael Jordan never began his ascent from a foul line with the intent of dunking a soccer ball through a peach basket, the appearance of some of today's commodities-related vehicles may at first seem dissimilar to the initial makings of the futures market. Nonetheless, they are rooted in the very same trade practices that were present in mid-nineteenth-century wheat trading. The commodities market is an avenue for sellers to meet buyers. And the lowest common denominator of commodities trading will always be supply and demand. A soccer ball in a peach basket is worth points for the offense, as is a 20-foot jump shot ending in "nothing but net" through a breakaway rim.

OILS WELL THAT ENDS WELL?

So the market vehicles available to the investor today are different than those of the nineteenth century, but the underlying fundamentals are much the same. To emphasize this point, let's recall the more recent debates from 2004 of what would happen to the price of everyone's favorite commodity (or at least the world's most heavily produced commodity), crude oil. In 2004 the investor who simply read the daily financial portion of his local fish-wrap was likely having difficulty remembering whether crude oil supplies were on the rise at the hands of OPEC's increased production promises, or whether increasing global demand from China would usurp any and all availability of oil, and drive prices ultimately higher. It was the classic supply-meets-demand quandary and the "panic in the streets" thesis was in vogue for quite a while. While a futures contract of crude oil was offered at less than $30 per barrel 12 months earlier, by September of 2004 prices were tickling the $50 mark, having traded everywhere throughout a 40 percent range in the two months prior. And if you were simply following the news headlines for the few weeks leading up to $50 and then $60 crude oil you saw more jukes than linebacker Ray Lewis did in the Baltimore Ravens' August training camp. Exhibit 8.1 provides but a taste of the headlines in the summer of 2004, any of which could have provoked an emotion-based decision from energy traders.

Oil is up, oil is down, reserves are found, reserves are depleted, Ivan the Terrible, Ivan the Not-as-Bad-as-It-Could-Have-Been! And that was just three weeks of time. Through it all, though, what was again glaringly obvious was that as the experts fall all over one another predicting where energy prices would go, the imbalance between supply and demand was the more accurate picture of where the price struggle was leading. Consider the Point & Figure chart of New York Mercantile Exchange (NYMEX) crude oil, which simply records the "spot" price of crude oil each day. Since peaking at $49/barrel, the price had consolidated nicely, forming a potential bullish triangle pattern from above the bullish support line. Exhibit 8.2, which is the very same that appeared in our *Daily Equity and Market Analysis* report on September 20, 2004, showed that potential breakout at $45.0 that would essentially end the "indecision" on a Point & Figure basis. The indecision between all buyers and sellers of crude oil futures contracts was ready to be resolved at $45, as that would once again produce a strong buy signal with trend already positive (as it had been for the

CBS MarketWatch, 8/20/2004:

Crude Oil futures peaked at a record above $49 a barrel Friday, but closed the session lower as Shiite militants in Iraq took steps to end their standoff with U.S. forces and local police, easing the threat to the nation's oil production.

CBS MarketWatch, 8/31/2004:

Oil futures fell again Tuesday, nearing a five-week low and ending the month with a loss of more than 2 percent amid new signs that key oil-producing countries will safeguard supply levels.

CBS MarketWatch, 9/10/2004:

Crude futures prices fell 4 percent Friday to close under $43 a barrel with most traders betting that Hurricane Ivan won't hurt output in the Gulf of Mexico and that OPEC will agree to raise its production quota next week.

El Universal Online, The Herald, 8-24-2004:

Three years of exploration has enabled Pemex to map oilfields that the state-owned oil monopoly believes will more than double the nation's (Mexico) known crude oil reserves. Luis Ramírez Corzo, Pemex's director for exploration, told EL UNIVERSAL that on a "conservative" estimate, almost 54 billion barrels lie underneath the oilfields. That would take Mexico's reserves to 102 billion barrels, more than the United Arab Emirates (which has reserves of 97.8 billion barrels), Kuwait (94 billion) and Iran (89.7 billion), and almost as much as Iraq (112.5 billion). Oil stocks closed lower Monday as crude futures settled at their lowest level in a week amid lessening concerns about world supplies.

CBS MarketWatch, 9/1/2004:

Crude-oil futures marked their biggest one-day gain since June on Wednesday, rising more than 5 percent to close at a one-week high of $44 a barrel after reports confirmed a hefty -- and unexpected -- drop in last week's U.S. inventories.

CBS Marketwatch, 9-17-2004:

Crude-oil futures prices climbed early Friday, edging toward $45 a barrel with many oil and gas operations in the Gulf of Mexico still at a halt and several days needed to assess and repair hurricane damage.

EXHIBIT 8.1 News on the Oil Front—2004.

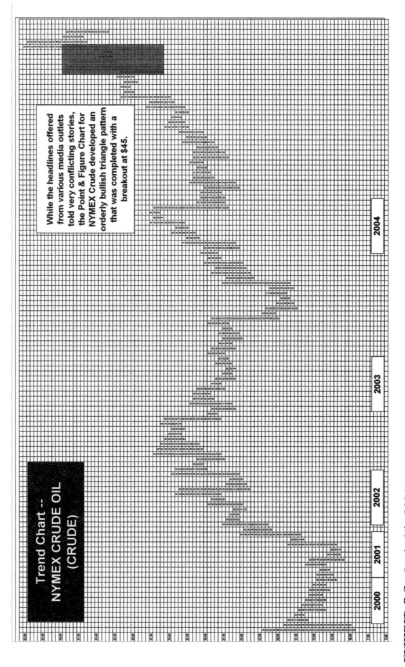

EXHIBIT 8.2 Crude Oil—2004.

previous year), a basic Point & Figure pattern you will recall being covered in Chapter 1. Perhaps this organized record of all buyers and sellers impacting the market was the best guide as to what "news" would prevail in terms of the eventual price action in crude oil.

While the average investor may not have the means, or perhaps the risk tolerance, to purchase oil futures contracts, commodity traders continued to see a bright outlook for energy prices. And, while in 2004 there weren't a great array of products that focused on energy prices on the equities market, there were a few open-end mutual funds that offered easy entry into the commodities market. The most applicable in this case, as it is the most highly correlated to the price of crude oil, is the Oppenheimer Real Asset Fund (QRAAX), which is a production-weighted raw materials mutual fund. The term *mutual fund* suggests that purchasing shares of the Real Asset Fund involves much the same process as buying shares of the Fidelity Magellan Fund or Vanguard 500, which the average investor very likely has some experience with, as these are the most widely held funds on the face of the Earth. The term *raw material fund*, on the other hand, identifies that this Oppenheimer Real Asset Fund invests its assets in raw materials rather than the equities (typically common stocks) that a fund such as Fidelity's Magellan Fund would own. So, rather than buying shares of Microsoft (MSFT), this particular Oppenheimer fund would invest in crude oil futures contracts, for instance. Meanwhile, the term *production-weighted* suggests that the Oppenheimer Real Asset fund invests in raw materials in a manner that favors the most heavily produced commodities first and foremost; of which crude oil is by far the most produced globally. This production-weighting practice is much the same as the capitalization-weighting practice of a mutual fund such as the Vanguard 500. The Vanguard 500 fund invests in 500 stocks, but invests most heavily in the largest companies of those 500. For instance, ExxonMobil was the largest holding within the S&P 500 Index at the end of 2006, constituting 3.5 percent of the fund. While ExxonMobil is only one stock out of 500 that the fund invests within and thus only one fifth of 1 percent of the total components of this fund, it gets 17 times the weighting of the average holding because it is the largest company in the fund. Capitalization weighting gives more votes to large companies and, similarly, production weighting allows a fund like Oppenheimer's Real Asset Fund to concentrate much of its fund on the most heavily produced commodity—crude oil.

As we have discussed earlier in this book, a commodities futures contract provides the owner leverage that is derived from the margin requirement to purchase a contract being significantly smaller in dollar value than the dollar amount of the raw materials that one future contract controls. The Oppenheimer Real Asset Fund is not designed to provide this same leverage, rather it provides investors with exposure on a dollar-for-dollar basis within the raw materials asset class. The fund will purchase investments in securities whose value is linked to the commodity markets, while offsetting that exposure with fixed income holdings to create a fund that carries the basic volatility of a commodity, but not a commodities contract. In short, it is designed to give the exposure of a commodities portfolio, while not the volatility of your average commodities account.

As mentioned, the fund is production weighted, making the exposure very similar to that of the Goldman Sachs Commodity Index (GSCI or GN/X), which was roughly 68 percent comprised in energy-related raw materials (crude oil, gasoline, heating oil, natural gas, etc.) going into 2007, the largest component of which is crude oil. While we will use the Oppenheimer Fund for example purposes because it has been in existence longer, we should mention that the Rydex Commodities Fund (RYMBX) is a very similar fund using the GSCI as its benchmark and maintaining a correlation of greater than 99 percent over the last three years with that bogey. While the Oppenheimer Real Asset and Rydex Commodity Funds are not strictly a "crude oil fund," per se, they are highly correlated to the energy futures market by virtue of their benchmark, and thus their internal weightings. The best illustration of this is provided very simply by reviewing the Point & Figure trend chart of QRAAX, which provided a very similar picture as that of crude oil back in September 2004 (Exhibit 8.2), thanks to that high correlation to the energy market. In Exhibit 8.2 we show the very same chart that we provided in our daily report on September 20, 2004. After reaching a high in August of that year at $9.90 the fund continued to look great and the ensuing consolidation was recorded as a simple pullback to support on this chart. Recall that the breakout on the chart of crude oil at $45 in Exhibit 8.1 was a strong signal to invest in crude, so too was it an indication to consider things that move like crude. The Oppenheimer Real Asset Fund had been trading in a strong bullish trend since late 2002, the pullback in late 2004 provided one of the many entry points along the way for those following the chart in Exhibit 8.3. As far as open-end mutual funds are concerned, this fund provides as close a play on crude oil as any other. So when the technical lineup for that heavily traded raw material, there is a high probability they will line up for the Oppenheimer Real Asset Fund as well.

Again, the Oppenheimer Real Asset Fund is not a direct play on the price of oil, but it is as close as there is within the mutual fund arena. It has a high positive correlation to the price of crude, qualitative reassurance of this can be seen in the coinciding peaks and troughs on the charts of QRAAX (Exhibit 8.3) and CRUDE (Exhibit 8.2), while quantitatively the Goldman Sachs Commodity Index (GSCI) (which QRAAX seeks to track) showed a correlation coefficient of 0.86 when compared to crude oil prices at the end of 2006. This suggests the Oppenheimer Real Asset Fund should

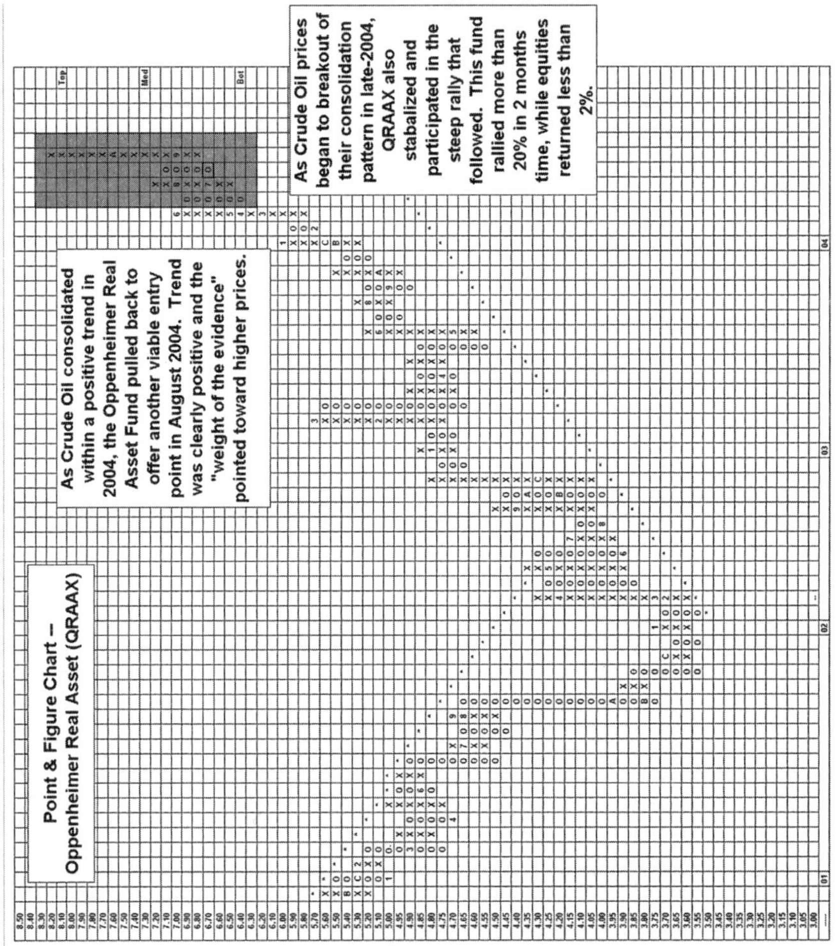

**Point & Figure Chart –
Oppenheimer Real Asset (QRAAX)**

As Crude Oil consolidated within a positive trend in 2004, the Oppenheimer Real Asset Fund pulled back to offer another viable entry point in August 2004. Trend was clearly positive and the "weight of the evidence" pointed toward higher prices.

As Crude Oil prices began to breakout of their consolidation pattern in late-2004, QRAAX also stabalized and participated in the steep rally that followed. This fund rallied more than 20% in 2 months time, while equities returned less than 2%.

EXHIBIT 8.3 Oppenheimer Real Asset Fund (QRAAX)—2001–2004.

Correlation to Goldman Sachs Commodity Index *(as of 12/29/2006)*	
Dow Jones–AIG Commodity Index	0.89
Goldman Sachs Crude Oil Index	0.86
S&P 500 Index	0.00
Lehman U.S. Aggregate Bond Index	0.05
MSCI EAFE Index	0.13

Data based on Monthly Returns.

EXHIBIT 8.4 Diversification through Noncorrelation.

have a high correlation to crude oil, and as Exhibit 8.4 depicts, virtually no correlation to domestic and foreign equities or bonds. Also, note that the similar overall trend of higher tops and higher bottoms has been in place for similar durations. While we don't choose to enter the game of predicting what will happen to oil fields in Iraq, the rigs in the Gulf, the findings in Mexico, or the tsunamis in the Pacific, the charts suggested back in September that oil still had an upside, and what followed was both successful for crude oil futures buyers as well as investors of the Oppenheimer Real Asset Fund.

Consideration toward investing in a fund such as the Oppenheimer Real Asset fund should be given for at least two other notable reasons: inflation and diversification.

Commodities exposure can help protect a portfolio against volatility in specific financial markets, such as equities, bonds, and even cash, which is as far as most investors think to diversify. The added diversification provided by tangible goods, such as agriculture or petroleum, is rooted in the premise that these goods are impacted by different factors than stocks or bonds. That doesn't mean that when stocks are going down, commodities will always go up, but it does mean that if they both go down it is likely for very different reasons, which is as far as diversification is meant to go. Consider a real estate developer who "diversifies" his holdings by owning some waterfront property in West Palm Beach, Florida, and others in the Outer Banks of North Carolina. In a worst-case scenario, that's not to say that a disastrous hurricane couldn't strike both, but it at least won't likely be the same hurricane. When we look at Exhibit 8.5, we see that there is little to suggest that the GSCI and S&P 500 will behave similarly for any extended period of time. More to the point, it is worth pointing out that there have only been two years since the GSCI was established that both stocks and commodities have been down in the same year using those two very popular benchmarks. The table in Exhibit 8.5 shows very clearly that especially in difficult equity markets, commodities can provide the benefit of true diversification to help smooth returns over time.

In 37 years there have been only two instances where both stocks and commodiites have finished the same year in negative territory.

Period End	SPX Total Return Growth of $10,000	SPX Total Return Percent Change	GSCI Growth of $10,000	GSCI Percent Change
1/31/1970	10,000	–	10,000	–
12/31/1970	11,224	12.24	11,309	13.09
12/31/1971	12,832	14.32	13,683	21.08
12/31/1972	15,262	18.94	19,502	42.43
12/31/1973	13,004	-14.8	34,120	74.96
12/31/1974	9,559	-26.49	47,602	39.51
12/31/1975	13,122	37.27	39,404	-17.22
12/31/1976	16,220	23.61	34,706	-11.92
12/31/1977	15,021	-7.4	38,305	10.37
12/31/1978	16,001	6.52	50,412	31.61
12/31/1979	18,968	18.48	67,467	33.81
12/31/1980	25,113	32.47	74,933	11.08
12/31/1981	23,870	-4.95	57,691	-23.01
12/31/1982	29,013	21.55	64,361	11.56
12/31/1983	35,557	22.56	74,824	16.26
12/31/1984	37,788	6.27	75,609	1.05
12/31/1985	49,777	31.73	83,180	10.01
12/31/1986	59,068	18.67	84,881	2.05
12/31/1987	62,170	5.25	105,061	23.78
12/31/1988	72,495	16.61	134,411	27.94
12/31/1989	95,466	31.69	185,885	38.28
12/31/1990	92,501	-3.11	239,906	29.08
12/31/1991	120,685	30.47	225,186	-6.14
12/31/1992	129,878	7.62	235,147	4.42
12/31/1993	142,999	10.08	206,157	-12.33
12/31/1994	144,858	1.32	217,072	5.29
12/31/1995	199,300	37.58	261,209	20.33
12/31/1996	245,060	22.96	349,800	33.92
12/31/1997	326,807	33.36	300,592	-14.07
12/31/1998	420,189	28.57	193,134	-35.75
12/31/1999	508,664	21.05	272,160	40.92
12/31/2000	462,339	-9.11	407,531	49.74
12/31/2001	407,392	-11.88	277,384	-31.94
12/31/2002	317,341	-22.1	366,341	32.07
12/31/2003	408,388	28.69	442,234	20.72
12/31/2004	462,780	10.87	518,652	17.28
12/31/2005	475,011	4.91	660,805	25.48
12/31/2006	**550,015**	**15.79**	**552,599**	**-15.09**

Average Annual Returns since 1970:	SPX	GSCI
	12.7	14.1

EXHIBIT 8.5 Historical Returns of S&P 500 and Goldman Sachs Commodity Index (GSCI).

There will be times when the inclusion of a raw materials vehicle within a portfolio will be very valuable, and there will be times where the added diversification results in the perhaps undesired underperformance when compared to an equities-only approach. Exhibit 8.5 illuminates how commodities have performed quite competitively with a buy-and-hold approach in the S&P 500, but that is certainly not to say commodities have outperformed every year. It is for this latter reason that it is extremely beneficial to add a tactical layer to your commodities involvement using relative strength, which will help guide which asset should be overweighted at any given time.

Consider the relative strength (RS) chart in Exhibit 8.6, which compares the QRAAX to the S&P 500 Index. While the QRAAX underperformed the S&P 500 throughout the late 1990s, the RS chart below shows the first buy signal was given for QRAAX versus the S&P 500 on September 6, 2000. This suggested the likelihood of this specific blend of raw materials to outperform the S&P 500 for the foreseeable future, and as long as that RS signal remained in force (11/16/2006) that is exactly what transpired. The QRAAX has outperformed the SPX by nearly 50 percent, while the RS chart in Exhibit 8.6 was on a buy signal, and 2007 was the first in seven years that began with the expectation that commodities would likely underperform.

The second valid reason to consider commodities as part of a portfolio is as a hedge against inflation. Typically, when inflation rises, the cost of both producing goods and borrowing funds increases, each of which can have a negative impact on stock and/or bond investments. Commodities, however, can benefit in this environment, as rising prices for raw materials (which are commodities after all) benefit the investor who owns a mutual fund invested in these same raw materials. As evidence here, consider two key observations back on Exhibit 8.5, showing the historical performance of both the GSCI and the S&P 500 dating back to 1970:

- Commodities tend to offer a high degree of noncorrelation to the equities market when played as an index. For instance, looking back to 1970 the GSCI and the S&P 500 Index have simultaneously only finished a calendar year in negative territory twice (1981 and 2001).
- Longer term, when we consider the returns over time from commodities versus stocks, the GSCI has performed better since 1970 than have stocks. A hypothetical $10,000 investment in each from 1970 through 2006 would be worth $552,599 through the GSCI, and $550,015 through the SPX total return index.

In such an environment, when inflation may or may not be led by rising energy prices, an investor may seek a commodity investment less correlated with crude oil at times, and more correlated to a broader investment

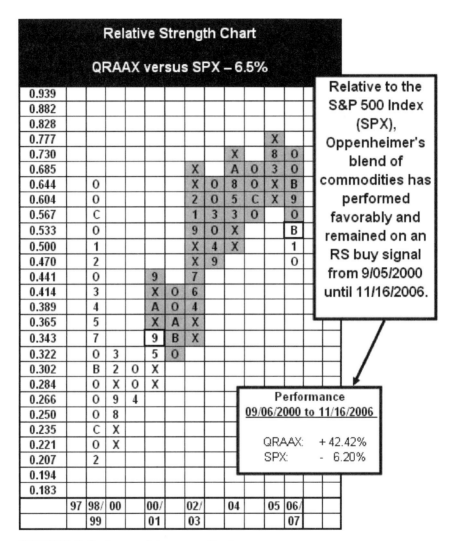

EXHIBIT 8.6 Commodities versus Stocks.

in raw materials. This end can be met within the mutual fund universe and as of early 2007 the most evenly diversified option for this within the mutual funds arena is the PIMCO Commodity Real Return Fund (PCRIX).

The PCRIX is not production-weighted fund (in contrast to QRAAX), but rather seeks returns more consistent with the broad raw material markets as it is benchmarked to the Dow Jones–AIG Commodity Index (DJAIG) that was discussed earlier in this book. We should mention that the Credit Suisse Commodity Return Fund (CRSAX) also provides an allocation benchmarked to the DJAIG, but because the PIMCO version has been available for longer we will use that for example purposes. Similarly to the approach used in managing the Oppenheimer Real Asset Fund, the PCRIX does not seek to pass on to the investor the leverage of commodity futures contracts, but rather invests in commodity-related instruments along with inflation-adjusted fixed income instruments such as Treasury inflation-protected securities (TIPS) to produce a dollar-for-dollar exposure within the commodities market. Both QRAAX and PCRIX funds are great tools to have at your disposal, and the proper fund to overweight will be determined by whether energy-related raw materials are outperforming a broader mixture of raw materials. The long-term crude oil chart (Exhibit 8.7) clearly shows a major change in trend for crude oil prices that occurred in late 2006. This is the equivalent of the winds moving into the face of those invested in energy-dominated vehicles, after it had been at the back, filling the sails of those same investors for a number of years prior. When crude oil prices are generally rising the QRAAX will likely be the more profitable holding, while the inverse would produce a scenario when the PCRIX provides a better investment opportunity within commodities.

Once again, RS provides a very straightforward analytical tool to help in this investment decision. Exhibit 8.8 compares PCRIX with QRAAX, as these two funds are similar in design they have a fairly high correlation and for this reason the RS chart below develops slowly. For this reason, we employ a 1.0 percent RS chart that is much more sensitive than those used to evaluate two investment vehicles that are not as correlated. When the RS chart in Exhibit 8.8 is on a buy signal, it suggests that a broader raw materials allocation with the PCRIX is our better option, and while on a sell signal it suggests that a more concentrated allocation in energy-related commodities is our better play. You will see that Exhibit 8.8 clearly depicts a relationship that favored QRAAX and energy-dominated allocations until roughly the same time period when crude oil (Exhibit 8.7) finally entered a negative trend in September 2006. From this point the relationship that is recorded on an RS chart comparing PCRIX and QRAAX moved to a buy signal, favoring PCRIX and more evenly balanced commodity exposure, the first such signal since these two funds have been available.

Another strong consideration that comes into play with the concept of commodities helping to protect a portfolio against inflation stems from the very definition of inflation, which is paraphrased by saying "things cost more dollars." You can look at this from the angle that production costs are rising, which leads to higher prices for the end user, or you can consider the other angle that sometimes other economic forces simply affect our currency (the U.S. dollar) adversely to make the dollars we use less, well, useful. This later symptom of inflation creates an entirely different role for today's mutual fund vehicles. There are now mutual funds available that al-

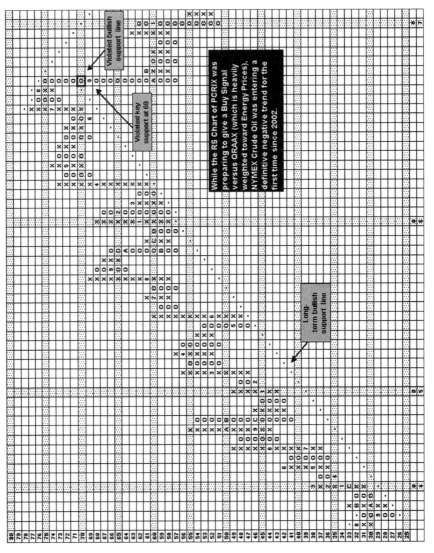

EXHIBIT 8.7 Long-Term Chart—NMEX Crude Oil (CRUDE).

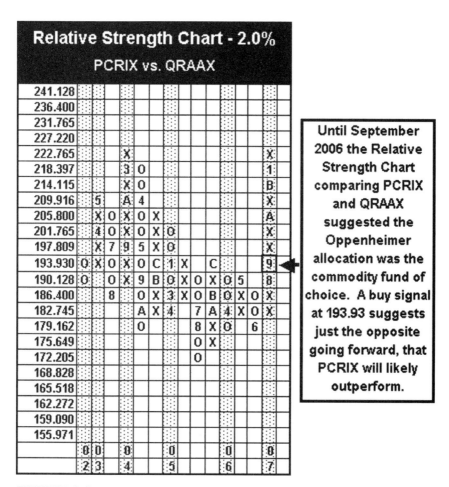

Until September 2006 the Relative Strength Chart comparing PCRIX and QRAAX suggested the Oppenheimer allocation was the commodity fund of choice. A buy signal at 193.93 suggests just the opposite going forward, that PCRIX will likely outperform.

EXHIBIT 8.8 The Weighting Game—PIMCO Real Return versus Oppenheimer Real Asset.

low an investor to speculate upon rising or falling U.S. dollar values when compared to a basket of foreign currencies. The fund families of Rydex and Profunds each offer strengthening/rising dollar funds, that benchmark the U.S. Dollar Index. The Rydex Strengthening Dollar Fund provides 200 percent leverage, while the Profunds offering is unleveraged in that respect. In addition, each family offers a weakening/falling dollar fund, which moves inversely with the value of the U.S. Dollar Index. If the U.S. dollar is falling in value versus a basket of foreign currencies, these funds will rise in value, and again the Rydex fund is 200 percent leveraged, while the Profunds fund is unleveraged to offer a 100 percent inverse correlation with the U.S. dollar. These funds can provide a speculative tool, or merely a hedge based on the larger picture for the U.S. dollar and your portfolio as a whole. Another very useful product comes from Franklin Templeton through its Hard Currency Fund, which we will take a closer look at now.

SOFT DOLLAR? TRY FRANKLIN TEMPLETON'S HARD CURRENCY FUND

Franklin Templeton's Hard Currency Fund, ICPHX, is designed specifically for this later scenario. While it's one of those funds that has a place in your playbook somewhere, it is not a fund that should be bought, or held, at all times, or for all instances, but it is one of those instruments that is unique and can add great value to an investment portfolio. Whether used as a growth idea or simply an alternative to cash, it's a managed fund option that you should become familiar with.

Briefly, the fund invests primarily in high-quality, short-term money market instruments (and some currency contracts) that are denominated in foreign currencies. The manager looks for currencies experiencing low inflation that may appreciate against the U.S. dollar, seeking to capture the relative move between foreign currencies and the U.S. dollar. The portfolio seeks to maintain 100 percent foreign-currency exposure (non–U.S. dollar). So, in other words, this is a mutual fund that generally goes up when the U.S. dollar goes down, and conversely, generally goes down when the U.S. dollar goes up. In a way, it gives the investor an option of keeping cashlike holdings in U.S. dollars (i.e., traditional money market), or cashlike holdings in foreign denominations that earn interest in euros, Japanese yen, or British pounds.

Is it a sound investment? That depends on your opinion of whether the U.S. dollar will rise or fall against other currencies going forward. On a technical basis, the fund has maintained a strong positive trend longer-term and has enjoyed a great deal of appreciation while the U.S. dollar has generally fallen versus foreign currencies. This fund is essentially a foreign fixed income fund, but as the dollar falls the interest that is generated within the fund is worth more and more when priced in dollars. When the U.S. dollar is out of favor, this is a mutual fund that should be considered by investors as a solution to hedge against inflation. Once again, let's go to the Point & Figure chart as Exhibit 8.9 shows the long-term chart of ICPHX.

Again, the key here is having some opinion of the picture of the U.S. dollar, and that chart will be a constant guide as to the helpfulness of ICPHX within your account. Let's first review the chart of the U.S. dollar September futures, DXU4, from July 2004. Exhibit 8.10 shows the near-month U.S. dollar contract in mid-2004, and one more test up at the bearish resistance line. While in a negative trend the U.S. dollar had approached

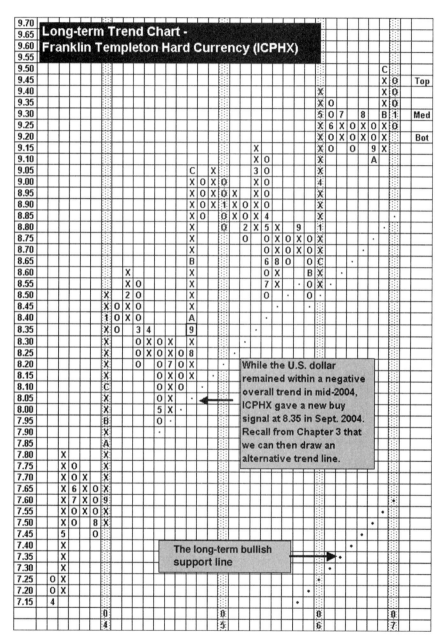

EXHIBIT 8.9 A Hard Currency Option for Soft Dollar Periods.

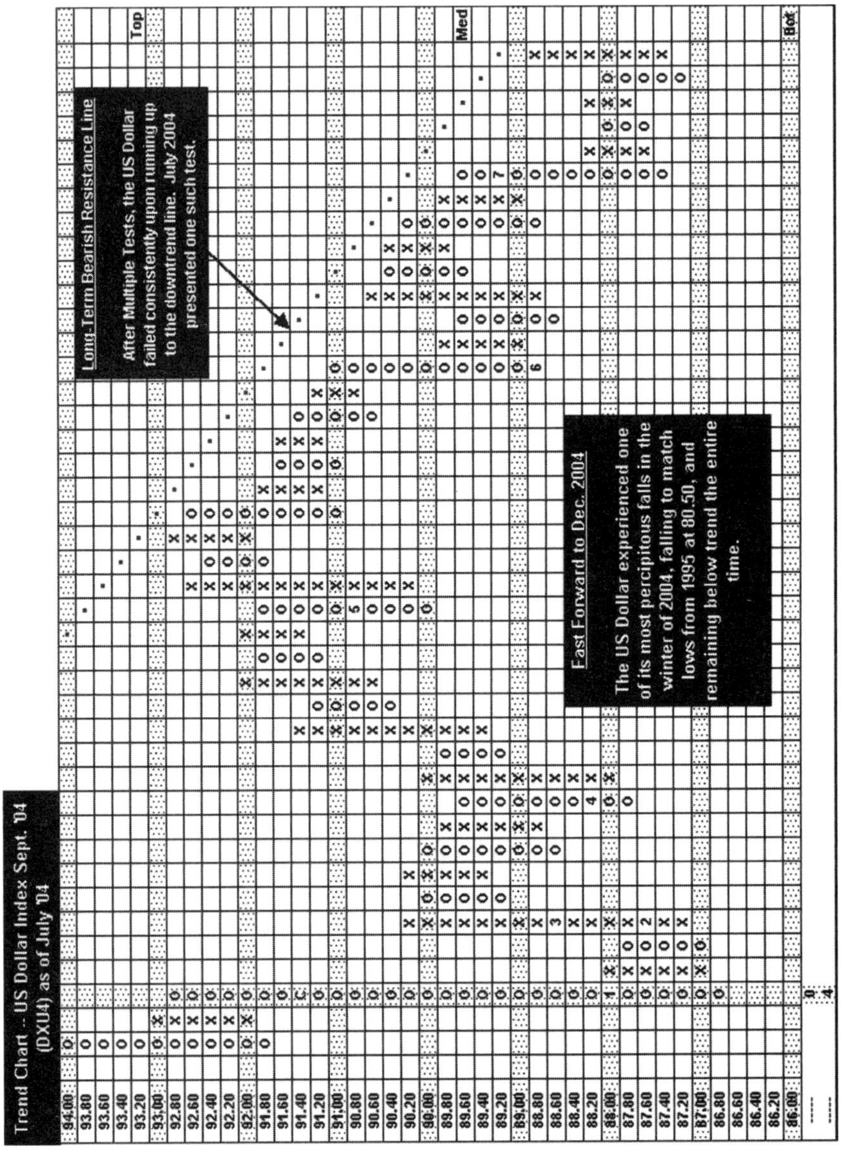
Trend Chart -- US Dollar Index Sept. '04
(DXU4) as of July '04
Long-Term Bearish Resistance Line
After Multiple Tests, the US Dollar failed consistently upon running up to the downtrend line. July 2004 presented one such test.
Fast Forward to Dec. 2004
The US Dollar experienced one of its most percipitous falls in the winter of 2004, falling to match lows from 1995 at 80.50, and remaining below trend the entire time.
Top
Med
Bot

EXHIBIT 8.10 A U.S. Dollar Debacle.

key resistance once again. The bearish resistance line was at 89.20 and was an important level to watch as far as a meaningful change for the investor. The long-term chart of the U.S. dollar spot was also on a sell signal and in a negative trend as well, so overall the bias of the U.S. dollar chart remained to the downside.

Clearly, the U.S. dollar, September 2004 chart was in a precarious position on a technical basis, and the ICPHX chart (shown in Exhibit 8.9) was contrarily in a positive trend and on a near-term buy signal in July 2004. The technical picture presented two opposing views, with the ICPHX clearly making the better investment at the time. The outcome in that case was a strong move higher in the Templeton Hard Currency Fund, while the U.S. dollar floundered for the next six months, enduring one of the most devastating losses in purchasing power ever, eventually matching levels not seen since 1995!

One consequence of the U.S. Dollar Index's falling is that cash holdings in accounts lose "real value" (read: buying power) even when held in "safe" places like a money market fund or even a safety deposit box. This doesn't often have a large effect on today, tomorrow, or next week, but over time inflation is a considerable adversary to any investor. In fact, a study by Dalbar, published by *CBS Marketwatch* in an article titled "Accidental Timers," showed that the average equity fund investor actually underperformed inflation in the years 1984 through 2002. According to that article during a vastly bullish stretch in the history of the U.S. stock market, the average investor didn't come close to keeping pace with an S&P 500 that was rising at a 12.2 percent pace each year, but more importantly the average investor couldn't outperform the forces of inflation. While Mr. Jones saw his account balances generally rising during that time, he wasn't necessarily able to buy more with that balance—in fact, he was able to buy less when all was said and done.

The ICPHX is a tool to consider when it appears evident that it has a good probability of outperforming the U.S. dollar, ideally when ICPHX is in a positive trend and the U.S. dollar is not. When this is the case, as it was for the vast majority of 2002 through 2006, the ICPHX is a valid idea for purchase either for potential capital gain, or for a simple alternative for cash. A trader has the option of seeking the most advantageous situations to move cash toward the ICPHX fund as the charts dictate, one example being the rally to strong resistance in the September 2004 U.S. dollar futures contract shown above. Meanwhile, an investor can simplify his or her approach by simply relying on the RS picture of the ICPHX versus DX/Y chart (Exhibit 8.11), which is the U.S. dollar spot chart (essentially a continuation chart of U.S. dollar futures contracts). Even in early 2007, the hard currency fund remained a valid alternative to a "soft dollar" that remained in a general downtrend. Exhibit 8.11 illustrates that RS depiction, which

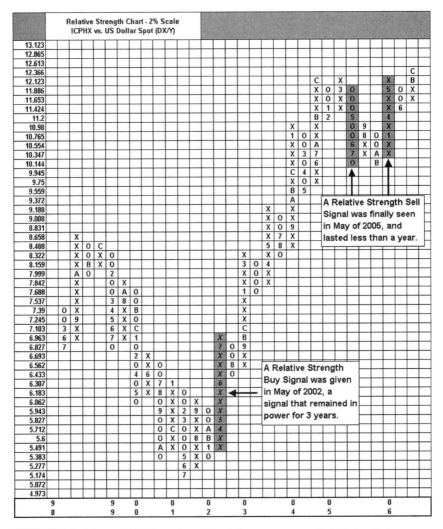

EXHIBIT 8.11 Franklin Templeton Hard Currency versus U.S. Dollar Index.

shows the ICPHX on an RS buy versus the DX/Y, and the fact that this has largely been the case since mid-2002.

THINKING TACTICALLY ABOUT CASH

What to do with cash? While not as tough as the answer of what to do without cash, it remains a formidable question for most investors, for the reasons that we have just discussed. For most of us, cash is always in limited supply and the sources of demand are painfully countless. The answer of what to do with cash in America is about the only thing the masses seem to agree upon. Americans decide to do something other than save 99 percent of their cash, as we have roughly a 1 percent savings rate in this country (or less, depending on the source). Be that as it may, in the investment world we constantly wrestle with the question of how much cash to raise at any given time, but rarely consider another important question, which is what to do with the cash. For the extremely risk-averse individual, your cash options are coffee cans buried in the backyard, or whatever room remains under the mattresses. Each of these is still susceptible to the erosion of inflation over time, but appears "safe" to many just the same. But for the savvy investor, the answer to the question of "what to do with cash" doesn't have to be your standard money-market fund. Sometimes that is a "right" answer, other times it is simply a hiding place, and yet other times it is a missed opportunity. You see, just as a handful of changes over the past decade as to whether you owned small-cap stocks versus large-cap stocks, or growth stocks versus value stocks, have netted major returns, the same is true as to how you have handled your cash position.

Certainly, there are enough decisions in this business without having to worry about where your cash sits, just drop it in a money market fund and leave well enough alone, right? Well, we've discussed the impact of inflation enough to understand that cash in a tin can is most often a losing proposition on a "real" basis, but add to that periods of a generally declining dollar and we reach periods where money market is also a losing proposition on a real basis even after factoring in the interest received in such funds. A money market fund is obviously a relatively low-risk proposition when compared to holding stocks or commodities, there is significantly less volatility. Still, as we grow closer to retirement, our tolerance for risk declines and we become more likely candidates for larger cash positions and this means that your cash position becomes a much more important slice of your investment pie and should thus be something you think more about in terms of protection. With today's investment vehicles, we don't have to surrender to the notion of negative real returns as a tactically minded investor. There are alternatives within the cash environment, one of them being in foreign currency, and we would like to show how Franklin Templeton's Hard Currency fund can be employed in a relatively simple, low turnover, manner.

As mentioned above, the hard currency fund invests primarily in high quality, short-term money market instruments (and some currency contracts) that are denominated in foreign currencies. The manager looks for currencies experiencing low inflation that may appreciate against the U.S. dollar, seeking to capture the relative move between foreign currencies and that of our own. The portfolio seeks to maintain 100 percent foreign currency exposure (non–U.S. dollar). So, in other words, this is a mutual fund that generally goes up when the U.S. dollar goes down against other currencies, and the fund will also generally go down when the U.S. dollar goes up, something not seen for prolonged periods since mid-2002.

That's the skinny on the fund, and we've discussed the performance of the fund versus the U.S. dollar in previous paragraphs. Let's consider another comparison, however, which is how this fund has acted as an alternative to a traditional domestic money market investment. The RS chart in Exhibit 8.12 compares the ICPHX to a simulated money market position, which includes interest payments that would be received in such an investment. You will see a very similar chart to that of Exhibit 8.11, the RS chart versus the DX/Y, as both charts suggest that since May 2002 the ICPHX has generally been our better alternative for cash. It has outperformed both the U.S. dollar and domestic money market accounts, and in some stretches by a very meaningful measure. From 1999 through mid-2006, the chart in Exhibit 8.12 gave only three signals, so they are long term in nature as well. This chart suggests that when on a buy signal, cash is better held in interest-bearing foreign currency positions, while cash positions are better left in domestic money market funds when on a sell signal.

In Exhibit 8.12 one can clearly see those three key changes, an RS sell signal back in February 1999, which suggested that a money market fund was likely to outperform the ICPHX, an RS buy signal in May 2002, which suggested the opposite, that ICPHX is a better alternative for cash, and finally the RS sell signal in May 2005. It can be seen clearly and obviously the signals have lasted years on end. What it doesn't show is how important taking these changes could have been for the account long term on an absolute basis. What we'd like to show is how a simple decision to afford some flexibility as to how you allocate "cash" can provide tremendous value to an account; and on a much larger level toward how you answer that question of what to do with cash. Consider Exhibit 8.13; where we begin to examine the impacts of incorporating the ICPHX into your business as a tool to use when domestic money market is simply out of favor when compared to money market exposure denominated in foreign currencies.

CONTEMPLATING CASH

Exhibit 8.13 examines a period (1) when the ICPHX is on an RS sell signal relative to U.S. money market accounts (a DWA index based on 13-week Treasury rates, designed to simulate real money market returns), a period (2) where the ICPHX was on an RS buy signal relative to U.S. money market accounts, and period (3) when the ICPHX reverted to an RS sell signal rela-

Relative Strength Chart - 1% Scale
ICPHX vs. DWA Money Market (MNYMKT)

Price																			
84.59																			
83.76																			
82.93																			
82.11																			
81.29														C	3				
80.49												X	O	X	O	5			
79.69	X											X	O	X	O	X	O		
78.90	X	O										X	2		5	4	O	B	
78.12	X	O	X								2		B		O	X	6	X	
77.35	X	B	C	O							1	O	X		O	1	9	X	
76.58	X	O	X	O								X	O	A	6	X	A		
75.82	A	O	X	1								X	3	9	7	X			
75.07	X	O		2								X	O	7	B				
74.33	X		O									C	4	X					
73.59	X		O									X	O	X					
72.86	X		3									B	5	X					
72.14	9		4	A								A	O						
71.43	X		O	8	O						X		X						
70.72	O	X		5	X	O					X	O	X						
70.02	O			6	X	B					X	O	X						
69.33				O	X	O					X	7	X						
68.64				7		C					5	8	X						
67.96				O					3			4	9						
67.29				1					2	O	X								
66.62				O					X	O	X								
65.96				O					X	O									
65.31				2					1										
64.66				O	X				X										
64.02				4	X	O			X										
63.39				O	6	O			X										
62.76				O	X	7			C										
62.14				5	X	8			X										
61.53				O		O				*X*	B								
60.92						O				7	O	9							
60.31						9	1			*X*	O	X							
59.72						O	X	O		*X*	8	X							
59.12						O	X	O		6	O	←							
58.54						O	C	2	X	*X*									
57.96						A	X	O	9	O	*X*								
57.39						O	X	3	X	O	5								
56.82						B		O	X	A	*X*								
56.25								O	8	B	4								
55.70								4	7	C	*X*								
55.15								5	X	1	*X*								
54.60								6	X	O									
54.06								O											
53.52																			
52.99																			

Bottom axis (years): 98 | 99 | 00 | 01 | 02 | 03 | 04 | 05 | 06

> The initial relative strength buy signal for ICPHX versus U.S. money market was given in June of 2002, lasting until May 2005.

EXHIBIT 8.12 Franklin Templeton Hard Currency versus U.S. Dollar Index.

tive to U.S. money market accounts. Period 1 encompasses the time frame from February 16, 1999, through May 30, 2002; period 2 encompasses the time frame from May 30, 2002, through May 13, 2005, while period 3 includes the time frame from May 13, 2005, until the study ended on April 18, 2006.

	Period 1 2/19/1999	Period 1 6/4/2002	Period 2 5/13/2005	Period 3 4/18/2006	Return Period 1	Return Period 2	Return Period 3
F.T. Hard Currency Fund (ICPHX)	7.57	7.00	9.57	9.26	-7.53%	36.71%	-3.24%
DWA Money Market Index (MNYMKT)	10.26	11.77	12.26	12.68	14.72%	4.16%	3.43%
S&P 500 CapWeighted Index (SPX)	1239.22	1040.69	1165.69	1307.65	-16.02%	12.01%	12.18%

EXHIBIT 8.13 Contemplating Cash—Examining Returns since 1999 for ICPHX, MNYMKT, and SPX.

Investment Allocation	Allocation Stock/Cash	Cum. Return 2/99 - 4/06
Using Positive RS Cash Option	(70/30)	21.93%
Using Negative RS Cash Option	(70/30)	2.04%
Money Market Only Cash Position	(70/30)	11.40%
Using No Cash Position	(100/0)	5.52%
Using Only "Strong" Cash Position	(0/100)	62.21%

EXHIBIT 8.14 Contemplating Cash—Hypothetical Returns of Tactical Cash Management.

We can clearly see that the ICPHX drastically outperformed money market, while the RS suggested that you own ICPHX, and meanwhile underperformed when the RS chart suggested that was likely to be the case. A better way to display the impact of this over the duration of our study period is to look at a few likely investment approaches over that time. We will use the S&P 500 as our "equities" proxy, and look at a few basic allocation alternatives to display how powerful a tactical approach toward managing cash can be.

We considered three basic allocations: a 70 percent equities and 30 percent cash portfolio, a 100 percent equities portfolio, and a 100 percent cash portfolio. Within the 70/30 split allocation we look at three management alternatives, using the positive RS cash option (either ICPHX or money market), using the negative RS cash option at the time (ICPHX or money market) and simply using money market (as your average investor would likely do). For example, the "positive RS cash option" example would keep the 30 percent cash allocation in money market from February 1999 until May 2002, because the RS chart of ICPHX was on a sell signal versus money market during that time. That account would then switch to investing all cash assets to ICPHX in May 2002 when the RS chart went to a buy signal, just as a tactical manager would likely do. It would then convert to money market in May 2005 upon seeing the RS sell signal for ICPHX versus MNYMKT that was shown in Exhibit 8.12. Each portfolio was rebalanced whenever a change was made. Exhibit 8.14 shows the returns of each approach from February 16, 1999, through April 18, 2006.

THE BIG PICTURE?

The best approach over the study period was indeed a tactically managed cash portfolio, or a blend of tactically managed cash and equities. This example took us through particularly strong years for equities (1999 and

```
Oppenheimer Real Asset Fund – QRAAX
Rydex Commodity Fund -- RYMBX
Pimco Real Return Fund -- PCRIX
Credit Suisse Commodity Return Fund -- CRSAX
Franklin Templeton Hard Currency Fund – ICPHX
Rydex Strengthening US Dollar Fund -- RYSDX
Rydex Weakening US Dollar Fund -- RYWDX
ProFunds Rising Dollar Fund -- RDPIX
ProFunds Falling Dollar Fund -- FDPIX
```

EXHIBIT 8.15 Commodities/Futures-Related Mutual Fund Lineup.

2003) and weak years as well (2000–2002), and gives us an idea of how important making major tactical decisions can be on a portfolio along the way. The least productive approach over that time frame was being either fully invested in equities, or having your cash position poorly managed.

While this study isn't the end all for cash management, it should give added reason to consider a tactical approach toward your overall portfolio management philosophy, and it certainly could point you toward adopting a more flexible approach toward managing your cash allocation. Today's mutual fund vehicles give you some powerful tools that can add a great deal of growth during periods where either low domestic interest rates and/or inhibiting inflation provide a tough test for investors who rely on heavy cash positions.

COMMODITY/FUTURES-RELATED MUTUAL FUND VEHICLES

Today's market is replete with products that allow the average investor admittance to areas formerly only accessible to commodity and currency traders, and the list is growing each year. This is perhaps more apparent in the ETF universe but is certainly the case within the mutual fund arena as well. Exhibit 8.15 provides a recap of the various commodity and futures-related funds discussed in this chapter should be added to the toolbox of the tactically minded investor. And while today's products may not greatly resemble those of years ago, their price fluctuations are still dependant upon the basic laws of supply and demand, meaning technical analysis adds a tremendous advantage to those willing to grasp it.

CHAPTER 9

Final Thoughts

We hope this book helps you become more successful and more organized in your commodity trading. I remember when I was first introduced to commodity trading back in 1987. I had been in the investment business for 13 years by then and specialized in the Point & Figure method of analysis, making it a natural extension to apply the Point & Figure methodology to my commodity trading. At this point I am sure your mind is racing with ideas and questions as we have covered a tremendous amount of material in this book. We have tried to harness what we have learned from our twenty years of experience in the commodity markets, and over 30 years of experience trading and researching the equity markets with the same tools. Amidst that, there are several crucial points that I don't want lost as you finish this book.

1. *Supply and demand drives it all.* And you don't have to look hard to find examples from your everyday life. Any parent knows this firsthand from inevitably spending a Christmas season looking for "Tickle Me Elmo" or a Sony PlayStation 3. You might have found yourself camping out with other moms and dads at your local Circuit City or Toys 'R' Us, or you might have latched onto the modern day equivalent of a farmer's market at eBay.com, bidding thousands for that perfect gift to place under the tree for Christmas morning. I have always viewed commodities simply as another investment vehicle, just like stocks, that adhered to the irrefutable laws of supply and demand—nothing more, nothing less. When I began my own commodity trading, I approached it as nothing more than trading IBM. All the techniques we used to trade equities

applied to commodities. To me orange juice was no different than live hogs and live hogs no different than rough rice. They all moved around like IBM or General Motors, in the sense that the very same forces affect them when we break price action down to the lowest common denominator. If there are more buyers than sellers willing to sell, then price must rise. When there are more sellers than buyers willing to buy, price must fall. And when buying and selling are equal, price will remain the same. But just like the produce in the supermarket, what is in season changes, though in the market it isn't determined by a calendar. Commodities will move in and out of favor, so you must construct a trading discipline that embodies both a buy and sell trigger. Many traders spend the bulk of their time crafting the buy decision, to the extent they never consider a sell discipline that is focused on limiting losses. The latter is essential to overall success; it must be central to all that you do in investments, especially in commodities.

2. *Commodities can have a place in any investor's portfolio.* If you have ever been canoeing with a friend you can probably recall at least a time or two that one of you leaned a little too far to the left, or a little too far to the right. It was up to the other person in the boat to compensate by leaning in the opposite direction to counterbalance that action. If they didn't, well, as Newton famously stated, an object in motion stays in motion until acted upon by an outside force. Adding commodities to an equity portfolio acts much the same way—balancing out the equity portion of the portfolio to keep the boat righted in many markets. As you read in Chapter 8, in the last 37 years, there have only been two years when both the equity markets and the commodity markets experienced down years simultaneously. All too often, U.S. investors tend to be quite narrowly focused with respect to the markets that are available to them. One area that should always at least be considered is the commodity market, if for no other reason than that which we illuminated in Chapters 6 and 8, the commodity market has a very low correlation to the equity markets. In other words, they each move to the beat of their own drummer and thus can compliment each other nicely in an investment portfolio. For instance, consider Exhibit 9.1, which shows how an account with pure equities versus one equally weighted with equities and commodities (rebalanced annually) shows less volatility, drawdowns that are typically more shallow, and long-term returns that are better than either asset class on its own.

3. *Like any investment, overleverage is typically what will precede any large losses.* This is not to be blamed on the underlying investment vehicle itself, as many mistakenly believe, but rather on the investor. As we pointed out in Chapters 7 and 8, one of the key differences between the commodity-related ETF market and the futures market

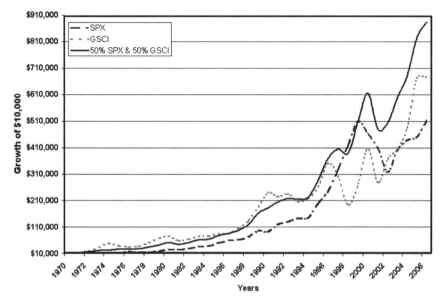

EXHIBIT 9.1 Best of Both Worlds: How Commodities Can Smooth Volatility.

is the lack of leverage in the former. This allows investors to access the commodity markets in accounts like individual retirement accounts (IRAs), 401(k)s, and other tax-sheltered accounts. This might be the equivalent of putting training wheels on a commodity investment, which may be the better path for many investors; you need to first be honest with yourself to determine your real risk tolerance and level of discipline. Take a look at our two hypothetical commodity traders in Exhibit 9.2. Trader A starts off with a good year, up 30 percent but then hits two losing years, falling 40 percent both years before recovering and making 30 percent two years in a row. Trader B starts off well too, up 20 percent. Then, the markets deal him a bad hand for two years in a row as well, but he contains his losses to 20 percent each year. Trader B also recovers during the next two years, up 20 percent in each of those years. Trader A's portfolio value has fallen from $100 to $79 during those five years, while Trader B has seen his portfolio value grow from $100 to $110. The lesson here is that you don't have to hit the ball out of the park to have a successful trading strategy. Consistent returns that limit losses will, in the end, allow you to score more runs.

4. *Follow the trend.* Sports fans will remember the football dynasty of the 1980s, the San Francisco 49ers. During their run, it seemed as if they were almost unstoppable. Then the head coach, Bill Walsh, retired and some of the players passed their prime; before long, the slide was on.

	Commodity Trader A		Commodity Trader B	
Beginning Balance	$100.00	Yrly Portfolio Return	$100.00	Yrly Portfolio Return
Year 1	$130.00	30%	$120.00	20%
Year 2	$78.00	-40%	$96.00	-20%
Year 3	$46.80	-40%	$76.80	-20%
Year 4	$60.84	30%	$92.16	20%
Year 5	$79.09	30%	$110.59	20%

EXHIBIT 9.2 A Tale of Two Traders.

The markets often move the same way—as the old adage says, "Don't fight the tape." Once a trend is established, that trend can be harder to stop than a freight train. Just as all good things come to an end, eventually, so do the bad things, and new trends will always be developing somewhere. I think you will agree that throughout this book, we have emphasized the importance of determining the trend of any commodity or currency and then playing that trend so long as it remains in force. Sometimes this is years, others it may be weeks, but we must change when the trend suggests so. The Point & Figure chart is amazingly versatile because it not only guides us toward areas of establishing trends, but also provides definitive levels at which trend has in fact changed. For instance, if gold is in a positive trend, and then we begin to see lower tops, followed by lower bottoms, those are the first warning shots across the bow. This tells us trouble is beginning to set in for the near term, and if the bullish support line is violated that provides the final signal that things have moved from a positive outlook to a negative outlook, dictating our range of action for the foreseeable future.

In addition to the overall trend, the individual Point & Figure chart along with other technical tools, can provide us with valuable insight into timing the entry and exit points. As pointed out in Chapter 1, entry points take on even more importance when you are looking at a shorter-term trade, as we often are with individual commodity contracts. Keep the following checklist handy whenever you evaluate any commodity position—and always remember that the goal of this entire process is simply to stack as many odds in your favor as possible (Exhibit 9.3).

5. *Relative strength (RS), as you have learned, is one of the cornerstones of Dorsey, Wright's technical research.* As the name implies, RS measures how one security is performing when compared directly with another; this comparison allows you to determine which security is outperforming the other. From this analysis, you want to invest in the vehicle that is outperforming the other, be it the market, another

P&F Chart Indicator	Pos.	Neg.	Comments
Overall Trend			
Point & Figure Pattern			
Price Objective			
Resistance			
Support			
Stop Loss Point			
Risk-Reward			
Relative Strength			
Weekly Momentum			
Trading Band			

EXHIBIT 9.3 Commodity Evaluation Sheet.

commodity or an index such as the CRB Index. However, we look to habitually steer clear of the underperformer. By focusing on strong RS commodities or currencies, for example, you put yourself in the position to capture large, positive outliers (winners), while avoiding big losers. The benefits of using relative strength in your analysis can be both short term and long term in nature, so RS can be applied by both traders and investors alike. One important aspect of relative strength to keep in mind is that it is a "relative" measurement. For this reason it is paramount that you use relative strength in conjunction with other "absolute" Point & Figure tools, such as trend and chart pattern analysis, especially when trading.

There are many ways to apply relative strength to the commodities landscape. The concept can be used for both broad and specific commodity-related decisions. For example, as previously discussed, RS can determine if the equity market is outperforming the commodity market, as measured by the S&P 500 versus the CRB Index. This allows you to make macro asset allocation level decisions. Furthermore, RS can pinpoint specific opportunities within a sector of the commodity market, such as grains, or can be used to itemize a specific foreign currency situation. This can be accomplished by comparing one commodity or currency to another with an individual RS chart, such as the U.S. dollar versus the euro, or can be visualized by constructing an RS matrix of all grains or all the CurrencyShares ETFs, for example.

When considering investing in commodities and currencies, it is important to rely on RS first in a very broad-brushed approach, as this will allow you to make sound asset allocation (big) decisions. It will

184 COMMODITY STRATEGIES

Total Market Asset Class RS Matrix

Rank	Ticker	Buys	X's	Combo	RYTPX	DBC	CL/	GSP	DJP	ICPHX	AGG	MNYMKT	GC/	SPX	RSP	EFA
1	EFA	11	10	21	BX	BX	BO	BX	BX	BX	BX	BX	BX	BX	BX	
2	RSP	10	9	19	BX	BX	BO	BX	BX	BX	BX	BX	BX	BX		SO
3	SPX	9	8	17	BX	BX	BO	BX	BX	BX	BX	BX	BX		SO	SO
4	GC/	8	8	16	BX									SO	SO	SO
5	MNYMKT	5	5	10	BX									SO	SO	SO
6	AGG	5	4	9	BX									SO	SO	SO
7	ICPHX	4	6	10	BX									SO	SO	SO
8	DJP	4	3	7	BX									SO	SO	SO
9	GSP	3	1	4	BX									SO	SO	SO
10	CL/	2	8	10	SX	BO		BX	SO	SX	SX	SX	SO	SX	SX	SX
11	DBC	1	2	2	BO		SX	BX	O	SO	SO	SO	SO	SO	SO	SO
12	RYTPX	1	1	2		SX	BO	SO	SO	SO	SO	SO	SO	SO	SO	SO

(Text box over rows 4–9, columns DBC–GC/): By comparing each asset to every other asset, we can construct an RS Matrix to determine which areas of the total market are performing the best compared to each other. As this matrix suggests, International, the US Market, and Gold should command your attention now. Conversely, the broad commodity indexes and Crude Oil reside at the bottom of the matrix, showing the poorest RS compared to other areas.

The above Total Market Asset Class RS Martix suggests that if you want to garner commodity exposure as an alternative asset class, your best bet is via Gold as is ranks the highest on the matrix

EXHIBIT 9.4 Total Market Access Class RS Matrix.

also minimize the number of decisions you need to make in the long run. First, answer the big questions, and from there you can use RS to pinpoint specific opportunities within that asset class. Exhibit 9.4 provides an example of how RS can be used in a very broad nature. As you can see, we have constructed an RS matrix that pits a number of different asset classes against one another. This allows us to determine which areas of the total market are performing the best. As this matrix suggests, International (EFA), domestic equities (RSP, SPX), and Gold (GC/) should command your attention first, given that they reside at the top of the matrix. Conversely, in this example, the broad commodity indexes (DJP, GSP, and DBC) and Crude Oil (CL/) should be avoided as they are exhibiting the weakest RS when compared to other assets. By consulting this single matrix you are provided with valuable information to make sound "big" investment decisions. Very clearly, within commodities specifically, a bet on gold rather than crude oil (or crude-dominated indexes) appears advisable based on this figure. (This posture was confirmed with a specific RS chart in Chapter 7, Exhibit 7.6.)

In Exhibit 9.5 we provide you with a summary table of RS applications. Hopefully, this information will allow you to easily remember the different uses and functions of RS.

6. *The list of commodity-related products currently available is growing nearly as fast as we can write this book.* Throughout the course of this text, we have spent considerable time educating with respect to the subject of commodity investing via futures contracts. It wasn't very long ago that this was the only way to garner exposure to this alternative asset class for most investors, short of literally purchasing a farm and managing your own crop of corn or soybeans! The average investor now has access to commodities markets in ways that before were only dreamt of; and these offerings are expanding rapidly, almost

Relative Strength Application Examples

	Macro Decisions	Micro Decisions
RS Matrix	Total Market Asset Class RS Matrix Dorsey, Wright Commodity Matrix	Commodity Sector Matrix (Grains) CurrencyShares ETF RS Matrix
Specific RS Chart	CRB Index vs. S&P 500 Basket of Currencies vs. US Dollar (ICPHX vs. DX/Y) Commodity Index vs. Commodity Index (GSCI vs. CRB)	Individual Commodity vs. CRB Index Currency vs. Currency (Dollar vs. Euro) Commodity vs. Commodity (Corn vs. Wheat)

EXHIBIT 9.5 Relative Strength Application Examples.

daily. After reading Chapters 7 and 8, you are likely more aware of the products now available to you. For example, the greatest expansion in product offerings comes in the form of ETFs (and ETNs). This particular medium has brought to your fingertips an array of choices, giving you the ability to play crude oil, grains, base metals, and the euro currency, to name a few, and to do so in much the same fashion as you would buy or sell a stock.

The existing mutual fund universe also permits investment into commodity indexes and currencies (as discussed in Chapter 8), though with some limitations compared to the ETF. As this book is being sent to press there are many new commodity-based ETFs in registration (pending approval from the Securities and Exchange Commission), with PowerShares due to launch two new ETFs that will allow access to the U.S. dollar (either long or short). Moreover, Barclays Global (BGI) is expanding their commodity-based ETFs, and is currently waiting approval on a handful of ETFs that will allow you to play natural gas and livestock, among others. *Bottom line*: As an investor you have the power to truly diversify your investment portfolio due to the plethora of commodity and currency-related vehicles now available. In Exhibit 9.6 we summarize the current commodity product offerings within the mutual fund and ETF universe. For a more complete list of futures contracts that are available for trading, consult the appendix at the end of the book.

It is up to you to harness the power of these products and bring this asset class into your investment spectrum. The DWA web site database can be a great advantage for you in doing so, as we offer an extensive array of tools that permit you to technically analyze commodity futures, ETFs, and mutual funds; and we constantly endeavor to offer up-to-date technical information on every commodity-related vehicle available. All Point & Figure concepts and indicators you learned throughout this text are available on our site—they are merely a mouse click away. Take advantage of the fact that you have such a powerful database of

Ways to Invest in Commodities/Currencies

Commodity Index	Futures Contracts	How to Invest	
		ETF's	Mutual Funds
Deutsche Bank Liquid Commodities Index (DBLCLX)	No	PowerShares DB Commodity Index (DBC)	
Goldman Sachs Commodity Index (GNX)	Yes	iPATH GSCI Total Return Index ETN (GSP) iShares GSCI Commodity (GSG)	Oppenheimer Real Asset A (QRAAX) Rydex Commodities Fund H (RYMBX)
Dow Jones AIG Commodity Index (DJAIG)	Yes	iPATH Dow Jones-AIG Commodity Index ETN (DJP)	PIMCO Allianz CommRealRetStr Insti (PCRIX) Credit Suisse Com Ret Str A (CRSAX)
Reuters Jefferies CRB Index (CR/Y)	Yes		
Continuous Commodity Index (UV/Y)	Yes		
Commodities *	Futures Contracts	How to Invest	
		ETF's	Mutual Funds
Energy	Yes	PowerShares Energy Fund (DBE)	
Crude Oil	Yes	PowerShares DB Oil Fund (DBO) Claymore MacroShares Oil Down (DCR) iPath Goldman Sachs Crude Oil ETN (OIL) Claymore MacroShares Oil Up (UCR) United States Oil Fund (USO)	
Metals	Yes	PowerShares DB Base Metals Fund (DBB) PowerShares Precious Metals Fund (DBP)	
Gold	Yes	PowerShares DB Gold Fund (DGL) streetTRACKS Gold Trust (GLD) iShares Comex Gold Trust (IAU)	
Silver	Yes	PowerShares DB Silver Fund (DBS) iShares Silver Trust (SLV)	
Agriculture	Yes	PowerShares DB Agriculture Fund (DBA)	
Currencies	Futures Contracts	How to Invest	
		ETF's	Mutual Funds
Basket of Currencies	Yes	PowerShares DB G10 Currency Harvest Fund (DBV)	Franklin Templeton Hard Currency Fund (ICPHX)
Australian Dollar	Yes	CurrencyShares Australian Dollar Trust (FXA)	
British Pound	Yes	CurrencyShares British Pound Sterling Trust (FXB)	
Canadian Dollar	Yes	CurrencyShares Canadian Dollar Trust (FXC)	
Euro	Yes	CurrencyShares Euro Trust (FXE)	
Swiss Franc	Yes	CurrencyShares Swiss Franc (FXF)	
Japanese Yen	Yes	CurrencyShares Japanese Yen Trust (FXY)	
Mexican Peso	Yes	CurrencyShares Mexican Peso Trust (FXM)	
Swedish Krona	No	CurrencyShares Swedish Krona Trust (FXS)	
U.S. Dollar	Yes	PowerShares DB US Dollar Bullish Fund (UUP)	Rydex Strengthening US Dollar Fund (RYSDX) ProFunds Rising Dollar Fund (RDPIX)
Inverse- U.S. Dollar	Yes	PowerShares DB US Dollar Bearish Fund (UDN)	Rydex Weakening US Dollar Fund (RYWDX) ProFunds Falling Dollar Fund (FDPIX)

* = Not all futures contracts are listed in this table. Consult the Appendix for a more complete listing.

EXHIBIT 9.6 Ways to Invest in Commodities/Currrencies.

commodity information at your disposal, at www.dorseywright.com. In Exhibit 9.7 we show you a small glimpse of the technical tools offered on our site.

7. *Think big—"big picture," that is.* You've learned a great deal by this point, especially if this is your first introduction to Point & Figure analysis, but that knowledge does nothing for you if you suffer from chronic "analysis paralysis." We've explained our process of commodity trading, but much of this book has focused upon using that asset class to produce an overall investment portfolio that better manages risk in the long run. Perhaps the greatest step for Dorsey, Wright in recent years has been our ability to refine relative strength into a systematic money management platform. Relative strength has been around in many forms for at least 70 years, we didn't invent it, but we have refined it into a powerful tool for overall portfolio management.

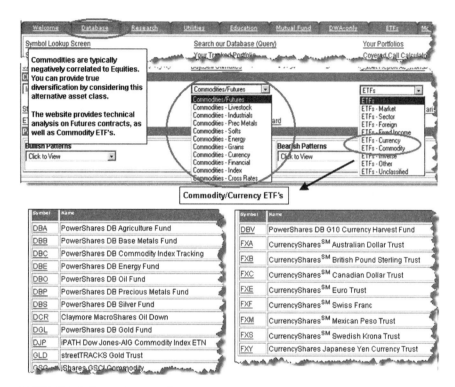

EXHIBIT 9.7 A Glimpse of DWA's Database.

The most widely known modern treatment of relative strength was offered by James O'Shaughnessy in his book, *What Works on Wall Street*. He tested, in a rigorous manner, what investing strategies can actually be proven to work in the stock market. He got access to the Compustat database and tested everything that had been purported to work—investing based on market capitalization, price-to-earnings ratios, price-to-book ratios, price-to-cashflow ratios, price-to-sales ratios, dividend yields, earnings per share, profit margins, return on equity, and relative strength—over a long period from 1951 to 1996. He tested them independently and in conjunction with other variables. He found that the market clearly and consistently rewarded certain attributes and consistently punishes others over a long period of time. His results were rather conclusive. He wrote, "Relative strength is one of the criteria in all 10 of the top-performing strategies, proving the maxim that you should never fight the tape." In addition, he pointed out that the worst strategy he tested was the anti-relative strength strategy of bottom fishing.

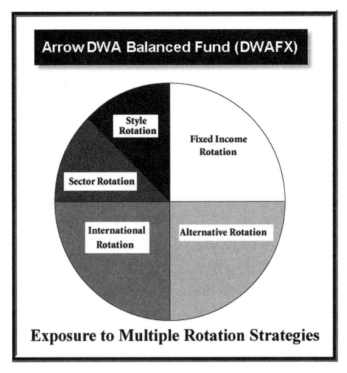

EXHIBIT 9.8   A Truly Global, Truly Balanced Option.

In 32 years in this business, I have found that there are no "get-rich-quick" schemes in the commodity or equity markets, none that have any staying power at least. Mr. O'Shaughnessy's findings speak directly to that point, though many would have you think otherwise. I also know that the commodity and equity markets have symbiotic characteristics within an investment allocation. This observation along with the advancements we have made in relative strength led to the creation of our first mutual fund, a global allocation fund titled the Arrow DWA Balanced Fund (DWAFX). I assure you this is no "get-rich-quick" fund, it is a fund that is truly balanced by always maintaining some level of exposure to U.S. equities, foreign equities, fixed income, and "alternative investments." The latter is where commodities often come into the equation (Exhibit 9.8).

Each quadrant invests in ETFs related to that asset class, but the first thing that happens in the management of the product is a tactical overlay to determine the allocation that is deserved by each of the four quadrants. Then, the tactical tools are applied to the inventory within each quadrant to determine which areas have the strongest relative strength of that asset grouping. Through relative strength, the portfolio is designed to become more defensive through bonds and alternative investments when the equity markets are not in favor. When equities have the strongest relative strength, the weightings will vary accordingly toward that group. This fund is essentially a summation of everything we have discussed to this point. It employs the latest, most innovative, products on Wall Street and the time-tested strategy of relative strength to create a managed product that is truly global and truly balanced. As the list of available ETFs expands, so too will the ability of this fund to enter new markets. DWAFX may be something that you decide to incorporate into your own investments, or it can simply serve as an example of how this methodology can work seamlessly for a total allocation answer. For us, this is a way to be certain we are always thinking "big picture."

For more information on the fund, visit www.arrowfunds.com, you can also call Arrow Funds directly at 301-260-0163 and ask for Jake Griffith.

Successful commodity trading takes dedication, patience, and a logical, organized method of recording the imbalance between supply and demand. Never forget, as I mentioned before, it is the irrefutable law of supply and demand that causes all price change. Embrace this basic economic law and you will be well on your way to consistent trading profits. Finally, I want to leave you with a quote from the late great investor Bernard Baruch (1870–1965), which speaks to the necessity of finding a trend following system that provides you with conviction in your actions. I hope Point & Figure analysis is that system for you.

> *If a speculator is correct half of the time, he is hitting a good average. Even being right 3 or 4 times out of 10 should yield a person a fortune if he has the sense to cut his losses quickly on the ventures where he is wrong.*
>
> ——Bernard Baruch

I invite you to utilize the commodity resources on the DWA web site. All of the tools discussed in this book are available on the web site—from charts, to relative strength tools to momentums to trading bands to matrix creation capabilities. I hope you have great success in trading. If you get a chance, let us know how you are doing; send me a note at tom@dorseywright.com. We'd love to hear from you, and we answer all e-mails.

Appendix
Commodity and Futures Reference Sheet

Contract	Root Symbol	Unit Size (per x)	Reg. Trading Hours (EST)	Trading Months	Contract Size	**Int. Margin Requirement
Currencies						
U.S. Dollar	DX	$1,000	8:05A - 3:00P	H,M,U,Z	$1,000 x Index	
British Pound	BP	$625 (.01)	8:20 - 3:00	H,M,U,Z	62,500 BP	$ 1,688
Canadian Dollar	CD	$1,000 (.01)	8:20 - 3:00	H,M,U,Z	100,000 CD	$ 1,148
Japanese Yen	JY	$1,250 (.01)	8:20 - 3:00	H,M,U,Z	12,500,000 yen	$ 2,160
Swiss Franc	SF	$1,250 (.01)	8:20 - 3:00	H,M,U,Z	125,000 SF	$ 1,485
Euro FX	EC	$1,250 (.01)	8:20 - 3:00	H,M,U,Z	125,000 Euro	$ 2,295
Australian Dollar	AD	$1,000 (.01)	8:20 - 3:00	H,M,U,Z	100,000 AD	$ 1,350
New Zealand Dollar	NZ	$1,000 (.01)	8:20 - 3:00	H,M,U,Z	100,000 NZ	$ 1,350
Financials						
30 Year T-Bond	US	$1,000	8:20 - 3:00	H,M,U,Z	$100,000	$ 1,350
10 Year T-Note	TY	$500	8:20 - 3:00	H,M,U,Z	$100,000	$ 878
5 Year T-Note	FV	$500	8:20 - 3:00	H,M,U,Z	$100,000	$ 540
Eurodollar	ED	$2,500	8:20 - 3:00	H,M,U,Z	$1,000,000	$ 743
10 Year Muni Bond	MB	$1,000	8:20 - 3:00	H,M,U,Z	$1,000 x MB Index	$ 878
Indices						
Dow Industrials	DJ	$10	8:20 - 4:15	H,M,U,Z	$10 x DJIA	$ 4,875
Mini-Dow	YJ	$5	8:20 - 4:15	H,M,U,Z	$5 x DJIA	$ 2,500
S&P 500 Index	SP	$250	9:30 - 4:15	H,M,U,Z	$250 x SPX	$ 19,688
Mini-S&P 500	ES	$50	9:30 - 4:15	H,M,U,Z	$50 x SPX	$ 3,500
Nasdaq 100	ND	$100	9:30 - 4:15	H,M,U,Z	$100 x NDX	$ 16,250
Mini-NDX	NQ	$20	9:30 - 4:15	H,M,U,Z	$20 x NDX	$ 3,250
NYSE Composite	YX	$50	9:30 - 4:15	H,M,U,Z	$50 x NYA	$ 12,000
S&P Midcap 400	MD	$500	9:30 - 4:15	H,M,U,Z	$500 x MID	$ 16,875
Mini-S&P 400	EW	$100	9:30 - 4:15	H,M,U,Z	$100 x MID	$ 3,375
Russell 1000	RX	$500	9:30 - 4:15	H,M,U,Z	$500 x RUI	$ 2,900
Russell 2000	RL	$500	9:30 - 4:15	H,M,U,Z	$500 x RUT	$ 16,875
Mini-Russell 2000	EZ	$100	9:30 - 4:15	H,M,U,Z	$100 x RUT	$ 3,375
Nikkei 225	NK	$5	9:00 - 4:15	H,M,U,Z	$5 x NK/	$ 4,688
CRB Index	CR	$200	10:00 - 2:30	F,G,J,M,O,X	$500 x CR/Y	$ 1,800
Continuous CRB Index	CI	$500	10:00 - 2:30	F,G,J,M,O,X	$500 x UV/Y	$ 1,800
Goldman Sach Commodity	GI	$250	8:55 - 2:40	All months	$250 x GN/X	$ 4,500
DJ AIG Index	AI	$100	9:15 - 2:30	F,G,J,M,O,V,Z	$100 x DJAIG	$ 1,418

EXHIBIT A.1 Commodity Futures Contract Specifications

Contract	Root Symbol	Unit Size (per z)	Reg. Trading Hours (EST)	Trading Months	Contract Size	**Int. Margin Requirement
Energies						
Crude Oil	CL	$1,000	9:00 - 2:30	All months	1,000 brls	$ 4,050
mini-Crude Oil	QM	$500	10:00 - 2:30	All months	500 brls	$ 2,025
Gasoline RBOB	RB	$420 (.01)	9:00 - 2:30	All months	42,000 gal	$ 5,400
Heating Oil	HO	$420 (.01)	9:00 - 2:30	All months	42,000 gal	$ 5,738
Natural Gas	NG	$1,000 (.10)	9:00 - 2:30	All months	10,000 MM Btu	$ 10,125
mini-Natural Gas	QG	$500 (.10)	10:00 - 2:30	All months	5,000 MM Btu	$ 2,531
Propane	PN	$420 (.01)	9:20 - 1:10	All months	42,000 gal	$ 2,363
Coal	QL	$155 (.10)	3:15 - 2:30	All months	1,550 Tons	$
Grains						
Wheat	W	$50	10:30 - 2:15	H,K,N,U,Z	5,000 bu	$ 1,553
mini-Wheat	YW	$10	10:30 - 2:15	H,K,N,U,Z	1,000 bu	$ 311
Corn	C	$50	10:30 - 2:15	F,H,K,N,U,X,Z	5,000 bu	$ 1,350
mini-Corn	YC	$10	10:30 - 2:15	F,H,K,N,U,X,Z	1,000 bu	$ 270
Soybeans	S	$50	10:30 - 2:15	F,H,K,N,Q,U,X	5,000 bu	$ 1,350
mini-Soybean	YK	$10	10:30 - 2:15	F,H,K,N,Q,U,X	1,000 bu	$ 270
Soybean Meal	SM	$100	10:30 - 2:15	F,H,K,N,Q,U,V,Z	100 tons	$ 1,080
Soybean Oil	BO	$60 (.001)	10:30 - 2:15	F,H,K,N,Q,U,V,Z	60000 lbs	$ 608
Oats	O	$50	10:30 - 2:15	H,K,N,U,Z	5,000 bu	$ 743
Rough Rice	RR	$20 (.01)	10:30 - 2:15	F,H,K,N,U,X	2,000 cwt	$ 675
Meats						
Live Cattle	LC	$400	10:05 - 2:00	G,J,M,Q,V,Z	40,000 lbs	$ 1,080
Feeder Cattle	FC	$500	10:05 - 2:00	F,H,J,K,Q,U,V,X	50,000 lbs	$ 1,620
Lean Hogs	LH	$400	10:10 - 2:00	G,J,K,M,N,Q,V,Z	40,000 lbs	$ 1,080
Pork Bellies	PB	$400	10:10 - 2:00	G,H,K,N,Q	40,000 lbs	$ 1,620
Milk	DA	$20	10:40 - 2:10	All Months	200,000 lbs	$ 1,013
Butter	DB	$400	10:30 - 2:10	G,H,K,N,U,V	40,000 lbs	$ 1,215
Metals						
Gold	GC	$100	8:20 - 1:30	G,J,M,Q,V,Z	100 troy oz	$ 2,700
mini-Gold	YG	$33.2	8:20 - 1:30	All Months	33.2 troy oz	$ 1,350
Silver	SI	$50 (.01)	8:25 - 1:25	H,K,N,U,Z	5,000 troy oz	$ 4,725
mini-Silver	YI	$10 (.01)	8:25 - 1:25	All Months	1,000 troy oz	$ 810
High Grade Copper	HG	$250	8:10 - 1:00	H,K,N,U,Z	25,000 lbs	$ 6,075
Platinum	PL	$50	8:20 - 1:05	F,J,N,V	50 troy oz	$ 3,375
Palladium	PA	$100	8:30 - 1:00	H,M,U,Z	100 troy oz	$ 2,025
Aluminum	AL	$440	7:50 - 1:15	All Months	44,000 lbs	$
Softs						
Cotton	CT	$500	10:30 - 2:15	H,K,N,V,Z	50,000 lbs	$ 2,025
Orange Juice	OJ	$150	10:00 - 1:30	F,H,K,N,U,X	15,000 lbs	$ 2,240
Coffee	KC	$375	9:15 - 12:30	H,K,N,U,Z	37,500 lbs	$ 2,700
mini-Coffee	MK	$125	9:15 - 12:30	F,J,M,Q,X	12500 lbs.	$ 840
Sugar #11	SB	$1,120	9:00 - 12:00	F,H,K,N,V	112,000 lbs	$ 1,190
Cocoa	CC	$10	8:00 - 11:50	H,K,N,U,Z	22,046 lbs	$ 1,120
Lumber	LB	$110	10:00 - 2:05	F,H,K,N,U,X	110,000 bd. Ft.	$ 1,650

** Margin Requirements last updated 2/10/2007

Please Visit us Online at www.dorseywright.com

Trading Months

F	January	N	July
G	February	Q	August
H	March	U	September
J	April	V	October
K	May	X	November
M	June	Z	December

EXHIBIT A.2 Commodity Futures Contract Specifications

Index